Yale College Series, 13

The French Communist Party

versus the Students

Revolutionary Politics in May–June 1968

by Richard Johnson

New Haven and London: Yale University Press

1972

This volume is number 13 in the Yale College Series of scholarly essays written by members of the senior class in Yale College. The series was begun in 1964.

Library of Congress catalog card number: 72–181533
ISBN: 0–300–01525–9 (cloth), 0–300–01563–1 (paper)

Designed by John O. C. McCrillis
and set in IBM Press Roman type.
Printed in the United States of America by
The Carl Purington Rollins Printing-Office
of the Yale University Press

Published in Great Britain, Europe, and Africa by
Yale University Press, Ltd., London.
Distributed in Canada by McGill-Queen's University Press,
Montreal; in Latin America by Kaiman & Polon, Inc.,
New York City; in India by UBS Publishers'
Distributors Pvt., Ltd., Delhi; in Japan by John
Weatherhill, Inc., Tokyo.

To My Parents

Contents

Preface

During the afternoon of May 3, 1968, a student political rally in the courtyard of the Sorbonne was broken up by the police. This proved to be the precipitating incident that touched off two months of intense student disorder.

That same morning the Communist newspaper, *l'Humanité*, published an extremely unfavorable article on student radicalism. The rebels were described as members of "certain groups (anarchists, Trotskyists, Maoists, etc.) composed in general of sons of the big bourgeoisie, and directed by the German anarchist, Cohn-Bendit." Needless to say, in the eyes of the French Communists there are few creatures more despicable than Germans, anarchists, and sons of the "big bourgeoisie."

It is hardly surprising, then, that the student rebellion subsequently took on a decidedly anti-Communist character. When the Party poet, Louis Aragon, went to the Latin Quarter to engage the rebels in a "dialog," he was hooted down. Cohn-Bendit advised his followers to be quiet: he pointed out that even "Stalinist slobs" had a right to be heard.

The battle between the French Communist party (PCF) and its adversaries on the extreme left was fought on many fronts. It began in the Party press and in the reviews and journals of the radical intelligentsia; it was later carried to the factories, universities, and meeting halls of France; and during the dramatic days of May and June, it was fought in the streets of Paris.

The question of ideology lay at the very heart of this struggle. The students and intellectuals argued that the leaders of the Party were unprincipled, incompetent theorists who were unable to use the insights of Marxism to create tactics and strategies appropriate to the existing situation. The Party, in turn, argued that the "adventurist actions" of the intelligentsia were manifestations of its essentially "petit-bourgeois" ideology.

Not only was ideology a major issue, but it also played an important role in determining the actual configuration that the struggle assumed. The leaders of the PCF perceived the actions of the student left through the perceptual categories posited by Marxism-Leninism.

Official doctrine focused their attention, organized their perceptions, and determined, to a large extent, what they actually "saw." As a result, the Party's response to its critics was shaped and formed by the concepts and formulas of its ideology.

In a similar manner, the leaders of the student radicals tended to view the Party and its policies in terms of the theories set forth by the oppositionist intellectuals of the Marxist movement—the doctrines of Trotsky and Luxemburg, as well as those of Jean-Paul Sartre and Louis Althusser.

This study attempts to describe the recurring patterns of interaction among the PCF, the radical intelligentsia, and the leftist students: it focuses on the double role of ideology, first as a subject of controversy and an object of debate, and second as a force that organizes perceptions and guides behavior.

Chapter 1 begins by examining the roles that the classics of Marxism-Leninism assign to ideology and the intellectual. It then analyzes the manner in which these classics have been adapted and revised as the Communist movement has transformed itself into a powerful system of hierarchical organizations, led by working-class functionaries.

Chapter 2 outlines the oppositionist theses set forth by the radical existentialists. It interprets existential Marxism as an expression of the classical dilemmas of the "alienated bourgeois intellectual"— who wishes to ally with the working-class movement, but who is reluctant to accept the role assigned to him by the proletarian apparatchik.

Chapters 3 and 4 examine the extent to which these theories have influenced the factional activities of the Communist students. These chapters also analyze the manner in which the student radicals have fused existentialism and structuralism with the more practical critiques of Trotsky, Luxemburg, Togliatti, and Mao.

The perceptions of the PCF leaders are framed by a doctrine that has been repeatedly modified in the course of its fifty-year history. These modifications seem to reflect the pattern of its organizational growth. Chapters 5 and 6 therefore argue that the PCF can be treated as a bureaucratic organism whose behavior is conditioned by an organizational ideology. The structure of this doctrine seems to reflect the capacities, needs, and tasks of the individuals who staff the Party's apparatus. This concept of the ideologically conditioned organism is set forth as an alternative to the theories of deradicalization and the decline of ideology, which are subjected to a critical analysis in chapter 9.

Chapters 7 and 8 describe the way in which the simplistic formulas of the Party's doctrine guided and shaped its reaction to the violent tactics and organizational innovations of the student left. Finally, chapter 9 interprets the revolutionary initiatives of the 1968 student revolt as attempts to translate the abstract theories of the oppositionist intellectuals into concrete political practices.

Acknowledgments

My research on French student radicalism was done in Paris in 1968 under a National Science Foundation grant obtained with the aid of Irwin G. Gertzog of the Yale University department of political science. This study began as an undergraduate essay, and my early efforts were guided by Sidney G. Tarrow, who taught me much of what I know about Marxist theory. My knowledge of Communist ideology and practice was also broadened by the excellent instruction of David Levey, Wolfgang Leonhard, Harry Magdoff, and Rudolf Tökes. In addition, I would like to thank James P. Sewell for all the help and advice he has given me during my stay at Yale.

While I was in Paris, the officials of the Communist Youth movement provided me with clear and frank explanations of their policies; I am particularly grateful to Claude LeCompte and François Rousel. I would also like to thank Claude Harmel of the Institut d'Histoire Social for allowing me to use his voluminous file on Communist student activity.

Isaac Kramnick and Phillip Shively read the first draft of my study and made many useful suggestions. Thomas Greene of the University of Southern California read the second draft and gave me a detailed critique that proved invaluable in my efforts to prepare my manuscript for publication.

Most of all, I would like to thank Joseph LaPalombara, who persuaded me to abandon a position of confused partisanship and patiently guided me to a perspective which I hope approaches objectivity. A young and inexperienced student of European politics could not hope for a better teacher and guide.

Finally, I wish to express my gratitude to Wendy C. Johnson for excellent meals, pleasant conversation, and fast, efficient typing.

R. J.

Organizations and Their Abbreviations

CGT — Confédération générale du travail: the Communist-controlled trade union federation; the largest labor union in France; Georges Séguy, a member of the PCF politburo, is its secretary-general.

CPSU(b) — The Communist Party of the Soviet Union (bolshevik), often listed as CPSU.

CRS — Compagnie républicaine de sécurité; the riot police controlled by the Ministry of the Interior.

ESU — Etudiants socialistes unifiés; the student organization of the Parti socialiste unifié (PSU), a splinter group on the extreme left of the social democratic spectrum; its leader is Michel Rocard.

FAU — Front anti-fasciste universitaire; an organization of leftist students formed to combat the Algerian war and the Secret Army Organization (OAS).

FER — Fédération des étudiants révolutionnaires; formerly the Comité de liaison des étudiants révolutionnaires; the student organization of the OCI (Organization communiste internationale)—a Trotskyist organization led by Pierre Lambert.

FLN — The National Liberation Front; the organization that led the struggle for Algerian independence.

JCR — Jeunesse communiste révolutionnaire; a Trotskyist student organization led by Alain Krivine (now called La ligue communiste); associated with the Parti communiste internationale, the Trotskyist party of Pierre Frank.

MJCF — Mouvement de la jeunesse communiste de France; the "umbrella organization" set up in 1965 to control the Communist student organization (UEC).

PCI — Partito comunista italiano, led by Palmiro Togliatti from the late twenties to 1964. Its youth journal, *Nuova Generazione,* exercised considerable influence among the Communist students of France.

PCF — Parti communiste français, led by Maurice Thorez and Jacques Duclos from 1934 to 1964, and by Waldeck Rochet and Georges Marchais from 1964 on. Its daily newspaper is *l'Humanité;*

its theoretical journal, *Cahiers du Communisme;* its economic journal, *Economie et Politique;* its intellectual revue, *La Nouvelle Critique.*

PCF(ML) Parti communiste français (marxiste-léniniste); the "official" pro-Chinese Communist organization; formerly the Fédération des cercles marxistes-léninistes and the Mouvement communiste français (marxiste-léniniste); its periodical is *l'Humanité Nouvelle.*

SNEsup Syndicat national de l'enseignement supérieur; the left-wing university teachers' union, led during the May revolt by Alain Geismar.

UEC Union des étudiantes communistes de France; the Communist-controlled student organization. Its journals were *Clarté* (1956-65) and *Le Nouveau Clarté* (1965-71).

UJC(ML) Union des jeunesses communistes (marxistes-léninistes); pro-Chinese student organization founded in 1956 at the Ecole Normale Supérieure by the followers of Louis Althusser

UNEF Union nationale des étudiants de France; France's largest national student organization. It is now controlled by left-wing socialist and Trotskyist students.

22 mars A student group with anarcho-Marxist orientations, started at the University of Nanterre by Daniel Cohn-Bendit. It was named for the date of a large, anti-Vietnam war demonstration in Paris in 1968.

SFIO Section française de l'internationale ouvrière; France's socialist party, led by the former premier Guy Mollet. It is presently part of the Federation of the Left (FGDS) led by François Mitterrand.

Chronology

1957   The Union des étudiants communistes de France (UEC) was founded in March.

1958   At the Second Congress of the UEC, delegates from Paris criticized the Party for not taking a more militant position against the Algerian war.

1961   High officials of the UEC are reported to have cooperated with Servin and Casanova, two members of the PCF central committee, in their attempt to unseat the PCF secretary-general, Maurice Thorez.

1962   At the Sixth Congress of the UEC, the revisionist program of the *italien* faction was overwhelmingly adopted. The PCF accused the students of "abandoning the positions of the working class."

1965   After a two-year struggle, the Party succeeded in reasserting its control over the UEC at its Eighth Congress. The *italiens* were ousted from leadership positions, and all factional activity was officially forbidden.

1966   *January:* After the Sorbonne-Lettres section of the UEC condemned the Party for supporting the presidential candidacy of Mitterrand, it was summarily dissolved by the pro-Party leadership.

March: Alain Krivine, former head of the Sorbonne-Lettres section, formed the Jeunesse communiste révolutionnaire. The group was Trotskyist in orientation.

October: The Amiens and Paris high-school sections of the UEC seceded and joined the pro-Peking Mouvement communiste français (marxiste-léniniste). Students at the University of Strasbourg bombarded a professor of social psychology with tomatoes to protest the "repressive ideological content" of his lectures. Soon after this incident, an anarcho-Marxist group called the "situationists" took over the student union and used its funds to circulate a manifesto attacking the school system, capitalism, the Church, the Communist party, and Alain Krivine's JCR. The union was closed by a court order on December 14.

November: The UEC expelled almost 600 members for pro-Peking factional activities.

December: The followers of Professor Althusser at the Ecole Normale Supérieure formed another pro-Peking group: the Union des Jeunesses communistes (marxistes-léninistes).

1967   The students at Nanterre started a sex education campaign and a drive against rules governing the visiting hours of males in female dormitories. By February most universities had abolished these rules.

1968   *March 22:* Daniel Cohn-Bendit led 142 students in the occupation of an administration building at the University of Nanterre. They were protesting the arrest of several of their compatriots during a Vietnam protest in Paris.

April 3: The government announced that it intended to introduce a selective admissions policy in order to reduce overcrowding at the universities. Under the new system, a high school diploma would no longer guarantee access to higher education.

May 2: The ultra-right group "Occident" set fire to the headquarters of a student union at the Sorbonne; at Nanterre the dean suspended classes because of militant leftist agitation. Cohn-Bendit was called to appear before a university disciplinary council because of his part in these activities. *L'Humanité* published an article that accused the leftist students of serving the interests of de Gaulle and monopoly capital.

May 3: Students gathered in the courtyard of the Sorbonne to protest the closing of the University of Nanterre. After extreme right-wing students threatened to attack the demonstrators, the dean decided to close the Sorbonne and called the police to clear the building. Their arrival sparked a riot in the Latin Quarter. Barricades were built, cars were turned over, and 596 students were arrested. The major student and faculty unions called for a strike.

May 4: L'Humanité condemned "political adventurism."
May 6: Approximately 20,000 students demonstrated on the Boulevard St. Germain. Three hundred forty-five policemen were injured and 22 hospitalized; 422 students were arrested; several hundred were wounded. The PCF softened its line; *l'Humanité* promised to help the students and teachers reopen the universities.

May 7: Thirty thousand students marched before the National Assembly. Peking hailed the "heroic battles" of the students and *Pravda* condemned their "irrational acts."

May 10: The Night of the Barricades. Students rioted throughout the Latin Quarter. Approximately 32 barricades were built, 367 students were injured, 460 were arrested, 188 cars were damaged.

May 11: The labor unions called for a 24-hour general strike and a mass demonstration. Pompidou disavowed the police violence and promised to reopen the universities on May 13.

May 13: Five hundred thousand workers and students marched across Paris. Many called for de Gaulle's ouster. ("Dix ans ça suffit.") Cohn-Bendit told the demonstrators to organize action committees in their factories and neighborhoods. At about 9:30 P.M. the students reoccupied the Sorbonne.

May 15: The workers at Sud-Aviation occupied their plant.

May 16: Occupations occurred at other large factories: Renault workers at Billancourt flew the red flag. The CGT, the Communist-controlled union, warned its members to remain "vigilant" against student "adventurism."

May 17: As the strike movement spread, de Gaulle decided to return from a state visit to Rumania. Student occupations occurred on even the most conservative campuses, including the law and medical schools and the "grandes écoles."

May 18: The CGT warned its members that adventurist slogans and calls for insurrection "played into the government's hands." *L'Humanité* argued that Pompidou's goal was to isolate the working class by exploiting the excesses of the ultra-leftists.

May 19: As the political situation deteriorated, Mendès-France called for de Gaulle's resignation; Waldeck Rochet declared that the PCF was "ready to assume its responsibilities." In almost all the universities, the principles of "autonomy" and "cogestion" (self-government by students and faculty) were overwhelmingly accepted by student-faculty assemblies.

May 20: The CGT stated that it pursued only "concrete demands" and denounced the concept of "autogestion" (workers' self-management) as a "stupid formula."

May 22: The government forbade Cohn-Bendit, who was lecturing in Britain, to reenter France. Protest demonstrations followed in the Latin Quarter.

May 23: L'Humanité argued that the demonstrations "played into the hands of the government."

May 24: De Gaulle announced that he would hold a referendum on *rénovation* and that he would resign if the nation's response was no.

May 27: Workers at Renault, Citroen, Rhodiaceta, and Berliet rejected tentative strike settlements reached by the government, industry, and the unions; the CGT called for de Gaulle's resignation and the formation of a "popular government."

May 28: Mitterrand called for an interim government with Mendès-France at its head; Waldeck Rochet demanded that the Communists be included in any government that might be formed.

May 29: De Gaulle secretly flew to Germany to consult with French army commanders and thus assured himself the support of the military.

May 30: De Gaulle dissolved the National Assembly and called for new elections on June 23 and 30. He warned of the dangers of "Communist totalitarianism." The Gaullists and Parisian anti-Communists staged a massive demonstration on the Champs-Elysées; the crowd was estimated at 100,000.

May 31: Communist representatives met with leaders of the Federation of the Left; they failed to agree on a policy of "single candidates" for the first round of the elections.

June 1: Forty thousand students marched from Montparnasse to the Austerlitz station, their slogan: "Elections, trahison" (freely: "elections betray the revolution").

June 6: CRS (riot police) occupied the Renault plant at Flins; a group of students and workers staged a counterattack. *L'Humanité* condemned the actions of the students as a "provocation" against the strikers.

June 10: The PCF began its election campaign with a massive rally in the Palais de Sport outside Paris; the same evening students staged a night-long riot in the Latin Quarter to protest the death of a Maoist high-school student at Flins. Three hundred fires were started, 75 cars were wrecked, and 100 police vans were destroyed. Seventy-two barricades were constructed.

June 12: The Minister of the Interior ordered that the JCR, UJC(ML), 22 Mars, FER, and other extremist groups be dissolved. All public demonstrations were banned.

June 17: The police reoccupied the Sorbonne and other university facilities.

June 23: In the first rounds of the legislative elections, the Gaullists scored massive victories; the PCF and other left-wing parties all sustained losses.

June 30: The second round of the elections gave the Gaullists 295 seats in the National Assembly (compared to the 197 it had won in the previous election), a 51-seat majority. The Federation of the Left kept 57 seats against 118 before; the PCF retained 34 seats against 73 before. The PSU lost its 3 seats.

1 The Apparatchik and the Intellectual

The belief that the working class is the fundamental revolutionary force in modern society is an inextricable element of the Marxist world view. Since the proletarian is exposed to "objective conditions" that become progressively more unpleasant, he develops the "subjective will" to destroy the capitalist system.

Although the working class finds temporary allies in other social classes, in the last analysis it alone accomplishes the revolutionary transformation of society.

> Of all the classes that stand face to face with the bourgeoisie today, the proletariat alone is a really revolutionary class. The other classes decay and finally disappear in the face of modern industry; the proletariat is its special and essential product.[1]

Even though the *Manifesto* is extravagant in its praise of the proletarian, it still contains hints that he will need substantial assistance if he is to accomplish his historical task. For example, in discussing the relationship between Communists and Proletarians, Marx points out that the former have over the "great mass of the proletarians the advantage of clearly understanding the line of march."[2] Another passage suggests that those blessed with this understanding are frequently of bourgeois origins. As revolutionary conditions develop, Marx says, the proletariat is ultimately joined by a portion of the "bourgeois ideologists, who have raised themselves to the level of comprehending theoretically the historical movement as a whole."[3]

One finds a similarly ambiguous attitude toward the proletariat in the writings of Lenin. On the one hand, he unequivocally asserts:

> The overthrow of the bourgeoisie can be accomplished only by the proletariat, as the particular class whose economic conditions of existence prepare it for this task and provide it with the possibility and the power to perform it.[4]

While Lenin states that the overthrow of capitalism can be effected *only* by the proletariat, he also insists that it cannot be accomplished

1

by the proletariat *alone*. For, "the history of all countries shows that the working class exclusively by its own efforts is able to develop only trade union consciousness."[5] In this respect, Lenin follows the teachings of the "renegade Kautsky." To achieve a truly "revolutionary consciousness," the working class needs the assistance of bourgeois ideologues.

> The theory of socialism . . . grew out of the philosophic, histori-
> cal and economic theories that were elaborated by the educated
> representatives of the propertied classes, the intellectuals. The
> founders of modern, scientific socialism, Marx and Engels,
> themselves belonged to the bourgeois intelligentsia.[6]

Some argue that this ambiguity in Marxism-Leninism amounts to a paradox. First, we are told that one's state of mind is a reflection of the material conditions in which one lives. "Your very ideas," says Marx to his bourgeois critics, "are but the outgrowth of your bourgeois production and bourgeois property."[7] "It is not the consciousness of men that determines their being, on the contrary, it is their social being that determines their consciousness."[8] But then we are told that the impoverished proletarian can achieve only an inferior level of trade union consciousness, while the relatively prosperous intellectual can achieve "true" or "revolutionary" consciousness.

The ideology of the French Communist party retains a measure of this ambiguity. The PCF insists on the "decisive role of the working class,"[9] and it emphasizes that this historical mission is the inevitable outgrowth of the "objective situation" in which the proletariat finds itself. "This is not a matter of dogma; it is so because it is the working class which submits most directly to capitalist exploitation."[10]

But the Party is equally adamant in asserting that the working class can fulfill its role only if it has the careful tutelage and guidance of the PCF. Waldeck Rochet, the Party's present secretary-general, contends that the Russian revolution demonstrated several "universal lessons." A primary one is "the necessity of a party which is the true, revolutionary vanguard of the working class."[11] The French Party, therefore, argues that the proletariat is naturally

revolutionary, while at the same time claiming that the proletariat
needs a vanguard to instill in it a revolutionary consciousness.

What equips an organization to fulfill a vanguard role is what
Marx calls a "comprehension of history" and a "clear understanding of its processes." Consequently, the French Communist party
justifies its leadership of the working class on the grounds that it
is thoroughly immersed in the "science" of Marxism-Leninism; as
Rochet says:

> It is because it is the party of the French working class, inspired
> by the great principles of Marxism-Leninism, that the French
> Communist Party is the only revolutionary party in France.[12]

The principles of Marxism-Leninism allow the Party to analyze a
given historical situation and, on the basis of its analysis, to provide the proletariat with a proper revolutionary strategy, "The dialectic," says Jacques Duclos, "is not merely a scientific theory, but
a method of knowledge and a guide to action."[13] Likewise, Rochet
emphasizes that Marxism-Leninism encompasses not only philosophy
and economics but also the "theory and strategy of the international
Communist movement."[14]

The Party can fulfill its mission as the vanguard of the working
class only if it assiduously follows the teachings of Marx and Lenin.
But these teachings must be applied in light of the concrete conditions which prevail in particular environments at particular times.
In other words, Marxism-Leninism must be carefully interpreted.
Rochet reminds us that Lenin stresses that tactics are not deduced
from general truths but are always propounded on the basis of
theoretical analyses of contemporary events.

> The only truly scientific way to approach problems is, in fact,
> to evaluate with precision the existing situation, particularly
> the relationship of class forces; it is to be able to know how to
> reveal and to predict the new tendencies in time to be able to
> determine on this basis the most correct political line.[15]

Since the Party can claim to be the true vanguard of the proletariat
only by virtue of the fact that its interpretation of Marxism-Leninism
is correct, the interpreter performs a key role within the Party. With-

out the theorist the Party could do nothing, it would be like a body without a head. "There is no revolutionary practice without revolutionary theory," Lenin declared; "the theory of Marx is omnipotent because it is true."[16] It is not surprising, then, that the leadership of most Communist parties is careful to claim ideological primacy: the leader is *the* ideologue.

Maurice Thorez, who was the PCF's leader for almost thirty years until his death in 1964, took great pains to stress his ideological expertise. In his autobiography he informs us that he spent his first prison term learning German, so that he could read the works of Marx and Engels in their original form and thus better apply their teachings to his political tasks. He makes it perfectly clear that his own tactical choices were deeply rooted in the classics of Marxism-Leninism.

> The analyses of the situation in France given by Marx in the *18th Brumaire* helped me considerably to understand the contemporary situation. . . . In Lenin's writings I discovered not only a striking picture of our own times, but also masterly directives for leading the proletariat to victory.[17]

When Marx and Lenin spoke of theorists, they were usually referring to the bourgeois intelligentsia. It seemed natural that the middle-class Communist might be better equipped to carry out theoretical analyses than his proletarian comrade. Having been raised in a more sophisticated cultural milieu and having attained a higher level of education, he would undoubtedly have less difficulty moving from the realm of the concrete to that of the abstract.

The Italian Communist party has been led since its inception by three highly articulate bourgeois—Antonio Gramsci, Umberto Terraccini, and Palmiro Togliatti. However, the French Communist party, which puts particular stress on ideological matters, has recruited almost all its leaders from the ranks of the proletariat. For the last forty years the French Party has been led by Maurice Thorez, the son of a miner; Jacques Duclos, a former chef's assistant; and Waldeck Rochet, a peasant from Burgundy. The French Party has never lacked intellectual militants. Its ranks include many prominent philosophers, economists, and scientists. But few have succeeded in insinuating themselves into the Party's policy-making inner sanctums.

It is likely that the relatively uneducated working-class leader feels somewhat uncomfortable in the role of theorist. It is also likely that he realizes he is vulnerable to the ideological challenges of his more intellectually oriented, middle-class comrades. The consequent insecurity of the PCF leadership might account for the fact that it has been so eager to defer to the ideological pronouncements of Moscow. It is obvious that the theoretically inept Thorez had a far greater need for a "strong papacy" than did the theoretically agile Togliatti. Since the Communist militants generally recognized the infallible nature of Stalin's and even Khrushchev's statements, the PCF leaders could remain reasonably safe from ideological criticism if they merely restated these pronouncements. It is not surprising, then, that Thorez strongly opposed Togliatti's concept of "polycentrism."[18]

Having achieved hegemony within the Party, the working-class leaders of the PCF have consistently discouraged their bourgeois comrades from engaging in "creative theorizing."* If the bourgeois members were allowed to undertake such activity, and if their conclusions differed from those of the leadership, the competence of the latter would automatically be called into question. In a Communist movement, *the legitimacy of authority rests largely on ideological expertise.* Consequently, the intellectuals have been assigned the task of documenting and generally "dressing up" the theoretical pronouncements of their leaders. In short, if the proletarian apparatchik is to feel secure in his position of political authority, *the bourgeois theorist must not be allowed to theorize.*

André Barjonet, a leading PCF economist who resigned his post during the May uprising, has aptly described the tasks of the loyal bourgeois intellectual.

---

*This is not to suggest that all Communist leaders of bourgeois origin are subtle and creative theorists, or that all working-class Communists are anti-intellectual ideologues. Marshall Tito, who was among the first members of the Communist movement to encourage innovative Marxist thinking, was of proletarian origins, while Molotov, a highly unoriginal Stalinist, was of cultured, bourgeois stock—a nephew of the composer Scriabin.

Economists and Communist sociologists refer to Marxism at every
turn—but for no real purpose. They do not analyze the facts, in
order to disengage from them general laws, on the basis of which
correct political directives can be drawn; instead, they depart
from the pre-established political line and justify it by means
of concrete examples.[19]

The French intellectuals have not, however, always been in positions
of subordination to their working-class comrades. This situation has
only gradually evolved, largely as a result of the influence which
Stalin exercised on the development of the PCF.

David Caute notes that of the thirty-two members of the executive committee of the First Congress of the PCF, four were workers;
the rest were "intellectuals . . . or those generally disposed in their
favor."[20] Likewise, the first council of ministers of the Bolshevik
government included eleven bourgeois intellectuals and only four
proletarians.

During the early twenties the policy-making organs of both the
PCF and the Communist Party of the Soviet Union were controlled
by elements of the bourgeois intelligentsia. But these were also the
years when Stalin was busily staffing the administrative apparatus
of the Soviet party and government with loyal, working-class subordinates. After the death of Lenin in 1924, Stalin was able to use
this bureaucratic power base in his efforts to purge the politburo
of its intellectual majority.

It is hardly an exaggeration to say that the great power struggles
of the twenties were essentially battles between the bourgeois intellectual elite and Stalin's newly recruited army of proletarian functionaries.

As a result of these power struggles, the classic tenets of Marxism-
Leninism were subjected to certain "historical determinations."
Marx's ambiguous attitudes toward the bourgeois intelligentsia were
clarified. By the mid-twenties the spokesmen for the bureaucrats
began to deemphasize the traditional Marxist view that the intellectual is the guide and tutor of the working class. At the Fifth
Congress of the Comintern, Clara Zetkin warned the assembled
delegates of the Communist parties that they must not let their
organizations become submerged by the intelligentsia, for this stratum
tended to produce unreliable Communists.

> In the course of the struggle, the proletariat will learn a thousand times that the intellectual is an inconstant ally. We must expect this and not be surprised if, at each perspective of the overthrow of the domination of the bourgeoisie, the intellectuals desert the camp of the revolution.[21]

By 1931 Stalin had carried the denigration of the intellectuals a step further. The intelligentsia, he declared, was totally incapable of understanding the basic policies of the proletariat. Therefore, a new stratum of intellectuals had to be recruited from the "factories, the mines, and the shock brigades." The "terror" followed, and the remnants of the prerevolutionary Russian middle class were all but eliminated.

During the late twenties the leadership of the PCF responded to Stalin's policies by purging the Party cadres of their most prominent intellectuals. By 1929, 70 percent of the central committee was of working-class origin. Since numerous members of the Trotskyist opposition were bourgeois intellectuals, the loyal Stalinists had an added incentive to rid the Party of its non-working-class elements.

In 1930 Maurice Thorez was appointed secretary to the PCF central committee. Although he was of impeccably proletarian origin, he seemed to take a somewhat conciliatory attitude toward the intelligentsia. Thorez's overtures were, however, largely of a tactical nature. He had no desire whatsoever to be guided by the intellectuals, and he continued to exclude them from the Party's deliberative organs. Instead, Thorez desired to use them, to transform them into political tools. In 1934 the Popular Front was born. The PCF forged a tentative alliance with the Socialist and Radical parties, and it set about to increase its influence among the middle class. Thorez seems to have viewed the intelligentsia as a perfect bridge between the Party and its new allies.

Caute analyzes the attitudes of the Party toward the intellectuals in terms of certain "principles of utility." The first involves the concept of "pure prestige reflecting favorably upon the Party." This notion is based upon the belief that the "average Frenchman" holds the intellectual in unusually high esteem. The French supposedly feel that once an individual has attained expertise in science, literature, or philosophy, he can apply it with equal facility to political and social matters. French political parties therefore assume that it is of particular importance to win the endorsement of prestigious intellectual figures.

In 1945, for example, Roger Garaudy proclaimed at the Tenth Party Congress that the PCF's recent electoral gains in urban, middle-class districts were due largely to its growing influence among the Parisian intelligentsia.[22] But while the Party used the intellectual, it continued to exclude him from the decision-making process. From the proletarianization of the Party in the late twenties to its partial liberalization in the late fifties, few intellectuals were chosen to serve on the central committee and none were put on the polit-buro.

From time to time, Thorez apparently sensed that the Marxist intellectuals aspired to reassume their role as "the brains" of the movement. He made no secret of the fact that he had an extemely low opinion of this prospect. In July 1948 he made a speech in which he asserted that "a certain number of intellectuals" had not yet "caught up with the political and ideological positions of the working-class."[23] He noted with displeasure that the intellectuals had also developed a tendency to try to "teach" Marxism-Leninism to the central committee. Thorez admitted that Marx and Engels were bourgeois intellectuals and that they had taught the principles of scientific socialism to the working class. But he insisted that the PCF had already succeeded in thoroughly internalizing these principles and had, in addition, tested and proved them in combat. He concluded that the working class must now guide the intellectual rather than vice versa. And since the working class and the Party were almost identical, that meant that the intellectual would have to submit without reserve to the political and ideological positions of the Party.

Laurent Casanova was given the task of expanding upon these themes in a book entitled *Le Parti communiste, les intellectuels et la nation* (1949). To illustrate his themes he employs a Socratic rather than a Marxian dialectic.* He has a hypothetical comrade

---

*During the Stalinist era, the Socratic dialectic we invariably used to refute theoretical criticisms of the Party leadership. The Stalinist ideologue would

put forth the following thesis: "there can be no revolutionary transformation of society without the active intervention of the intellectuals." He responds by outlining the consequences and implications of
this demand that "the working class and its Party should share with
the intellectuals the leadership of the revolutionary movement, for
reasons which deal directly with the revolutionary content of the
tasks which have been set by the proletariat."[24] According to Casanova this would be a blatant contradiction of the basic Leninist
tenet that the proletariat is the only true revolutionary class. The
idea that the intellectual should share in the direction of the Communist movement is said to be "an unsupportable proposition from
the moment that it is stated in all clarity."[25]

Casanova's book makes it clear that although the ideology of the
PCF reproduces Marx's ambiguous attitude toward the working
class, it suppresses the corresponding ambiguity toward the intelligentsia. To thwart the challenges periodically posed by the Party
intellectuals, the proletarian leadership unequivocally rejects the
original Marxist notion that the intellectual guides the working class.

Casanova explains that the proper task of the intellectuals is to
fulfill secondary, service functions. First, they must support the
Party line among their colleagues. "It is in this way that the Communist intellectuals actively militate in unions or groups of writers,
artists, scholars, doctors, lawyers—and often in positions of authority."[26] Second, the intellectuals serve the Party by periodically assuming the task of the political journalists. "They contribute to
periodicals edited by the Party in order to treat questions of interest to the intelligentsia or to debate certain important ideological
problems."[27] Finally, they help the Party spread its doctrine, and
they assist it in its efforts to raise the level of mass consciousness
and win the ideological struggle with the bourgeoisie.

Casanova fails, however, to mention the two specific functions
that he, as an intellectual, is performing by writing *Le Parti com-*

---

extract a proposition from the position of his opponent and would then
list its logical consequences. The proposition was "disproved" if it could be
shown that any of these consequences "contradicted" any of the "unquestionable" postulates of Stalinist theory.

muniste. The first entails translating the ex cathedra pronouncements of the Party leadership into somewhat subtler and more sophisticated terms. Casanova tries to transform Thorez's demand that
the intellectuals "stay in their place" into an acceptable theoretical
statement—a thesis that appears to be in accord with the basic principles of Leninism. The second function involves polemicizing against
those who would challenge the ideological supremacy of the Party
leadership. His own book, for example, bitterly denounces the theoretical pretensions of Jean-Paul Sartre. Existentialism, Casanova asserts, "in its present form appeared alongside the decomposition of
the bourgeoisie, and its origins are bourgeois."[28]

Casanova's offensive against the existentialists was in part a response
to Soviet prompting. In the late forties Stalin's trusted aid, Andrey
Zhdandov, had begun an intensive campaign against all "non-Communist
ideological influences." The movement had entered a period of harsh,
theoretical sectarianism. But the polemics against Sartre also represent a long-established element of French Communist tradition. They
provide an ideal example of the proletarian leadership's ritualistic
reaction to bourgeois intellectuals who refuse to fulfill their assigned
roles and who, instead, insist upon engaging in "creative theorizing."

2 Existentialism and the Dilemmas of the Intellectual

The PCF mobilized its most prominent intellectuals in an effort to discredit Sartre. Henri Lefebvre, dean of the French academic Marxists, noted that Sartre had been "a disciple of the Nazi Heidegger."[1] Jean Kanapa, editor of *La Nouvelle Critique* and a former student of Sartre, referred to him as a "Fascist abscess" and a "cop-intellectual." Roger Garaudy expressed his disgust over the "intellectual fornications" of the existentialists.[2] In 1947 *Pravda* accused Sartre of being "a servile executor of a mission entrusted to him by Wall Street." Not to be outdone, *l'Humanité* darkly hinted that he was in the pay of the American ambassador.[3] (The insults of the Communists were almost indistinguishable from those of the extreme right; pro-Gaullist Claude Mauriac characterized Sartre as an "excrementalist.")[4]

The Party occasionally halted the polemics and cautiously extended an olive branch. It welcomed Sartre's participation in the World Peace Movement, for example, and at the time of the Vienna Conference, *l'Humanité* forgot its former rancor and noted approvingly that the congress had given him a standing ovation.[5] At one point, Kanapa was prevailed upon to apologize for the excesses of his previous insults; and at one of the first mass rallies for disarmament and peace, Sartre was given a place of honor on the speaker's platform, next to Jacques Duclos.[6]

The PCF's treatment of Sartre followed a long-established pattern. When he agreed to fulfill what it considered to be the proper functions of the bourgeois intellectual, it patted him approvingly on the head; but when he tried to fulfill the role of the creative Marxist theorist, it reacted with insults and vicious innuendo.

If the Party manifested a definite ambivalence in its treatment of Sartre, he manifested a similar ambivalence in his treatment of the Party. Early in 1956 he defended the PCF from the criticisms of Pierre Hervé, a former Communist journalist. While he noted his disagreement with certain aspects of its doctrine, Sartre pointed out that the Party, as a political entity, displayed an extraordinary intelligence and realism. Its tactical decisions, he asserted, were rarely mistaken.[7] Yet six months later, after the Hungarian invasion, he

11

wrote that the PCF was absolutely incompetent, totally impotent, and completely cut off from the masses.[8]

The interaction between the Communists and the radical existentialists has been characterized by a curious symmetry. Since the end of World War II, they have alternately courted and attacked one another. The source of this symmetry seems to have been the tendency of each to regard the other in essentially utilitarian terms.

As far as the PCF is concerned, the bourgeois intellectual fulfills certain useful functions. He is one of the many means the Party employs to gain its *political* ends. For the Sartrian intellectual, on the other hand, the socialist movement is a political means to *ethical* ends. Sartre, Merleau-Ponty, and Simone de Beauvoir regarded the proletariat and its party as "historical agents," whose practical activity would lead to the actualization of a particular normative vision. When the existentialists refused to fulfill their instrumental functions, the Party reacted angrily. Likewise, when the PCF violated existentialist morality and refused to fulfill its role as an ethical agent, Sartre and his followers responded with bitter disillusionment.

THE PROBLEM OF CHOICE

Most commentators stress the discontinuity between the young and old Sartre. The existentialism of the thirties and early forties is said to have been radically individualistic in its focus and fundamentally aesthetic in its preoccupations. Sartre supposedly compromised his earlier convictions by embracing Marxian collectivism and by turning from art to politics.[9]

The opposite view can also be argued. Sartrian politics can be seen as a logical consequence of the basic metaphysical assumptions of the *Transcendence of the Ego* (1936) and *Being and Nothingness* (1943). In both of these early works, Sartre insists upon bifurcating man into consciousness (being for itself: the *pour-soi*), and being (being in itself: the *en-soi*). Consciousness is equated with nothingness, for Sartre defines consciousness in terms of what it is not: that is, everything that "is" and can therefore become an object for consciousness. The reflective consciousness, he argues, can always detach itself from any particular object. It has no content; it is an "emptiness," a "crack in being." In its ability to turn away from, or negate, any possibility which confronts it lies the foundation of human freedom.

In Sartre's fictional works the images associated with consciousness are "clear" and "translucent," while those used to describe being are "heavy" and "dense." For the *en-soi* is opaque to the light of the *pour-soi*. When man confronts the world of being and asks for its meaning, the world remains silent. Existence has no intrinsic value; any meaning that it appears to possess has been imposed upon it by the human imagination. "Existence precedes essence," in the sense that the reality of one's physical existence precedes one's decision to pursue the goals and objectives that give one's life its direction and purpose.

Although consciousness is sharply distinguished from the "things" of being, it always has a "thing" as an object. The light, translucent *pour-soi* is invariably trapped in the dense, opaque world of the *en-soi*. Likewise, freedom always expresses itself as a specific choice in a particular situation.

From the radical opposition of consciousness to being, and from their perpetual juxtaposition, the essential problematic of Sartrian existentialism emerges. If freedom is the essence of man, then to become truly human he must make choices. But on what basis can one choose if the world of being is one of meaningless contingency? Why is one choice any better than another? Do the meanings of one's choices have any foundation outside one's own being? If not, how can one recommend—or justify—them to others?

Sartre has never provided a satisfactory answer to these questions; that is, he has never produced an existentialist ethic. In its place he has posited an existentialist politics. By accepting certain political assumptions, he has transformed the world of being from an arena of absurd opacity into a set of clear, relatively unambiguous situations. In the words of one of Simone de Beauvoir's fictional characters: "On the one side, you have the proletariat which wants reforms; and on the other, the bourgeoisie, which doesn't."[10] "American domination meant the perpetual oppression and undernourishment of all the oriental countries. Their only hope is the Soviet Union."[11] If one insists upon describing human society in this fashion, then choices and commitments are relatively easy to make.

Like the Marxists, the radical existentialists view politics in terms of sharp contradictions. Every time one makes a political decision, he assists one of the parties in conflict. A particular course of action favors either the USA or the USSR; the proletariat or the bourgeoisie; the Gaullists or the PCF.

It is impossible, the existentialists argue, to remain aloof from this struggle. By refusing to act, one invariably lends de facto support to the existing balance of forces. After Word War II Sartre rejected his earlier thesis that one can give satisfactory meaning to one's life through pure aesthetic activity.[12] Art-for-art's-sake is, in fact, art in support of the bourgeois order. By remaining apolitical, the artist implicitly accepts the reality of capitalist oppression; in addition, by creating a world of artificial beauty, he diverts attention from the actual sordidness of a system based on mass poverty and exploitation.[13] Literature must engage itself in the ongoing process of social conflict.

It can therefore be argued that Sartrian Marxism provides a solution to a dilemma created by Sartrian existentialism. In Sartre's early works, we learn that if the individual is to be truly human, he must be free; and if he is to be truly free, he must choose. We are not, however, told how he is to make meaningful choices in a world devoid of meaning. In the later works, this problem is resolved through political commitment—a commitment justified by a Marxist analysis of the "historicity" of man.

THE PROLETARIAT AS "MORAL AGENT"

Martin Heidegger, the German existentialist, also fused the notions of "freedom" and "resolve" with a commitment to radical political action. In 1933 he told his students: "From now on every matter requires decision and every action responsibility." At the same time, he declared: "The Führer himself and himself alone is the German reality, present and future, and its law."[14] Responsible action became possible once the Heideggerian resolved to accept the will of the Führer as his own law; for "to give oneself a law is the highest form of freedom."[15]

Both Sartre and Heidegger actualized their freedom by making decisive choices in the social world; both sought to justify their choices by appealing to the political configuration of their historical situations. While Heidegger defined his in nationalist terms, Sartre chose to employ the categories of Marxist theory.

Sartre's postwar alliance with the proletariat can be viewed as a logical consequence of his prewar rejection of the bourgeoisie. Almost all his fictional works ridicule and denounce middle-class life. In *La Nausée* (1936) the heavy, the dense, and the opaque are associated with the metaphysical category, "being," but they are also associated with the life of the provincial bourgeoisie, the citizens of Bouville ("mud city"). The latter spend their week at dull, routine jobs and give meaning to this drudgery by looking forward to "their lovely Sunday." When it finally comes, they find that they have nothing to do. They parade up and down the boulevards, pompously tipping their hats to one another; then they go home and wait restlessly for Sunday's empty and oppressive freedom to slowly pass.[16]

For Sartre, the middle class is characterized by its hypocrisy and self-deception. Instead of recognizing the vacuity of his existence, the shopkeeper takes pride in his dignity as a respectable citizen. But beneath his slogan, "liberty, equality, fraternity," lie the actual pettiness, greed, and selfishness of the world of business.[17]

As far as the radical existentialists are concerned, the history of modern France embodies the gradual decline and decay of bourgeois civilization. For the past thirty years the middle class has repeatedly betrayed the ideals of its own republicanism: from the Vichy collaboration to the immobilism of the Fourth Republic; from the brutality of the Algerian campaigns to the Bonapartism of the Gaullist state.

Becoming a writer and an intellectual is a way of rebelling against both the style and the substance of bourgeois existence; it represents a rejection of both the crass materialism of the middle class and the hypocritical idealism which disguises it. "In 1930," says Sartre, "there was only one counterfeit currency for us to destroy; the intellectual had as his mission to twist and tangle the strands of bourgeois ideology."[18]

The existentialist claims to discard the comforts of bourgeois illusion. He calmly confronts both the opacity of being and the nothingness of death; he insists upon remaining "lucid to the end." Unfortunately, the rejection of the bourgeois order and the subsequent acceptance of the intellectual's vocation produce certain difficulties. Although the intellectual consciousness is pure and translucent, it is also empty. The bourgeois cloaks his actions in false values, but at least he acts. The intellectual, on the other hand, enjoys his lucidity in an impotent, inactive isolation. His only weapon is the pen; and in a world of mass parties and nuclear weapons, the pen is hardly the equal of the sword.

After the war, the socialist movement rescued the Sartrian intellectual from this frustrating predicament. Within the schema of left-wing existentialist thought, the proletariat emerged as a powerful social force whose *praxis,* it was hoped, would actualize the moral vision of the alienated bourgeois intellectual. This is particularly apparent in the work of Maurice Merleau-Ponty, Sartre's political mentor. In *Humanism and Terror* (1947) Merleau-Ponty wrote:

> If [Marxism] accords a privilege to the proletariat it does so because on the basis of the internal logic of its condition, and its least settled mode of existence—that is, apart from any messianic illusion—the proletarians "who are not gods" are the only ones in a position to realize humanity. . . . That means that the proletariat, if we take its role in the given historical constellation, moves towards the recognition of man by man.[19]

According to Merleau-Ponty, the bourgeoisie view their fellow businessmen as competitors, as hostile "others"; they view their workers as "things," as instruments to increase their profits. Only the proletarian recognizes the humanity of his comrades. As he engages in the class struggle, he comes to regard his fellow worker not as an "other," but as one who is essentially like himself, that is, as one who faces the same threats and enemies and who holds the same interests and goals. Most important, in the course of the collective struggle, the worker comes to realize that his own liberation is inextricably bound up with the liberation of his fellowman. "What he hopes for is that the relationships of solidarity which he maintains with his other workers will become the very model of human relationships."[20]

In *Being and Nothingness* the individual consciousness perpetually "wished the death of the other." Every "I" tended to regard every "thou" as an object—and at the same time struggled to avoid becoming "objectified" for the "thou's" consciousness. In the Marxism of Sartre and Merleau-Ponty, this existential battle is said to be constitutive not of human existence in general, but only of the epochs of presocialist society. Communism, achieved through the class struggle and based on socialist productive relations, will introduce a form of human solidarity that will permit each consciousness to recognize the autonomy of the consciousness of the "other."

In addition, the *praxis* of proletarian politics leads to the immediate realization of human freedom. To overcome its material need, the proletariat must struggle against the bourgeoisie; to do so successfully, it must unite into a collective movement—one which is guided by a coherent strategy. "It is precisely in becoming revolutionaries," Sartre has written, "that is, in organizing with other members of their class to reject the tyranny of their masters, that slaves best manifest their freedom." Concrete liberty is realized in consciously evolved plans, designed to "supersede" the limits of particular situations. Through proletarian revolution the free consciousness affirms itself by negating the "unfreedom" posed by the scarcity and oppression of the world of being. "This possibility of rising above a situation in order to gain a perspective on it (a perspective which is not pure knowledge, but an indissoluble linking of understanding and action) is precisely what we call freedom."[21]

UNEASY ALLIES

Sartre shares Lenin's conviction that the proletariat cannot emerge as a self-conscious class unless it is led by a vanguard party. "Les classes ne sont pas, on les fait."[22] Classes have no a priori phenomenal existence; they are created. The task of the Party, Sartre argues, is to engage the worker in collective revolutionary action and thereby make him aware of his identity as a proletarian. Only in the risks, dangers, and conscious cooperation of the class struggle is freedom realized and humanity recognized.

Sartre also suggests that the intellectual plays an important role in this enterprise. In a revealing passage in the *Critique de la raison di-*

alectique (1960), he describes a petit-bourgeois intellectual looking out a hotel window at an adjacent field and observing two workmen who are separated by a fence. The intellectual knows that he is different from the two "objects" that he is studying; he realizes that he does not share their hopes, worries, skills, and aspirations. But by virtue of the fact that he can grasp their "differentness," he can categorize them as a unity; he can conceive of them as a distinct group. Only an individual standing outside a region can grasp its limits and hence "define" it.

One might conclude from this that only a petit-bourgeois intellectual, who is alienated from his own class, but who nevertheless stands outside the working-class community, can conceive of this community as a coherent totality.[23] Only he can perceive its salient characteristics, observe its role in society, and define its mission. Sartre recognizes, however, that it is not easy for the intellectual to ally himself with the working class. It is natural for the worker to become a Communist; it is his sole means of overcoming alienation. In addition, the proletarian is compelled to become a Party member by the most authentic of motives: concrete, material need. The intellectual's motives, on the other hand, are somewhat dubious. Given his striving for universality, he naturally longs to identify with Marx's "universal class." But Sartre argues that this identification is basically "inauthentic." This is apparent in his characterization of Hugo, the bourgeois Communist in *Dirty Hands* (1948). Since the worker is driven by need, he willingly accepts the discipline of the Party. But Hugo has never experienced need; not only has he never been hungry, but when he was a child his parents had to force him to eat. In the obstinate individualism of Hugo, in his rebellion against the harsh discipline of the Party, one senses the inevitable bad faith of the bourgeois Communist.

One of the reasons the Sartrian intellectual joins the socialist movement is that he regards it as the antithesis of middle-class existence. While the bourgeoisie disguises its materialism with a false idealism, the proletariat bases its activity on "true" ideas—that is, it engages in *praxis*. After achieving a lucid conception of its own situation, it employs this conception to transcend that situation.

Sartre was convinced, however, that the materialism of the PCF was just as false and ideological as the idealism of the bourgeoisie. He could not accept the Stalinist dictum that ideas were merely the reflection of material reality. For him, revolutionary activity was not a Pavlovian response to environmental stimuli; on the contrary, it was a consciously evolved *projet,* an undertaking, an endeavor, a conscious commitment. Man revolted because he freely chose to do so. In the long run, Sartre argued, Stalinist determinism would have a debilitating influence on the class struggle. "We cannot indiscriminately form the young by teaching them successful errors. What would happen if materialism one day stifled the revolutionary project?"[24] Mechanistic fatalism, he asserted, was inimical to the essence of the socialist enterprise.

The existentialists were willing to ally with the proletariat and its party—but only under certain conditions. First, they insisted upon retaining their authenticity as petit-bourgeois intellectuals—and thus upon remaining beyond Party discipline. Second, they asked the Party to reject its Stalinist determinism and accept a philosophical perspective that recognized the crucial importance of freely and consciously created "projects"—which, it just so happened, the petit-bourgeois intellectual would play a definite role in devising.

THREE DILEMMAS

In the context of this study, the immediate importance of Sartrian existentialism lies in its widespread influence among radical students. But the political theories of the existentialists are also of interest because they provide a number of significant insights into the classical dilemmas faced by the alienated bourgeois intellectual.

The intellectual's first act of revolt is often a moral one; it frequently involves the rejection of socially accepted norms, goals, or taboos. Sartre, for example, discovered a radical freedom by denying the philosophical legitimacy of all social restraints. This denial was based on a thorough critique of the very concept of morality—a critique which seemed to banish all values to the contingent realm of the *en-soi.*

Unfortunately, this negative movement, which created freedom by destroying restraints, also made it difficult to justify any positive affirmation of freedom. Having accepted the existentialist position, one finds it hard to present objective criteria for choice or rational bases for action.*

A similar dilemma has faced many twentieth-century intellectuals. Philosophical and artistic movements which begin with an unequivocal rejection of tradition often have difficulty moving beyond their initial negativism. This is not because options are lacking; on the contrary, it is because there are *too many* options—and no firm foundation, no solid criteria that can be used to justify the choice of one option over the others. The initial critique of tradition, if it is a radical and rigorous one, almost invariably calls into question the possibility of a value foundation—the very possibility of a transcendent basis for moral choice.

At first, the discovery of freedom is exhilarating, but soon it becomes burdensome and problematic. As a result, the intellectual revolutionary often makes the transition from liberation to choice—from negative to positive freedom—through what appears to be a Kierkegaardian "leap of faith." Heidegger sought resolve in a quasi-mystical commitment to the "Right Man." Breton and Aragon turned from Dada and surrealism to Trotskyism and the Party. Likewise, Sartre found the will to act in a Marxist description of social conflict. Merleau-Ponty's interpretation of Marx, he tells us, brought him from the anguished inaction of early existentialist thought to

---

*Sartre initially denied that the existentialist critique precluded the possibility of a coherent ethical system—but he repeatedly abandoned his efforts to construct such a system. Simone de Beauvoir tried to do so in her *Ethics of Ambiguity* (1948) but subsequently admitted that this work achieved only an ambiguous success. She also reports that André Gorz, who was later to become coeditor of *Les Temps Modernes* and one of the existentialists' chief political strategists, immediately realized the ethical vacuum created by Sartre's metaphysics. "At a party in Lucerne, Sartre had met a young man called Gorz, who knew all his writings like the back of his hand and talked very knowledgeably about them. In Geneva we saw him again. Taking *Being and Nothingness* as his starting point, he could not see how one choice could justifiably be given preference over another and, consequently, Sartre's commitment troubled him. 'That's because you're Swiss,' Sartre told him." *Force of Circumstance*, p. 92.

the passionate commitment of the postwar years. "It was *Humanism and Terror* which caused me to make an important decision. . . . It gave me the push I needed to release me from my immobility."[25]

This first dilemma of the alienated intellectual might be called "the problem of choice." Its resolution lies in the acceptance of an ideology which clarifies one's situation in a manner that sanctifies decisive action.

This is not to suggest, however, that existential Marxism is merely an "inauthentic leap." Sartre and Merleau-Ponty tried to interpret Marxism in a manner that preserved their original commitment to the belief that all men should be regarded as autonomous centers of consciousness. In doing so they hoped to provide a basis for the *positive expression* of freedom, that at the same time incorporated their concept of the *negative essence* of freedom—that is, individual liberty. The future Communist society would be a "realm of freedom"; it would be a community of real, concrete liberty for all, achieved through the mutual recognition of man by man—that is, the universal recognition and respect for man's capacity for free and independent choice. By virtue of this ultimate ethical objective, Marxist theory allowed Sartre and his disciples to affirm in a positive manner the radical freedom discovered in their initial act of intellectual rebellion.

Existential political thought also reflects a more practical dilemma, one which emerges from the unequivocal rejection of the bourgeois order. The alienated intellectual tends to define his role as an intellectual in terms of his condemnation of bourgeois life. The bourgeois person is typically portrayed as dishonest and deluded. He uses words to disguise the reality of his existence; his moral convictions serve to mystify and thus preserve the inequities of the existing order. The authentic intellectual, on the other hand, is often defined as one who uses words to criticize, to lay bare the essential configuration of his situation and guide his subsequent attempts to transcend or change it.

By defining himself in sharp opposition to the bourgeoisie, the alienated intellectual places himself in opposition to capitalist society. But as an intellectual, as a user of words and a pursuer of clarity, he can do virtually nothing to alter this society. He soon discovers that intellectual revolt, by itself, is an impotent rebellion. Little is accomplished through words, declarations, manifestos, and satirical attacks. "For a long time I took my pen for a sword," Sartre confesses; "I now know we're powerless."[26]

To succeed in his rebellion, the intellectual must ally himself with a powerful, antibourgeois force. In other words, to overcome this dilemma of powerlessness, he must throw in his lot with the proletariat and its party. Only the actual political practice of a social class can bring his words to life and give his thoughts a concrete, objective existence. According to Simone de Beauvoir:

> Ideologists of the right have explained (Sartre's) alliance with the Communists by psychoanalytical jargon. . . . What nonsense! The masses were behind the Communist Party; socialism could triumph only through the Party. . . . The universality to which he as a bourgeois intellectual aspired could be bestowed on him only by the men who incorporated it on earth.[27]

Consequently, the proletariat often provides the alienated intellectual with a sort of metaphysical construct which permits him to theoretically resolve certain dilemmas that emerge from the manner in which he defines his situation as an intellectual.

However, a third dilemma arises as his theoretical conception of the proletariat comes into conflict with the stubborn realities of working-class politics.

The existentialists, for example, justified their cooperation with the PCF by arguing that (1) the proletariat was the only true revolutionary class in modern society; (2) in France the majority of the working class supported the Communist party; and (3) the Party, by virtue of its commitment to Marxism, pursued correct goals, even if its tactics were questionable. According to Merleau-Ponty:

> We have the same values as the Communists. . . . We may think that they compromise them by incorporating them into today's Communism, but they still remain ours, while on the contrary, we have nothing in common with the majority of Communism's enemies. . . . Whatever its crimes, the Soviet Union has this enormous advantage over bourgeois democracy: revolutionary aims.[28]

It could not be denied, however, that the actual practice of the Party was radically contradictory to the existentialist moral vision. Simone de Beauvoir says of Sartre:

> What he held against them most of all was treating people as things; if you didn't believe in their right to freedom, in their judgment or their good will, then individuals weren't worth bothering about.[29]

The class struggle was supposed to actualize freedom and bring about the mutual recognition of man by man. Yet freedom of discussion—usually the liberty most prized by the intelligentsia—was virtually absent in the Party. In addition, the news of Stalin's forced-labor camps cast grave doubts on the hypothesis that the Soviet proletariat would introduce the universal recognition of man's humanity.

It also became apparent that the Party used words in much the same manner as the bourgeoisie—to hide the often unpleasant reality of its activities. Just as the court intellectual is an apologist for the ruling class, the Communist intellectual appears to be the apologist for the elite that rules the Party. As far as Sartre was concerned, the Party and the bourgeois intellectuals were frequently indistinguishable. "The most generous of them," he says of the postwar Communist writers, "had given themselves to the Party, which had restored to them everything: a family, monastic rule, a tranquil chauvinism, respectability. The day after the war this youth went mad with pride and humility. It found its pleasure in an orgy of obedience."[30]

The first two "dilemmas of the alienated intellectual" pushed Sartre and his followers toward an alliance with the working class. "We had to affirm," Simone de Beauvoir tells us, "in spite of our solitude, that we were marching at their side, at the side of the working class."[31] The third dilemma kept them from consummating this alliance by joining the PCF. Sartre wanted to be "an intellectual dedicated to the revolution without compromising himself as an intellectual."[32]

FELLOW TRAVELING

At first the existentialists tried to surmount these dilemmas by setting up independent Marxist organizations. During the Resistance, Sartre,

Merleau-Ponty, Simone de Beauvoir, and Jean Pouillon joined to form "Socialism and Liberty." After the war they cooperated with other leftist intellectuals to establish the Rassemblement démocratique révolutionnaire.[33]

Both of these initiatives failed, largely as a result of the unrelenting hostility of the PCF. The intellectuals soon realized that they lacked both the skills and the resources to construct an effective mass organization. Launching a political party proved considerably more difficult than writing a treatise on ontological phenomenology.

Sartre came to appreciate the realism and competence of the Party leaders. Thorez and Duclos were indifferent to ethical niceties and ignorant of the subtleties of metaphysics, but they undoubtedly possessed a definite aptitude for organizing, inspiring, and guiding the working class. After comparing the professionalism of the PCF campaigns with the amateurism of their own efforts, Sartre and his followers reluctantly decided to defer to Communist leadership.

Unable to establish a third force, the existentialists assumed the roles of critical fellow travelers. In their journal, *Les Temps Modernes,* they generally supported the Party line but continued to maintain a cautiously critical posture. They supported the Soviet-led peace movement, condemned the American "invasion" of Korea, and opposed the Marshall Plan. But they also published articles on the Soviet prison camps and repeatedly criticized the "dogmatism" of dialectical materialism.

An attempt was made to reach a modus vivendi with the Party. The existentialists wanted the right to set forth ethical critiques of Party practice and philosophical critiques of its ideology; but at the same time, they were generally willing to accept the practical, day-to-day guidance of the politburo. According to Simone de Beauvoir, Sartre felt that "Communist sympathizers should play a role outside the Party similar to that played within other parties by the opposition, a role which combined support with criticism."[34]

Unfortunately, an understanding of this sort was unacceptable to the Party. For reasons outlined in the previous chapter, no ideological criticism could be tolerated. The proletarian leadership insisted on exercising ultimate authority on moral, metaphysical, and even epistemological issues. Documents on the prison camps were labeled "vile slander" and Sartre's efforts to existentialize Marxism were dismissed as "hopeless bourgeois idealism."

Sartre responded with considerable restraint. Unlike Raymond Aron, he refused to be driven into the enemy camp. He pursued what he considered to be a middle course between intellectual purism and unprincipled submission. He rejected Camus's position of aloof moralism, but he also rejected the servile collaboration of Kanapa and Garaudy. He cooperated—at times; and he criticized—to a certain extent.

Sartre's course of action has often been criticized as indecisive and compromising. But it was a comprehensible and perhaps justifiable one—given the immediate realities of French politics and the eternal realities of the alienated bourgeois intellectual's situation.

The revolutionary intellectual must affirm his freedom, but he must also preserve it. He rejects the bourgeois order, but he accepts the fact that he himself is its product. His heritage, his upbringing, and his style of life invariably set him apart from the worker and the proletarian Communist. He realizes that unless he comes to terms with an effective social force, he will never be able to actualize his own normative vision. He also respects the experience and expertise of the professional politician. But, at the same time, he refuses to surrender principle to efficacy. He insists that the practical politician recognize the importance of both philosophical perspective and ethical considerations. Action that is not guided by sound ideas is just as superfluous as a correct idea that can never be translated into action.

Reconciling these conflicting realities is as difficult as finding a mediating term between the *pour-soi* and the *en-soi,* as difficult as discovering the illusive intersection between the purity of consciousness and the heavy opacity of being.

3 A Year of Transition: 1956

From 1946 to 1956 Sartre and the *Temps Modernes* group adhered
closely to Party policy. After the outbreak of the cold war, every
attempt was made to combat the devisive effects of anticommunism
so that the French left could form a united front against the colonial
wars in Indochina and North Africa.

In 1956, however, the unity of the left was subjected to a number
of serious strains. In January, Pierre Hervé, one of *l'Humanité*'s leading journalists, broke with the Party. In a book entitled *La Révolution et les fétiches* (1956), he attacked the PCF's "dogmatic intellectual style" and attempted to expose the general "degeneration"
of its theory. As an example of the latter, he cited Maurice Thorez's
theory of "the absolute pauperization of the working-class," in which
it is argued that the worker's standard of living inevitably declines
as capitalism develops. In 1955 this theory seemed to be blatantly
contradicted by the fact that the French proletariat possessed more
cars, appliances, and TV sets than ever before. Hervé regarded theoretical incompetence of this sort as inexcusable. To guard against
dogmatic errors, he demanded that the Party leadership become
more responsive to criticism from the base.

In addition, he set forth an alternative to the strategy then being
pursued by the PCF. He reread the texts of Marx and Lenin, emphasizing the passages which seemed to favor a peaceful road to
socialism. Stressing the absolute necessity of avoiding a nuclear war
between the United States and the Soviet Union, he concluded that
the goal of violent revolution might have to be set aside in certain
countries, including France. He argued that instead of fighting for
an abrupt seizure of power, the Party should strive for reforms which
were "provisionally inapplicable in the present political situation"
but which could serve to "push the struggle forward." By virtue of
their attraction for the masses, these reforms would help the Party
assemble the political base necessary to secure their actual implementation.[1]

The PCF found Hervé's ideas just as objectionable as those of Sartre.
Six leading intellectuals were mobilized to discredit his book. The
style of their arguments is typified by a remark of Guy Besse: "Mr.
Dulles could not find a more docile commentator."[2]

It is interesting to note that the *Temps Modernes* group also criticized Hervé's assault upon the PCF. In the eyes of Sartre and his colleagues, Hervé's attack was exceedingly ill-timed. It disrupted the current efforts to nurture an atmosphere favorable to a united front.

Nevertheless, when taken together, the theses of Sartre and Hervé provided the basis for what later came to be known as French "revisionism." Sartre contributed the ethical component: the concern for moral principles and socialist humanism. Hervé contributed the strategic aspect: the concept of Communist revolution through the gradual reform of structures.

The Party's ability to fight revisionist critiques was severely hampered by the Twentieth Congress of the Communist Party of the Soviet Union. In February 1956, Khrushchev made a series of pronouncements on the "peaceful road to socialism" and "peaceful coexistence" that seemed to legitimatize the essential aspects of Hervé's program. In addition, the Soviet leader's firm attack on the excesses of Stalinism seemed to lend support to Sartre's concept of an ethical Marxism.

The PCF was deeply committed to Stalinism. Thorez's ideological, strategic, and tactical policies were, in most cases, faithful imitations of those of the Soviet leaders. Thorez could not condemn Stalin without calling his own past into question. Consequently, he was extremely reluctant to follow the guidelines set forth at the CPSU's Twentieth Congress.

Nevertheless, it was difficult to disregard the example set by Krushchev. Within the PCF the leading role of the Soviet Union was an inviolable principle. As a result, cautious steps toward liberalization were initiated. *La Nouvelle Critique* published articles critical of the Party's position in the Lysenko controversy; and a retreat was made on the question of socialist realism in the arts.[3] At the Fourteenth PCF Congress in July, a number of reforms were discussed, although few were subsequently put into practice.

These mild concessions to self-criticism and open debate might have satisfied the intellectuals had it not been for the dramatic events of the fall. The hopes which had been raised by the CPSU's Twentieth Congress were cruelly shattered by the Russian invasion of Hungary.

Sartre abruptly ended his uneasy courtship of the Party:

> From every point of view, the intervention was a crime. It is an abject lie to pretend that the workers are fighting side by side with Soviet troops. . . . What the Hungarian people teach us with their blood, is the complete failure of socialism as a merchandise imported from Russia.[4]

He attacked not only the Soviets but also the French Party. In a special issue of *Les Temps Modernes* on the revolt in Hungary, he wrote:

> For our part we have engaged in dialogue with the Communists for twelve years. At first fiercely and then in friendship. But our aim has always been the same: to collaborate as much as possible, in establishing unity among leftist groups which alone can save our country. Today we return to the opposition for the simple reason that there is no alternative. Alliance with the Communist Party as it is and intends to remain can have no other effect than compromising the last chance for a common front.[5]

As far as Sartre was concerned, the PCF's support of the Hungarian invasion represented clear evidence of its stubborn refusal to de-Stalinize. "The structure of the Party is in flagrant contradiction to its policies; consequently, the latter remain inoperative and unrealistic."[6]

The year 1956 marked a decisive split between the radical existentialists and the Party. As Sartre moved away from the PCF, however, he moved closer to Marxist theory. After studying the theories of historical materialism and Marxist economics, he modified his original conception of human freedom. He began, he tells us, "to feel the physical weight of his chains."[7] In his *Critique de la raison dialectique* he attempted to adapt existentialist thought to the general framework of Marxist social and historical analysis.

This double movement is highly significant. During the second half of the fifties, one discerns a progressive divergence between Marxist thought and the established Communist movement. Intellectuals had defected before, now, however, they left the Party but retained their commitment to a socialist moral vision and their faith in the efficacy of the Marxist method. The PCF was no longer regarded as the only legitimate embodiment of Marxist theory. *Praxis* was possible outside the Party, and, indeed, many intellectuals began to argue that it was possible *only* outside the Party.

THE EXODUS

On November 7, 1956, four Communists—Claude Roy, Roger Vailland, J.-F. Rolland, and Claude Morgan—joined Sartre and Simone de Beauvoir in signing an open letter that denounced the use of tanks and guns to "break the revolt of the Hungarian people and its will to independence."[8] On November 21, a second letter of protest was written, and its signatories included some of the PCF's most prestigious intellectuals: Picasso, Besson, Marcel Cornu, Wallon, Pierre Lazz, and Hélène Parmelin.[9] Aimé Caesar, the poet of *négritude,* angrily resigned as a Communist deputy from Martinique. In 1958 two of the Party's leading philosophers, Jean-T. Desanti and Henri Lefebvre, also left the Party.

Despite this unrest among its intelligentsia, the PCF made no concessions. Garaudy accused Sartre of "proud individualism" and warned the other intellectuals not to attempt to "turn the party into a debating society." Servin reinforced the warning: "We will not tolerate and the working-class will not tolerate the action of termites who try to undermine the Party from within."[10]

The intellectual opposition evoked almost no response among the Party's proletarian rank and file. François Fejto assumes that the leaders of the PCF "were strongly helped by their appeal to the traditional reflexes of the workers, expressed in this simple argument: since the Poles and the Hungarians are applauded by the bourgeoisie, they must be traitors to Communism."[11] In addition, the anti-Soviet demonstrations which followed the invasion of Budapest were frequently led by the virulent anti-Communists of the extreme right. Anyone who sided with these "vicious proto-Fascists" could be accused of aiding and abetting the most execrable of the class enemies.

While failing to arouse the workers, the intellectuals did win considerable support among the student clientele of the PCF. In the spring of 1957, the Communists at the Sorbonne launched the *Tribune de Discussion,* an opposition journal with apparent Trotskyist sympathies. This activity caused Servin to complain of the laxity and indiscipline prevalent among the 1,000 Communist students in Paris;

he called for less arguing in Party cells and more action. Thorez responded to the student unrest with open anti-intellectualism. "The best," he said, "is not necessarily he who speaks the best or he who knows the best." [12]

THE COMMUNIST STUDENT

In July 1956, after the Twentieth Party Congress of the CPSU but before the Hungarian invasion, the PCF restructured its youth organization, dismantling the Union de la jeunesse républicaine de France (UJRF) and creating in its place the Union de la jeunesse communiste de France (UJCF). The latter was intended primarily for working-class youth; it was announced that a separate organization for students, the Union des étudiants communistes de France (UEC) would hold its constitutive congress after the universities opened in the fall. Probably as a result of the crisis surrounding the Hungarian events, the congress was not held until March 1957. At its founding the UEC claimed to contain 2,000 members, about 1,500 of whom were Parisians. It was made up of university cells, student members of the Party, and the "circles" from the old UJRF.

Some have argued that the PCF created these new structures in order to isolate the student dissidents from the parent Party so the students would not corrupt the workers. According to Trotskyist oppositionists within the UEC:

> The Union of Communist Students was created by the leadership of the PCF to regulate the violent conflicts which had developed in the student cells over the problems of de-Stalinization after the Twentieth Party Congress. In dissolving the opposition into a mass organization, the Party leaders succeeded in isolating it from the regular Party structures. [13]

An examination of the history of the PCF's youth organizations calls this interpretation into question. The restructuring which occurred in 1956 was essentially a return to the pre-Word War II state of affairs, in which the students were mobilized in the Fédération des étudiants communistes and the young workers in the Fédération des jeunesses communistes, both of which were established in 1921.

These organizations had grown significantly during the popular front phase: from a combined membership of 3,500 in 1933 to 100,485 in 1936.[14] After the Liberation, the Party apparently decided to exploit the success of its "frontist" organizational strategy. It consolidated its two youth groups into the UJRF, which was designed, according to *l'Humanité*, to mobilize "les masses les plus larges."[15] It seemed that the Party hoped to create a vast "popular front of youth" analogous to the Combattants de la paix or the Confédération générale de travail (CGT). It would welcome all "patriotic youth" of a "republican" persuasion, regardless of specific political or religious affiliation—but would, of course, be controlled by a Communist fraction.

For a brief period the UJRF succeeded in fulfilling its assigned function. In 1946 it boasted 300,000 members. But as the PCF moved into political isolation during the late forties, its membership rapidly declined. By 1956 it claimed only 35,000 members.[16]

As early as 1951, elements within the Party felt that the amorphous popular front movement should be abolished and an overtly Communist organization established. Roger Garaudy, in a report to the politburo, wrote: "In 1945 . . . the national spirit overshadowed the class spirit, consequently, it was possible to organize large popular masses in great unity movements such as the National Front." Garaudy argued, however, that by the early fifties the situation had reversed itself. The class spirit now had the upper hand. As a result, the UJRF was no longer a functional form of organization. "Before the war we had more members in the Communist Youth than now in the UJRF. . . . In order to reverse this movement, in order to reawaken enthusiasm, it is necessary that the name correspond with the content. It isn't necessary to put old wine in new bottles. There is a prestigious name, with a great heritage of struggles. . . . It is the name 'Communist Youth.' "[17]

The Party rejected Garaudy's suggestion and continued its efforts to build a broad, popular front structure. At the Fifth Congress of the UJRF in 1955, the organization was encouraged to deemphasize its political character and to increase its membership by "responding to all the preoccupations of the young." It was suggested, for example, that dances be held to attract new recruits. "Dances," Guy

Ducoloné declared, "are one of the favorite distractions of the youth. The UJRF must satisfy this need the same as all the others."[18]

But even fun and games failed to transform the UJRF into a viable popular front organization, and the Party was eventually compelled to accept the Garaudy position. On May 25, 1955, *l'Humanité* frankly stated that the UJRF had failed in its efforts to become a true mass organization. It simply did not attract non-Communists. Georges Rubrola concluded that the youth movement should openly proclaim and pursue its specifically Communist goals.

> As far as I can see, the UJRF is only an organization of young Communists and Communist sympathizers. If this indeed is the case, then I see no reason not to give it back the name "Union of Communist Youth."[19]

The First Congress of the new organization was held on December 14, 1956. It was emphasized that the UJCF was not to concern itself with sports, games, patriotism, or dances. It would concentrate on Communist political action. Marcel Cachin told the delegates:

> Work with all your energy for the definitive victory of Communism in our country of France, so that we, your elders, might have the joy, before we die of entering the promised land with you.[20]

Henri Martin declared that there were no exclusively "youth" problems—there were only class problems. Consequently, the UJCF and the PCF had to be closely linked to one another. "Without the Party, the young people of our country would be defenseless in the face of the propaganda of the exploiters."[21]

The stress on the overtly Communist nature of the UJCF reflected the Party's decision to abandon its efforts to create a massive youth front. The failure of this effort had been noticed as early as 1951, and the final decision to restructure was apparently made in 1955. It is therefore difficult to argue that the new format was created specifically in reaction to the outbreak of student oppositionism in 1956.

Yet in one sense, this decision does indicate that a certain malaise existed among the younger comrades. As Rubrola points out, the only people who entered the UJRF were avowed Communist militants. They joined in order to engage in Communist political action, they apparently resented being denied recognition as Communists. It would also seem that they resented the fact that they had been assigned to the secondary, bridge-building function of creating an amorphous coalition of patriotic and republican youth. Rather than ally with the bourgeois democrats, they wanted to share the vanguard tasks of the working class.

The decision to create a separate organization for students also seems to have been a reaction to the dissatisfaction of the Party's university clientele—but not simply the immediate dissatisfaction aroused by the Twentieth Congress of the CPSU and the events in Hungary. Communist strength in the university community had been steadily declining since the end of the war. In 1946, 25 percent of the students at the Ecole Normale were members of the PCF; by 1956 only 5 percent were members. The Communists have always felt that the way to increase their strength among a given clientele is to appeal to the interests and aspirations peculiar to that group. To show that it was specifically concerned with student problems, the Party established a special student organization, ostensibly devoted to the struggle for larger university budgetary allocations, the construction of more university restaurants, and similar objectives.

It must be remembered that the utility of the student Communist is different from that of the young proletarian. The student is viewed as a potential Marxist-Leninist intellectual. Consequently, a special organization is needed to develop the skills and attitudes that the Party feels its intellectuals should possess. The statutes of the UEC made it clear that the Party was no longer interested in using its students to further popular front objectives. Article 2 stated that the organization was to combat "all forms of bourgeois and petit-bourgeois ideology, especially the ideology of the social democrats"; in addition, the UEC was to remain vigilant against the "obscurantist undertakings inspired by the Vatican." In other words, little emphasis was to be placed on overtures to the SFIO or to the progressive Catholics.

In his address to the First Congress of the UEC, Thorez made it clear that these bridge-building functions were to be superseded by educational ones. In essence, the UEC was to become an ideological training program.

Thorez began his discourse by enumerating the "evils" of the contemporary world: the dangers of war, the threat of fascism, the "decadence" of contemporary culture, etc.; then he stated that "only Marxism-Leninism can renew human society. Only it offers solutions to the questions which disturb the young."[22] He listed the basic strengths of Marxism: that it is based on a "faithful" analysis of reality; and that its tenets have been "proved" by the accomplishments of the Soviet Union. Communist theory, he said, is "the fruit of the historical development of all the sciences."[23]

After this eulogy to scientific socialism, he returned to the specific problems of the French youth: the Algerian war, the need for world peace, and the inadequacy of educational facilities. He encouraged the students to grapple with each of these problems; but he reminded them that their efforts would be doomed to failure unless they utilized the tools of Marxism-Leninism:

> In order to accomplish their great tasks, the members of the Union of Communist Students . . . will have to learn Marxism-Leninism by heart, and study the classics of our doctrine, and always be careful to link the science of socialism to their practice, reminding themselves that our theory is not a dogma, but a guide to action.[24]

Thorez concluded by pointing out that the UEC should be a twofold organization: first, a mass organization with an "independent character"; but also "an organization for the preparation of Communists, in which its members assimilate and spread the science of Marxism-Leninism."[25] On the one hand, then, the UEC was designed as a channel for student political action; on the other, it was set up as a school for potential Party intellectuals.

Thorez reconciled these two goals with the following argument. The student has certain specific problems and aspirations, which can be dealt with through political practice; Marxist-Leninist theory is the key to successful political practice; the Party is the correct interpreter of Marxism-Leninism, hence, the student must carefully study and adhere to the ideological pronouncements of the leaders of the PCF.[26]

The orthodox anti-Communist would argue, with some justification, that this was typical Communist duplicity. To the anti-Communist, the student movement is a traditional Leninist front. It poses as an articulator of student interests in order to mobilize the student masses and place them at the disposal of the revolutionary vanguard. Thus, in the "rightest" view, the UEC has an *ostensible* function and a *real* function: The first is to channel student protest; the second is to produce skilled, orthodox, and, above all, obedient Communist intellectuals. The first disguises the second.

But from the beginning the disguise was thin. The PCF made it perfectly clear that the independence of the UEC was purely formal. It was to be a typical "organization de masse communiste." During the free discussion period of the Fourteenth PCF Congress, a delegate asked if the UEC statutes would prevent the development of future discord between the student organization and the Party. One speaker even proposed an "autonomous line" for the Communist students. The leadership declared this proposition absolutely invalid. There could never be "two Communist parties," for two independent organizations would pose different slogans (*mots d'ordre*) which would inevitably confuse and disorient the masses.[27]

The statutes of the UEC make it clear that the students are expected to espouse Marxism-Leninism exactly as it is set forth by the leaders of the PCF. The UEC is described as a "Communist organization and a school for communism." Its members must "educate themselves in the spirit of democratic centralism," and "assure their unity in the struggle at the side of the working class and its Party."*

ROOTS OF REBELLION

The PCF assigns both its students and its intellectuals to secondary, functional roles. The latter have well-defined boundaries, which it is impermissible to transgress. The bourgeois theorist does not theorize; instead, he concentrates his energies on lending style and ele-

---

*See Léo Figuères, ed., *La Jeunesse et le communisme* (Paris, 1963); for a complete text of Communist student union statutes, see *Clarté,* numbers 6 and 7, March and May 1966.

gance to the authoritative pronouncements of the Party's proletarian leaders. The student is viewed as a potential Party intellectual; consequently, the primary function of the UEC is to train its members in the habit of skillfully and unquestioningly justifying the existing Party line.

Despite the unequivocal attitude of the Party elite, the role definitions of the student and the intellectual still contain disturbing ambiguities. According to the Marxist-Leninist classics, the bourgeois intellectual is basically an apologist for the ruling class, and his consciousness is permeated with its reactionary ideology. Nevertheless, both Marx and Lenin stress that certain intellectuals can guide the working class by providing it with a "clear comprehension" of the historical process.

The PCF leadership chooses to emphasize the negative side of this definition; understandably, many intellectuals prefer to stress the positive side. Sartre, for example, used his own existentialist assumptions to construct a mission for the petit-bourgeois intellectual that was remarkably similar to the one found in the texts of the movement's founders.

The proletarian apparatchiki have adamantly refused to accept any redefinition that endows the intelligentsia with a vanguard role. Within a Communist organization, political and ideological authority are intimately linked. When a philosopher of Sartre's stature questions the theoretical competence of the Party leadership, he poses a serious threat to the legitimacy of its rule. As a result, the challenges of a Sartre or a Hervé have to be energetically repulsed.

Just as the ideological expression of the intellectual's function is characterized by ambiguity, so is its institutional expression. The students and the intellectuals are mobilized in distinct, subsidiary organizations. These organizations possess dual functions. For example, the apparent role of the UEC is to help students fight for their rights and for social justice; but its real function is to prepare docile Party ideologues. Likewise, the ostensible goal of the Party journal, *Economie et Politique,* is to undertake creative analyses of the French political and economic structures; but its actual task is to document and dress up the theses of Thorez, Rochet, and Marchais.

There is little doubt that the Party originally created the UEC, its publications, Les Combattants de la paix, and its trade unions as instruments. The day-to-day tasks of these organizations were regarded as tactical objectives—and all good Marxist-Leninists know that tactics must always be subordinated to long-term, overall strategy.

But the dedicated member of the mass organization inevitably invests a great deal of time and effort in his routine assignments. As a result, he becomes committed to his organization's aims, and he tends to identify with its specific objectives. For example, Charles Tillon became so involved in the "struggle against war" that he set the Communist peace movement on an independent course, one that ran counter to the Party's aims.[28] Moreover, Party trade union officials often become so wrapped-up in their efforts to win incremental gains for their clientele that they seem to forget the basic strategic goal of the PCF—the achievement of political power. In a similar manner, Jean Pronteau, a prominent Party theorist, tried to transform *Economie et Politique* into a journal devoted to truly independent and creative analysis. Developments of this sort almost always lead to sharp conflicts within the movement. Tillon and Pronteau were both forced to resign from the Party; and many "opportunist" trade unionists have been rebuked and demoted.

The UEC has found itself in just such a situation. Its members have become extremely concerned with the need to transform the group into an effective mass organization. They have consequently set about to improve its image and revise its policies. As shall be shown in the next chapter, bitter struggles with the Party leadership have resulted.

The ambiguity of the intellectual's role and the problem of dual functions provide the basis for potential revolts against the authority of the Party's leaders. There is, however, another important basis for such revolts. Just as the PCF views its students and intellectuals in essentially instrumental terms, the alienated bourgeois intellectual frequently sees the proletariat and its party as tools that can be used to actualize his own antiestablishment normative vision.

Consequently, the intellectual's relationship with the Party is generally a frustrating one. At times, it becomes painfully apparent that the Party has little interest in realizing the lofty ethical principles of the moralist and philosopher. Instead, the Party seems to exploit

Marxist theory for its own national or organizational interests. This
appeared to be the case in 1956, when, under the cover of international solidarity, the Russians crushed the Hungarian insurrection; and
when, in the name of doctrinal purity, the PCF refused to de-Stalinize. Under circumstances such as these, many intellectuals reach the
bitter conclusion that the Party is just as "inauthentic" and "hypocritical" as the bourgeoisie.

In the postwar period, one of the ways in which one could show
one's disillusionment with the Party, but still maintain a radical posture, was to adopt an existentialist political perspective. Existentialism,
in its popularized form, became an ideology. In fact, it achieved a status
somewhere between an intellectual fashion and a passionate religion.
Sartre became a cultural hero; in the words of one student: "I became a victim of Sartrolatry; I was at once Sartrist, Sartrian, Sartro-
logue, and Sartrizing."[29]

It was probably not coincidental that between 1946 and 1956,
during the height of Sartre's influence, Party membership in the
Parisian faculties fell drastically. The PCF correctly regarded existentialism as an ideological challenge to its own official doctrine.
Sartre was therefore viewed as a corrupting influence among the
youth of France. Garaudy told him, "You are preventing people
from coming to us."[30]

Sartre was indeed a "corrupter"; both his writings and his own
career called into question the so-called dilemma of the Stalinist alternative. They suggested that one does not have to be *either* an un-
questioning adherent of the Party *or* a servile tool of Wall Street.
According to Sartre, critical independence is not only possible, but
it is also the only authentic posture that a petit-bourgeois intellectual can assume. Although he is obliged to take responsible and progressive political stands, he should not—and probably cannot—become a loyal Communist or a true worker.

Just as the students were interested in Sartre, he was also interested in the students. Both he and Simone de Beauvoir enjoyed the
freedom of student life, and both continued, well into their thirties,
to make close friends among high-school and university students.
According to Mme. de Beauvoir: "Sartre couldn't resign himself to
moving on to the age of reason, to adulthood."[31] Growing old and

becoming a responsible adult meant accepting the conventions of the hated bourgeoisie. Conversely, clinging to the bohemian style of university life meant winning at least a temporary respite from this fate. Sartre, Simone de Beauvoir, and their young acquaintances all shared a disdain for "Sunday crowds, proper ladies and gentlemen, the provinces, families, children, and all humanisms."[32]

After the war, Sartre was acutely aware of his influence among the students. In fact, his sense of responsibility to the younger generation seems to have caused him considerable anguish.[33] But in 1956 he and his followers began to view student radicalism with a new interest, for it seemed to provide a new solution to what has been referred to as the "dilemma of powerlessness."

During the Algerian crisis and the early revolts of the UEC, the student left emerged as a distinct and self-conscious social force. The *Temps Modernes* group soon realized that the revolutionary youth could be utilized as a vanguard, that is, as shock troops whose political activity could at least begin the difficult task of translating their theoretical visions into concrete political practice.

4 The Student-Intellectual Opposition

Soon after the Twentieth Party Congress of the Communist Party of the Soviet Union, the PCF began to adhere assiduously to the Khrushchevian theses of peaceful coexistence and "the peaceful path to socialism."

When he addressed the Congress, Khrushchev declared that "in certain capitalist countries, the working class, rallying around itself the peasantry and the intellectuals and all the patriotic forces, can conquer a solid majority in parliament and transform this organ of bourgeois democracy into a true instrument of the popular will. . . . This instrument, traditional in many highly developed countries, can become an organ of true democracy, a democracy for workers."[1]

Thorez wholeheartedly embraced this "rightist" revision of Marxist-Leninist theory. In 1958 he sternly rebuked the leftist opposition in his own Party, saying, "We will not let ourselves by turned away from our theses . . . on the possibility of a peaceful road to socialism or on the role that a true parliament can play, a true expression of popular sovereignty based on the masses." This appropriation of Soviet theory had profound tactical consequences. The PCF could never travel the parliamentary road to socialism unless it succeeded in effecting an alliance with the Socialist and Radical parties. Thorez therefore followed Khrushchev's advice and sought a rapprochement with the once-hated Social Democrats.

> We are ready to meet with all republicans who do not share our opinions on the necessity and certain coming of socialism in France, but who understand and admit that we have the legitimate ambition to lead the working class and the people of our country to this goal.[2]

The acceptance of this tactical stance helped determine the PCF's reaction to the Algerian war. For the Radicals and the SFIO were participating in the very governments that were perpetrating imperialist adventures in North Africa. If the PCF wanted to win the support of its republican allies, it naturally had to moderate its attacks on the war. Therefore, in 1956 the Communist deputies in the National Assembly voted to give Premier Guy Mollet's government emergency powers to deal with the Algerian insurrection. Throughout the conflict the Party maintained an equivocal position. Although it ostensibly opposed the war, it never called for victory by the National Liberation Front (FLN); it merely demanded a negotiated settlement of the hostilities.

The Party realized that many of its voters were far from "enlightened" on the Algerian question. As Raymond Guyot candidly stated, "We must recognize that one part of the working class has remained restive to our explanations; this social strata does not support our position on the independence of Algeria."[3] A sizable segment of the proletariat refused to abandon the notion that Algeria was French. The Party was therefore ambivalent in its demands for Algerian freedom. It clung to the "French Union" formula, and contented itself with insisting that "such a union must bring together free people with equal rights; it must guarantee the respect of their mutual interests; it must be based on voluntary ties and lasting friendship."[4]

In addition, the PCF obstinately refused to sanction the violent and terroristic tactics of the FLN. Thorez claimed that his objection centered around the fact that the Algerian rebels were "digging their own grave." "If the FLN thinks that it's winning public opinion, it's mistaken; it turns opinion against itself."[5] But Thorez clinched the argument by declaring that "such methods open the door to all sorts of provocations against *us.*"[6] The PCF's position was hardly one of international self-sacrifice. Thorez was demanding that the Algerians sacrifice their struggle for independence to the PCF's efforts to maintain its strength in the parliament.

This opportunism, this apparent betrayal of the spirit of internationalism, does not necessarily indicate that the PCF was no longer guided by the tenets of Marxism-Leninism. It cannot be inferred that the Party had become a pragmatic, nonideological institution. The PCF was merely putting into practice ideological criteria which had been set forth by the Moscow "papacy" as early as 1925. Thorez's treatment of the Algerian revolutionaries demonstrated that he had thoroughly internalized the logic of "building socialism in one country." As Stalin felt that the members of the Comintern should always act to defend the interests of the USSR, so Thorez felt that revolution-

aries in the French colonies should always act to defend the interests of the PCF. Obviously, Thorez's policy was based on ethnocentrism—but it was ethnocentrism that was deeply rooted in orthodox Stalinist ideology.

The proletarian leaders of the PCF obediently followed Soviet
strategic theory. There does not seem to have been any serious effort
to adapt this strategy to the peculiarities of the French situation. The
Algerian war was virtually ignored. The Party attempted to forge an
immediate alliance with the Radical and Socialist parties—regardless
of the moral and ideological implications.

As a result, the tactical choices that the Party made during the Algerian period infuriated the intellectual purists. Sartre was one of the
first to react. "In the face of the surrender of the left," he said, "we
must forge a radical position."[7] The radical existentialists stepped
forth to defend the humanist ethics and the Marxist principles that
they felt the politicians of the Party had betrayed.

The *Temps Modernes* group was merciless in its criticisms of the
government pacification program—a policy which had been instituted
thanks to Communist votes in the National Assembly. "Voilà l'évi-
dence, voilà l'horreur, la notre, nous ne pourrons pas la voir san
l'arracher de nous et l'écraser."[8] In 1957 *Les Temps Modernes* was
seized four times in Algeria; in June of that year it was seized for
the the first time in metropolitan France. While the PCF courted the
Socialists, Sartre unequivocally condemned them. In June 1957 he
published an article on the SFIO leader, Guy Mollet, entitled "He
Disgraces the Name of Socialism." In 1960 Frances Jeanson, a close
associate of Sartre, established an underground network in France
to aid the FLN.

The students soon responded to Sartre's lead. An organization
called Jeune résistance was formed to urge young men to refuse
military service. In 1960 the Union nationale des étudiants françaises
(UNEF) passed a resolution at its national congress calling for a cease-
fire and negotiations. In the same year six students were arrested for
complicity in FLN terrorism; four were UNEF activists.

Simultaneously, dissident groups began to appear within the Party.
In January 1958 *La Voie Communiste,* a new opposition paper, was
published. A few months later *La Voie Nouvelle,* a theoretical journal with a similar orientation, appeared. Two leading Communist

philosophers, Henri Lefebvre and Jean Desanti, joined Sartre in contributing articles to these publications. In May the UEC Parisian philosophy circle disseminated a text written jointly with the Socialist and Radical students. The statement reprimanded their parent parties for voting additional "special powers" to the Pflimlin government.

After de Gaulle's 1958 referendum, the Sorbonne-Lettres cell of the University of Paris issued a resolution that held the Party leadership responsible for the Party's crushing electoral defeat. It argued that the leaders had committed "very grave errors" on the Algerian question. It also censured them for their "uncritical acceptance" of Khrushchev's peaceful-road-to-socialism thesis and for their mechanistic attempts to forge an alliance with the bourgeois parties. It charged that Thorez had "resisted a genuine analysis of the French situation"; it accused him of talking about a French road to socialism but failing to "take this concept seriously." Finally, the resolution condemned the apparat for its general unresponsiveness to suggestions from the "base" and for its habit of condemning all criticisms as "coming from the enemy."[9]

The Algerian crisis created a new pattern of opposition in French politics. The student and intellectual left emerged as an independent force—one that insisted upon distinguishing itself from all established political parties, including the Communists. The existing organizational structures, both proletarian and bourgeois, were viewed as "immobile" and "sclerotic." As a result, the concept of the "avant-garde detonator" emerged. According to Francis Jeanson, the task of the radical intelligentsia was to engage in exemplary acts of militant protest, which, it was hoped, would prod the traditional forces of the left into decisive action.

Although the *Temps Modernes* group and their student followers clearly differentiated themselves from the "old left," they felt that little could be done without its active assistance. Militant action, Jeanson argued, "would make sense only in dialectical perspective, as a complement to official political action."[10] Through their "exemplary protests," the intelligentsia hoped to stimulate similar activities by the established leftist organizations.

But instead of provoking the PCF to adopt a more radical stance, the intellectuals merely caused a split in the Party. The Communist students placed themselves in opposition to the policies of the Party leaders. The dissidence of the Communist students became an echo of the dissidence of the leftist intelligentsia. The student Party members eagerly adopted the criticisms of Sartre and Jeanson; they embraced the theses of the revisionists, and set about to translate the counterstrategies of the older oppositionists into actual political practice.

This pattern repeated itself several times between 1958 and 1968. The Union des étudiants communistes became the principal arena for factional struggles within the Party. The students became the featured actors in the battles between the proletarian apparatchiki and the bourgeois intellectuals. To grasp the dynamics of this student-intellectual alliance, it is necessary to examine the twelve-year history of the UEC.

THE RIGHT OPPOSITION

From 1956 to 1958 the UEC passed through a brief "pre-opposition" phase. During these years the Communist students were generally quiescent. The UEC seemed to function as a reliable school for Communism. In 1957 the SFIO dissolved its student group as a result of its opposition to the Algerian war. Edouard Daladier, the leader of the Radicals, castigated his party's student organization for similar reasons. But it seems that the UEC was totally submissive. As Leo Figuères somewhat cynically remarked: "It is not in our camp that one sees the dissolution or condemnation of student organizations."[11]

The second phase lasted from 1958 to 1962. This was in the midst of the Algerian war, during which the PCF found itself challenged by oppositionists on both the left and the right. At the Second Congress of the UEC these factional conflicts surfaced. A minority composed essentially of Parisians fought to achieve an intensification of the struggle against both the Algerian war and the renascent, proto-Fascist organizations. But their positions were rejected as a result of the more moderate stands taken by the provincial delegates.

However, between 1960 and 1962 the UEC continued to exploit the Algerian war to broaden its base of support. In particular, it tried to establish close relations with the Union nationale des étudiants françaises. The Party leadership had ambivalent feelings about the

UEC's overtures to the UNEF. On the one hand, it was eager to politicize the student union: when the UNEF lost its government subsidy as a result of its opposition to the war in Algeria, the Communist trade unions offered generous financial assistance. But at the same time, the Party seemed wary of a UEC-UNEF alliance. In October 1960 it ordered the UEC not to participate in a mammoth antiwar demonstration organized by the UNEF. The Communist students reluctantly obeyed, but several months later their journal, *Clarté*, published an extensive interview with the UNEF president. Much to the Party's displeasure, the editors failed to preface the article with a critical commentary distinguishing the UNEF's views from those of the Communists.

In its efforts to ally itself with the student union, the UEC began to deemphasize certain aspects of the Party program. The apparat was extremely displeased with this development. At the Sixteenth Congress of the PCF in 1961, Paul Laurent accused the UEC delegates to a recent UNEF conference of succumbing to an opportunist attitude toward economic planning. The delegates, he pointed out, had made no effort to criticize the "nefarious character of the motion of general orientation, which in fact supported the idea that economic planification was possible under a Gaullist regime."[12] Roger Garaudy also attacked the students for misinterpreting the results of the CPSU's Twentieth Congress by overemphasizing the de-Stalinization aspect of Khrushchev's speech and failing to pay sufficient attention to the positive achievements of the USSR. In addition to being disturbed at the overwillingness of the students to reach agreements with non-Communist groups, the Party was also annoyed at the UEC's tendency to "underestimate the class struggle" and "overestimate the conflict of generations."

The leaders of the student organization succumbed to Party pressure. Jean Piel, the UEC's secretary-general, admitted that his policy toward the UNEF had been erroneous.

It put a one-sided emphasis on the need for Communist students to participate in mass organizations successfully, without underlining the importance of educating our members in the spirit of Marxism-Leninism.[13]

In essence, Piel was apologizing for placing the ostensible function of the UEC above its real function. By trying to cement an alliance with the UNEF, he was attempting to engage the UEC in an effective mass organization. But in so doing, he weakened its ability to educate its members in the "true principles" of PCF ideology. He failed to inculcate the student Communists with the essence of democratic centralism, namely, the necessity to forcefully and obediently justify the Party line.

After 1960 the problems posed by the UEC oppositionists became complicated by the emergence of divergent trends within the world Communist movement. As long as international communism maintained its monolithic façade, discipline was relatively easy to maintain. The working class was viewed as a single, organic entity; it was represented by an indivisible international movement which had one, universally applicable line. Anyone who opposed this line placed himself against the working class and, hence, against the will of history.

As has been emphasized, to strengthen discipline within the PCF, its leadership continually stressed the infallible nature of decisions emanating from the Soviet Union. There was no greater defender of monolithism than Thorez. But, ironically, after the Twentieth Congress of the CPSU his attitude began to undermine the autocratic powers of the PCF leaders. Since Thorez had been an undeviating Stalinist, the condemnation of Stalin brought his own past into question. Yet he could hardly challenge Khrushchev's position, for Stalinism posited the leading role of the Soviet Union as a basic, unquestionable tenet. Therefore, if Moscow declared that Stalinists were scoundrels, all good Stalinists had no recourse but to agree.

In 1960 elements within the PCF apparently took advantage of this situation to challenge the hegemony of Thorez. According to Fejtö, Laurent Casanova used his position as PCF representative at the World Peace Conference to "slip into Soviet ears" rumors of Thorez's anti-Khrushchev and pro-Peking tendencies. He and his fellow politburo member, Marcel Servin, also supposedly used their friendship with Soviet Ambassador Vinogradov to accuse Thorez of "sabotaging," by his systematic opposition to Gaullism, "all possibilities of a 'national' policy for France."* The Russian "papacy" was thus enlisted in an effort to dethrone Thorez.[14]

It is interesting to note that the supporters of Servin and Casanova were almost all bourgeois intellectuals. One of the brightest rebels was Jean Pronteau, editor of *Economie et Politique.* He took advantage of the conflict to chart an independent course for his journal. Instead of merely documenting and dressing up the official positions of the PCF leadership, he began to present original and innovative interpretations of the existing economic and political situation. He rejected Thorez's notion that de Gaulle was not really a nationalist, since the general was "objectively" the tool of "cosmopolitan, internationalist monopoly capital." Instead, *Economie et Politique* interpreted de Gaulle's nationalistic hostility to the United States as a manifestation of significant contradictions *within* the world capitalist camp.

Unfortunately, the leadership refused to accept Pronteau's efforts to reassume the creative, critical functions of the original Marxist intellectual. He was denounced by the central committee in July 1960 and removed from his post. In January 1961 the editor of *France Nouvelle* suffered the same fate.

By 1961 Casanova had managed to win the support of between fifteen and twenty-one "intellectual" members of the central committee. Besides Pronteau, the group is said to have included the poet Louis Aragon, the physician, Jean-Pierre Vigier, and the writers Jean Kanapa and André Stil. The positions of these young revisionists were soon adopted by elements within the UEC. *Clarté* began to echo the Casanova line, and in the midst of the factional struggle, the journal's editors had the audacity to publish an article by Aragon which described Casanova as "advisor and defender of the French intellect." Vigier, who virtually controlled the Party's university cells, had little difficulty in mobilizing the clientele to support the "anti-Party group."

---

*For a conflicting account of the "Servin-Casanova Affair," see Jacques Fauvet, *Histoire du Parti Communiste Français*, vol. 2, pp. 311-17. Fejtö's reports of possible Soviet "intervention" should perhaps be interpreted with caution, since he is a Hungarian emigré, works for the pro-regime French Press Agency, and has the reputation of a "cold warrior."

Ultimately, the efforts of the oppositionists were thwarted. But it took Thorez approximately a year and a half to restore discipline. The struggle revealed deep-seated divisions within the Party, antagonisms which could not be easily resolved. The conflict was not, as some have suggested, a generational battle. The old, proletarian leaders like Thorez and Duclos were joined by young, working-class protégés like Georges Marchais, 39, an ex-steelworker, and Roland Leroy, 33, a former railroad man. Their opponents, on the other hand, were almost all of bourgeois origin, including both the 63-year-old Aragon and his 20-year-old student comrades. In essence, the Servin-Casanova affair was a battle between the Party's working-class leaders and its bourgeois intelligentsia.

Until the late fifties the latter had been almost totally excluded from the Party's inner circle. No sooner had several bourgeois intellectuals been admitted to the central committee, however, than they joined in a conspiracy to unseat the proletarian establishment. This lesson has certainly not been lost on Thorez's successors. The Party's working-class leadership was once again reminded of the intellectuals' persistent "usurpation" impulse. And it was also reminded that the intellectuals' most constant allies are to be found in the bourgeois university community.

The Servin-Casanova affair also illustrates the difficulty which the leadership had in imposing discipline, given the divergent tendencies within the international Communist movement. Thorez could no longer excommunicate his opponents on the grounds that their oppositionism placed them outside the world Communist community. The student-intellectual alliance may have strayed from the orthodox line of Thorez, Molotov, Ulbricht, and Novotny, but its positions appeared quite consistent with those of Tito, Togliatti, and even Khrushchev. This placed Thorez in a dangerous dilemma. He could not defend his legitimacy on the grounds of his undeviating loyalty to the Soviet Union while simultaneously ousting the "Khrushchevites" within his own Party.

THE ULTRA-RIGHT

In 1962 the UEC again took advantage of the divided nature of the world Communist movement to reassert its independence from the

PCF. In February, many statements of Palmiro Togliatti and Giorgio Amendola, two PCI leaders, and numerous articles from the Party's youth journal, *Nuova Generazione,* were circulated and discussed in UEC circles, apparently under the benevolent eyes of the organization's leaders.[15]

By the time the Sixth Congress of the UEC opened in January 1963, the pro-Italians had managed to take complete control of the organization. The Congress wildly applauded the Italian delegation, while the official representatives of the PCF sat with their hands crossed. The applause turned into a standing ovation, and the delegates on the floor booed the PCF representatives and demanded that they join in.

The Congress then approved an unabashedly revisionist, Italian-inspired program that proclaimed that the ideology of the Communist movement had become completely distorted by Stalin. "The dogmatic and mechanistic deformation of theory which dominated the Stalin epoque has considerably harmed research and the production of Marxist works." The UEC thus joined Hervé and Sartre in condemning the "simplistic dogmas" of the working-class ideologues and in simultaneously calling for a complete revision of Marxist theory. The Congress also demanded more internal Party democracy. It supported the Italian thesis that different tendencies be allowed to co-exist within the Party.

Italian colonization of the UEC represented a serious threat to Maurice Thorez. In 1956 Togliatti had proposed the doctrine of "polycentrism," according to which the Communist movement could not be led by a single center but rather must be led by a proliferation of regional centers. Moscow represented the natural center for Slavic communism; Havana for Latin American communism; Peking for Asian communism. And, if one followed the logic of Togliatti's arguments, one was led to the conclusion that Rome was the natural center for European communism. Thorez could hardly have looked upon this conclusion with equanimity. The PCI's growing influence within the UEC undoubtedly appeared to be the first step in the "Romanization" of the French Communist party.

The oppositional activities of the UEC rightists provided a good illustration of the general pattern of student dissidence. First, the themes set forth were essentially reflections of those previously formulated by rebellious intellectuals. In this case, the intellectuals were primarily French revisionists, who had been influenced by Togliatti and the Italian Communist party. The *Temps Modernes* group figured prominently in this regard. Sartre and his followers were largely responsible for popularizing the ideas of the Italians. "If I were in Italy," Sartre has said, "I would join the PCI."[16] His magazine frequently printed articles by Togliatti, Amendola, and Giancarlo Pajetta. And Sartre, in turn, has made a number of contributions to PCI reviews and periodicals.

It is not surprising, then, that Sartre gave his blessing to the UEC revolt. In 1964 he, Simone Beauvoir, and several other Parisian intellectuals participated in a UEC-sponsored colloquium on the "functions of literature." The purpose of this event was to raise money for *Clarté*, which the PCF was trying to starve out of existence.

The November 1964 issue of *Clarté* contained a most comprehensive statement by the *italiens* of the UEC. It was entitled "An Open Letter to the Central Committee of the French Communist Party." Like most student and intellectual dissidents, the student revisionists placed a strong emphasis on the theoretical inadequacies of the PCF leaders. The open letter completely rejected Thorez's contention that the reign of Stalin was either a transient period of "socialist illegality," or "a simple departure from principles." Instead, it argued that Stalinism was a serious *ideological deviation*, which had managed to permeate the entire world Communist movement. As a result, the strategies of both ruling and nonruling Communist parties had been adversely affected.

> For the offensive strategy of Leninism which includes tactical retreats, Stalin substituted the retreat and the "status quo" as the general line not only of Soviet diplomacy, but also of all the various Communist parties; the latter have tended to form themselves into impregnable citadels, in imitation of the Soviet state.[17]

From this general critique of the Stalinist party, the open letter passed to specific attacks on Thorez's alleged theoretical blunders. It argued that his analysis of the existing economic and political situation was totally inadequate, since it rested on the monotonous repetition of certain simplistic Stalinist formulas (for instance, "the imminent crisis of capitalism" and "the absolute pauperization of the working-class"). Armed with these hopelessly outmoded concepts, Thorez was incapable of dealing with such innovations of neocapitalism as wage-price guidelines and central planning. These developments— according to the students—called for original and creative contributions to Marxist theory.

Like most dissident intellectuals, the UEC rebels buttressed their critique of Party theory with "a true Communist strategy." The students began from the assumption that a Bolshevik-like seizure of power had become inconceivable, for the prevailing situation "is not revolutionary in the classical sense which Lenin gave to this word." Since a sudden, cataclysmic revolution was not a realistic possibility, a gradual evolution toward socialism was the only acceptable strategic alternative. The UEC therefore suggested that the Party set forth a series of "intermediate democratic objectives," which would (1) rally larger and larger segments of the population behind the PCF; and (2) objectively bring France closer and closer to socialism.

In this respect, the students' program resembled the classical revisionism of Bernstein and Hervé. But the UEC added an Italian innovation. The *objectifs démocratiques* of the Communist trade unions, said the UEC spokesmen, should be "worker's self-management" or "autogestion." The open letter quoted approvingly the strategic aims of Bruno Trentin, one of the PCI's leading theorists.

> One of our fundamental goals should be the conquest of workers' autonomy (in terms of revenues, of qualifications, of trade union prerogatives) in relation to their particular enterprises and to the conduct of business carried out there.[18]

Thus, the Party would fight on two independent fronts: economic and political. While its trade unions were struggling for autogestion, the Party itself would fight for basic structural reforms such as nationalization schemes and *planification démocratique.* These specific proposals would be set forth as integral parts of a program of profound social, political, and economic changes, which could be fully consummated only as the nation evolved into a truly socialist society. Thus, UEC strategy did not imply simple "reformism"; on the contrary, the "objectives, no matter how partial they might be," would "pose the necessity of the democratic and socialist transformation of the nation."

This strategy was virtually identical to that propounded by André Gorz, a disciple of Sartre and a co-editor of *Les Temps Modernes.* Both juxtaposed a trade union struggle for workers' self-management with a political struggle for structural reforms. Both argued that the natural result of these programs would be a gradual evolutionary movement toward socialism. Gorz's book *Stratégie ouvrière et néo-capitalisme,* [19] was published in 1964, several months before the appearance of the open letter. As usual, the dominant trends in student oppositionism were "reflections" of the dominant trends in intellectual oppositionism.

One of the immediate goals of the UEC strategy was to enlarge the base of the Party's support—to win bourgeois sympathizers. Without them, a Communist electoral victory would be impossible. The open letter therefore called for a forceful popular front policy. The UEC saw itself as a vital, vanguard element in this policy. It argued that if the working class were to win control of the French state, it had to demonstrate that it was interested in more than simply improving its own economic well-being. It had to prove that it was capable of governing society as a whole. An ideal way for it to do so was to present a comprehensive reform program for the educational system—which serves *all* elements of society.

> Educational reform—isn't that an excellent territory where the working class could show its capacity to manage all national problems in a manner conforming to the general interests of the country?[20]

The UEC argued that it was ideally suited to carry out the fight for "democratic reform" of the educational system. But in order to fulfill this function, it claimed that it needed autonomy, for the necessity of adhering to the Party line seriously inhibited its tactical flexibility. For example, in 1958 UNEF put forth a demand for *allocations d'études,* which were government subsidies for individuals engaged in higher learning. This proposal was enthusiastically welcomed by the great mass of French students. But the Party ordered the UEC to oppose it on the grounds that workingmen's taxes should not be used to finance the education of rich *fils de bourgeois.*

The UEC also argued that the dominantly bourgeois university provided the Communists with a perfect environment in which to forge links with progressive elements of the middle class. But it complained that the PCF constantly interfered when the UEC attempted to initiate cooperative projects with non-Communist groups. The UEC demanded real autonomy so that it could effectively carry out its role as an "organization de masse indépendent."

The open letter argued that the UEC's program should cease to be a simple echo of the Party line; instead, different tendencies should be allowed to coexist within the organization. The UEC should be allowed to adopt as its own those proposals democratically selected by a majority of its members. The students totally rejected their submissive, secondary position. They declared their firm intention to play an independent and vanguard role in the struggle for socialism.

After the publication of the open letter, 100 Communist intellectuals sent a sympathy letter to the influential *Le Monde.* They argued that the student crisis was "the expression in student quarters of the general malaise which French Communist intellectuals, on the whole, have felt for several years." The *Le Monde* letter underscored the fact that Stalinism was largely responsible for this "malaise," in that it had rendered the Party's decision makers generally unresponsive to criticism from the base. In the future, it argued, the elaboration of doctrine should be the object of "large discussion."[21]

Student and intellectual dissidence had become intimately fused. While revisionism was au courant among the Parisian intellectuals, student oppositionism took on a decidedly rightist flavor. The PCI became the "ideal party" to the Communist student.

But intellectual fashions change quickly, and Sartrian revisionism soon found itself passé. In 1964 a new fad emerged. Bernstein ceded to Trotsky, and Rome was replaced by Peking. The patrons of the Café Flore stopped discussing autogestion and structural reforms and turned instead to the more exciting themes of left-wing Communism.

THE LEFT OPPOSITION

At the Seventh Congress of the UEC, a new group of dissidents appeared. A motion calling for internal party democracy was introduced not by an *italien* but by Alain Krivine, a leader of the left opposition. "It is necessary," he stated, "that the Congress say yes or no to the question of whether it is possible for Communist minorities to express themselves in the UEC. . . . Yes or no, have the French Communists broken with Stalinist practices?" On this issue, the left and right stood united. Both defended the sacred principles of socialist democracy against the "unprincipled" Stalinists of the PCF apparatus.

But during the Congress the leftists made it perfectly clear that they opposed the essential strategic orientations of both the PCF and the *italiens.* Krivine predicted that the newly elected leadership of the UEC would effect no significant changes. "Inactivity will be just as great with the leadership elected by the majority as it was with the old National Bureau."[22] The leftists therefore circulated a tract in which they promised to intensify their efforts to lead the PCF back onto the "true revolutionary path." The reformist aspects of the new leadership would, it was claimed, become increasingly evident in the coming months; consequently, Krivine promised to initiate a new phase of oppositional activity.

Indeed, the period from 1965 to 1968 represents the final phase of the UEC's history, the phase dominated by the left and the ultraleft. What immediately distinguished the left oppositionists from the right oppositionists were their respective attitudes toward the Party's popular front strategy. While the revisionists thought this strategy should be more forcefully pursued, the *gauchistes* adamantly condemned it. In January 1966 Krivine's *secteur* (Sorbonne-Lettres) publicly attacked the PCF for endorsing the presidential candidacy of François Mitterrand. This cooperation with the bourgeois socialists was viewed as an unforgivable betrayal of revolutionary principles.

But the motivations of the right and the left seemed markedly similar. Both felt frustrated and unfulfilled. The revisionists were annoyed because the Party would not let them play a vanguard role in the creation of an effective popular front; and the leftists were annoyed because the Party would not allow them to participate in what they considered true revolutionary activity. For example, the Party condemned the militantly antiwar Front anti-fasciste universitaire (FAU) as vanguardist and adventurist. The FAU had succeeded in organizing almost 8000 Parisian students who opposed the Algerian war. Nevertheless, the Party refused to support the Front and ordered its militants not to participate in FAU demonstrations. According to the leaders of the Sorbonne-Lettres section, the FAU, "because it was sabotaged by the Party," was "a powerful revelation of the Stalinist direction of the Party and a decisive element which carried the crisis to a higher stage in its development."[23]

Like the revisionists, the *gauchistes* echoed themes already voiced by dissident intellectuals. But Krivine and his followers found their inspiration in the traditional heroes of the *opposition de la gauche.* Soon after its dissolution, the Sorbonne-Lettres section joined with dissidents from Cannes, Rouen, and Caen to form a new organization, the Jeunesse communiste révolutionnaire (JCR). The delegates at the JCR's First Congress "sat in front of the portraits of Engels, Marx, Lenin, Rosa Luxemburg, and Trotsky."[24] The JCR was essentially Trotskyist in its orientation. It seems to have been closely linked with the French section of the Fourth International, the Parti communiste internationale. The JCR's secretary-general, Alain Krivine, was a member of the International's politburo. Of the other eight members of the JCR executive committee, it is known that at least one is a member of the International's central committee.[25]

The contemporary intellectual guru of the leftists is Ernest Mandel, one of the triumvirate which directs the official Trotskyist movement in Europe. Mandel is a highly respected socialist scholar who has written numerous books and articles on Marxist economics, politics, and revolutionary strategy. In May 1968 he was invited to Paris to help lead the "revolution." After addressing the young radicals on May 10, he is rumored to have enthusiastically pushed his own car into a barricade on the Boulevard St. Michel. His appeal to student leftists undoubtedly rests on his eagerness to combine Marxist theory with revolutionary action.[26]

Like almost all student and intellectual dissident groups, the JCR began its attacks by questioning the theoretical competence of the

PCF leaders. It put forth the Mandellian argument that by rejecting Trotsky's theory of the permanent revolution and by accepting Stalin's theory of "building socialism in one country," the international Communist movement had set itself on unstable ideological foundations. In the JCR's view, Stalin's policy kept foreign Communist parties from evolving theoretical and strategic solutions appropriate to their own settings. Instead, it made them into mere pawns of Soviet diplomacy.[27] The prime goals of foreign parties did not entail "making revolution" but, rather, looking out for the interests of the USSR. According to the JCR, the PCF based its tactical choices not on correct analyses of French conditions but on directives from Moscow. Hence, after Khrushchev's development of the peaceful coexistence doctrine, Thorez responded by transforming the French Party into a peaceful, social-democratic movement.

Since they were ardent Trotskyists, the JCR militants maintained their faith in the revolutionary character of the working class. "The increasing divergence between the policies of the PCF and the spontaneous consciousness of the working-class tends to make the Communist party particularly vulnerable." According to the JCR, the bureaucratic structures of the Party will inevitably be bypassed by the instinctual revolutionary will of the proletariat. The JCR strives to prepare for this event by constructing the groundwork for a truly revolutionary organization. It feels that the youth are ideally suited to this task; since they have not "submitted to the glorious hours of Stalinism . . . they are particularly receptive to the development of the world revolution."[28]

The Jeunesse communiste révolutionnaire thus stands and waits. It feels that someday the working class will rise in spontaneous revolt; and when this fateful day comes, it feels that it must be ready with at least the foundations of a true revolutionary organization.

During the Algerian war, another Trotskyist organization had emerged, the Comité de liaison d'étudiants révolutionnaires (CLER). Its founders were the sons of Pierre Lambert, the head of the Organisation communiste internationale, a factional offshoot of the French section of the Fourth International. CLER sought to substitute revolutionary action for the revolutionary verbiage of the UEC and the JCR. It transformed approximately 300 Parisian students into well-equipped commandos, trained in judo and karate,

and prepared to participate in "véritables expéditions puni-
tives."[29]

Trotskyism provided the CLER and the JCR with strategic perspectives radically different from those of the Sartrian revisionists.
While the rightists envisioned a long, gradual, evolutionary path to
socialism, the Trotskyists anticipated an imminent revolutionary
situation.

On the eve of the May revolution, CLER* commanded cadres of
revolutionary storm troopers who were ready and eager for violent
action. The JCR, too, had a tightly knit revolutionary organization,
with agents in a number of factories. Unlike other Marxist groups,
it was fully prepared for the May uprising—for like all good Trotskyists, it assumed that the proletariat was always on the verge of a
massive, spontaneous outburst.

THE ULTRA-LEFT

In addition to having to deal with the student "trots," the Party
also had to confront the challenge posed by the pro-Chinese professors of the Ecole Normale Supérieure. In 1960 Louis Althusser
and a number of his enthusiastic followers began to publish a series
of articles which seriously questioned the theoretical basis of the new
popular front strategy. The chief target seemed to be Roger Garaudy,
who was, at the time, the Party's chief ideologue. In his recent writings, Garaudy seemed to have appropriated a great deal of Sartre's
thought. Both concentrated on the humanistic works of the young
Marx; both emphasized Marx's Hegelian background, his ethical
values, and his analysis of alienation. Both also stressed the Marxist-
existentialist notion that man is, above all else, a "creative being,"
who "makes his own history."

Garaudy fulfilled the typical popular front duties of the Party intellectual. He strove to make communism appealing to the sympathetic bourgeoisie. His *De l'anathème au dialogue* (1965) was essentially an attempt to convince the progressive Catholic that Marxists
are basically benevolent, humanistic reformers. He repeatedly stressed

---

*Renamed FER—*Fédération des étudiants révolutionnaires.*

that both the Party and the Church were committed to the same fundamental goals and the same human values.

His next book, *Marxisme de XXe siècle* (1966) seemed to be directed primarily at the bourgeois intellectual. In it, Garaudy emphatically rejected the rigid dogmatism of the Stalinist era; and he exorcised socialist realism, intolerant atheism, and mechanistic determinism. In addition, he argued the necessity of assimilating the positive contributions of existentialism and structuralism into modern Marxist theory.[31]

Louis Althusser and his colleagues set about to destroy the theoretical basis of Garaudy's popular front overtures. In "Surdétermination et contradiction," Althusser tried to show that the Marxist concept of the dialectic has literally nothing in common with its Hegelian counterpart.[32] In "Sur le jeune Marx," he attempted to demonstrate that the economically oriented, mature Marx repudiated most of the notions of the ethically oriented young Marx.[33] In "Marxisme et humanisme," he argued that Marxism had virtually nothing in common with the humanistic conceptions of the existentialists and the progressive Catholics.[34] In *Lire le capital* (1965) he strongly suggested that the structuralism of Lévi-Strauss cannot be reconciled with the Marxist notions of dialectic and contradiction.[35]

In the opinion of many French intellectuals, the rigor and brilliance of Althusser's work make Garaudy's efforts look exceedingly dilettantish. If one were to apply the criteria of logical consistency, faithfulness to texts, and general erudition, one would have to concede that Althusser put on a superior intellectual performance.*

Nevertheless, at a special 1966 meeting, the central committee vindicated the revisionist line and sternly reprimanded Althusser. Garaudy's approach was accepted not because it was theoretically superior, but because it was tactically more useful. By opening a Christian-Marxist dialogue, for example, Garaudy had significantly

---

*See Annie Kriegel's judgment in *Le Socialisme Français et le Pouvoir,* pp. 211–12. For other accounts of the Althusser "affair," see François Fejtö, *The French Communist Party and the Crisis of International Communism,* pp. 202–04, and François Furet, "The French Left: from Marxism to Structuralism," *Survey,* January 1967. For a critical view of Althusser and his followers see Raymond Aron's *Marxismes Imaginaires.*

increased the PCF's potential vote. The pious Frenchman would no longer view the Party as the embodiment of the devil—for the Archbishop of Paris would certainly never let his priests enter into a dialogue with the Prince of Darkness. For many Frenchmen, voting Communist might soon become a viable possibility.

The Garaudy-Althusser affair illustrates once again the secondary, subordinate role of the bourgeois theorist. Creative theoretical activity no longer guides strategic and tactical decision making. Instead, theory is used to justify and facilitate the execution of a predetermined political line.

It is interesting to note, however, that Althusser was not completely condemned. He served a functional popular front role, and, since his brilliance was widely recognized, he was extremely useful as a prestige symbol. The central committee therefore recommended that he continue his work as a specialist in philosophy but that he avoid controversies with strategic and political implications.

The Party's reaction to Althusser bears close examination, for it gives us some interesting insights into the basis for the Party's persistent fears of the bourgeois intelligentsia. The aspect of Althusserism that the PCF found most disconcerting was his bifurcation of science and ideology. The Party itself usually draws no such distinction. It claims to be the true vanguard of the working class because it is guided by the "scientific ideology" of Marxism-Leninism. This ideology is scientific in that its principles are continuously subjected to empirical verification—and affirmed, rejected, or revised accordingly. In *Marxisme du XXe siècle,* Garaudy defines the scientific method of Marxism in the following manner:

> The materialist moment of understanding according to Marx and Lenin is dominated by empirical criteria (the criterion of practice), the experimental verification of our theories, of our models, alone can guarantee to us, in the last analysis, that our conceptual construction corresponds to an objective reality.[36]

But Althusser seriously questions this conception. The Marxist scientist, he argues, is not an empiricist; the empirical method is a bourgeois mode of inquiry, an intrinsic part of the capitalist ideology. The empiricist is deluded when he conceives of himself as a dispassionate subject objectively viewing material reality. The specific problems to which he chooses to address himself are determined by his "problematic," that is, the structure, or the underlying, unconscious configuration of the ideology that he has internalized. This structure also determines "what he sees;" in other words, it posits the symbolic formations that guide and distort his empirical perceptions.

The capitalist mode of production has a corresponding ideology; this ideology contains certain notions and categories: profit, rent, interest, wages, etc. But the inner structure of capitalism can never be grasped in terms of these ideological categories. For the very purpose of an ideology is to disguise and "mystify" the exploitive nature of the capitalist system. To comprehend the essence of this particular mode, Marx rigorously criticized these ideological notions, and through his theoretical practice he transformed them into scientific categories: exchange value, surplus value, price of labor, organic composition of capital, etc. Using these categories, Marx was able to construct the structure underlying all capitalist systems.

Althusser's theoretical-scientific method has no place for the empirical experimentation of political practice. Althusser does not build models and test them through their practical application in the real world. His conclusions and theories are justified on the basis of criteria internal to his theoretical practice—not by external criteria borrowed from political practice. Rather than compare himself to an applied physicist or chemist, Althusser compares himself to a mathematician.

> No mathematician in the world expects that his theorems have to be applied by the physicist before they are declared verified by the facts. The truth of its theorems are completely furnished by the internal criteria of mathematical practice. . . . We could say the same of all the sciences.[37]

Althusser's definition of "science" seems to represent, in its purest form, the bourgeois intellectual's challenge to the proletarian apparatchik.

Garaudy clearly recognized this; for in one of his latest books, *Peut-on être communiste aujourd'hui*? (1968), he condemns this conception unequivocally by pointing out that it suggests that "ideology is good enough for managing the masses, but that theory should be reserved for the technocrats of philosophy."[38] In other words, in Garaudy's view Althusserism seems to lead invariably to a form of intellectual elitism. The outlook of the ordinary man is always polluted by the prevailing ideology. To rise above this ideology, one must possess certain theoretical skills—for one must be capable of mastering the rigorous methodology of pure theory.

Althusser states that "Marxist philosophy is one of the indispensable theoretical weapons in the proletariat's class struggle."[39] All Communists agree: a clear theoretical comprehension of existing conditions must inevitably precede the making of tactical choices. But Althusser implies that this theoretical comprehension can be achieved only by the professional logician—the militant thoroughly trained in the *science* of Marxist-Leninist thought. Who then is more capable of formulating a strategy for the working class—Waldeck Rochet, a former Burgundian peasant, or Louis Althusser, a brilliant scholar of Marx?

The threat posed by Althusser was enhanced by the fact that he had become the nominal leader of a faction that strongly criticized the current Party strategy. Althusser was identified with the leftist tendency within the PCF. He apparently agreed with the Maoist contention that the peaceful-road-to-socialism thesis was opportunistic. But his oppositionism was discreet. He obeyed the principles of democratic centralism and never publicly attacked the Party's policies. Likewise, the Party itself did not acknowledge his oppositionist position. One must, therefore, infer the general character of his views from oblique hints. For example, in one of his latest books, Garaudy argues that Althusser's theories "risk becoming the foundation of political adventurism."[40] One cannot help but notice that Althusser's writings are sprinkled with numerous allusions to the theories of Mao Tse-tung.[41] Since the present PCF leadership is Moscow's most ardent supporter in the Sino-Soviet split, such references are hardly politic.

And although Althusser never publicly attacked the Party leadership, his disciples did. His most ardent followers were his students at the Ecole Normale Supérieure. In 1964 the cercle d'ulm of the UEC undertook a study of Marxist theory under the leadership of Althusser. Gradually, the group adopted a leftist, pro-Chinese position. But the students apparently decided to follow the example of their teacher and observe strict Party discipline. Thus, although they deplored the Party's support of Mitterrand, they refused to oppose it openly. When in 1965 the PCF summarily dissolved the leftist Sorbonne-Lettres section of the UEC, the Althusserites merely pointed out that this action was contrary to the organization's statutes. They issued no formal objections and even went so far as to condemn the rebellious section for violating the sacred norms of Party life.

But when, in March, the central committee partially vindicated Garaudy and reprimanded Althusser, the cercle d'ulm could no longer contain its revolutionary indignation. Althusser's students came to his defense by publishing a brochure, "Faut-il réviser les théories de Marx?" Widely circulated in the ranks of the UEC, this brochure attacked the PCF leadership in a style that Annie Kriegel calls "charming in its poetic irreverence, but atrocious in its dry and arrogant disdain."[42]

The arrogance is particularly apparent in the Althusserites' insistence upon the prime importance of their own preoccupation: the rigorous, disciplined study of Marxist scholarship. Their opposition to the PCF leadership seemed to rest in large measure upon the latter's neglect of theoretical tasks. They tell us that from 1964 to 1966 the entire Ecole Normale Communist "circle" was united on a number of propositions, including "the recognized importance of theoretical work and theoretical education" and "the absence of theoretical work in the PCF and its general ideological degeneration." They also agreed on the need to struggle against "Garaudyism" or, as they put it, "the struggle against revisionist, humanist and eclectic ideologies which are gaining more and more influence in the organizations of the French Communist party."[43] (In fact, the struggle against "Garaudyism" seems to have taken precedence over the struggles against both the bourgeoisie and the capitalist state.)

The Althusserites' admiration for Mao appears to have grown almost inevitably out of their intense preoccupation with theoretical and ideological problems. During the initial period of the Sino-Soviet split, the theoretical writings of Mao and his *Red Flag* comrades were infinitely more sophisticated than the "goulash Marxism" espoused by Khrushchev. The Althusserites therefore came to support the "theory and practice of the revolution in China, the laws of ideological transformation, and the cultural revolution put into practice in China."[44]

It is hardly surprising that the Althusser followers found the "great proletarian cultural revolution" extremely attractive. It subordinated all tasks—even the construction of a socialist economic base—to the maintenance of the revolutionary purity of Marxist theory. The prime goal of both the Althusserites and the Maoists was to effect a thoroughgoing ideological revolution. Both argued that basic political and economic changes cannot be brought about until the masses have been thoroughly permeated with true Marxist-Leninist principles.

In October 1966 the left oppositionists succeeded in provoking a general crisis within the UEC. Eight Parisian militants issued an appeal. "Réjoignons le mouvement communiste français (marxiste-léniniste)." The MCF(ML) was France's new "official" pro-Chinese organization. It received both ideological and material support from Peking.* Two bureaus of the UEC responded to the appeal. The Parisian lycée sector and the Amiens sector went over to the MCF (ML) en masse.

But the Althusserites continued to agitate within the UEC. In the summer of 1966 the cercle d'ulm formed a clandestine underground to seize control of the student organization. Members of this underground rebuked the MCF(ML) for encouraging students to break openly with the UEC.

> The eight resignations of the members of two Parisian sections of the UECF have rendered more difficult the organized struggle of Marxists in these organizations. They risk disorganizing the struggle in the lycée section at a decisive moment.[45]

When the UEC leadership became aware of the factional activities of the pro-Chinese, they initiated another mass purge. Four circles

---

*Evidence of Peking aid can be found in *France Nouvelle,* 21 juillet, 1965; *l'Humanité,* 17-7-65; and *Cahiers du Communisme,* September 1965. The PCF journals reprint a report from the Swiss government register that on June 19, 1965, the Swiss sureté arrested three leaders of the Fédération des cercles marxistes-léninistes. According to the Swiss, they had visited the Chinese embassy and had received political instructions, documents, and $600 (US).

were dissolved, including the cercle d'ulm. During October and November some 600 students were exluded.

In December many of these *exclus* joined together to form the Union des jeunesses communistes (marxistes-léninistes). The UJC(ML) refused to merge with the MCF(ML)—which seems to have been composed largely of working-class defectors from the PCF. The students apparently had a very low opinion of the theoretical capabilities of these proletarian Marxists and therefore stated that "the moment to create a new Communist Party has not yet come." They retained their autonomy and continued to expend most of their energies in an almost scholastic preoccupation with theoretical tasks. The official pro-Chinese organization responded by labeling the Althusserites "a nest of young intellectuals totally cut off from social reality."[46] As Jean-Luc Godard shows in *La Chinoise,* this description is not altogether inaccurate.

The Maoists of the university community thus manifested the usual characteristics of student dissidents: disgust with the Party's "theoretical ineptitude"; disillusionment over the PCF's betrayal of "revolutionary principles;" and a general tendency to echo the theses set forth by their adult intellectual mentors. But their strategic alternatives were definitely unique. As a result of Althusser's influence they placed an inordinate importance on theoretical practice. Until the May revolt, the Maoists seem to have spent most of their time polemicizing against their enemies and polemicizing among themselves.

But Mao's teachings also left their mark. The young Althusserites invested a startling amount of hope in the revolutionary potential of the French peasantry. After the outbreak of the spontaneous farmers' strikes in 1967, they predicted that the coming revolution in France would be fought largely by peasant guerrillas. In the wake of the abortive revolt of 1968, the Maoist students decided to spend their summer vacations on a so-called long march. They took to the countryside, intent upon explaining the May uprising to the "revolutionary" peasants (whose votes had just given de Gaulle an overwhelming endorsement.)

GENERAL PATTERNS OF STUDENT DISSIDENCE

Certain distinct patterns underlay the activities of the various student opposition groups. First, each group was composed largely of protégés of prominent bourgeois intellectuals. Piel's clique responded to the initiatives of Casanova, Aragon, and Pronteau; the *italiens* were disciples of Togliattism—as interpreted by Sartre and the *Temps Modernes* group; the left opposition was Trotskyist—its contemporary mentors being Frank and Mandel; and the ultra-left was Maoist—its guru being Professor Althusser of the Ecole Normale Supérieure.

The students and the intellectuals were brought together by mutual frustrations. The Communist philosophers, sociologists, and economists hoped to make original contributions to Marxist-Leninist thought. They wanted to engage in creative and innovative activity. But the Party's proletarian leadership constantly relegated them to secondary and seemingly insignificant tasks. Instead of acting as critical theorists, the intellectuals were forced to act as blind, obedient servants.

The students suffered a similar fate. Ostensibly the UEC was designed as an effective channel for student protest. But when the group tried to take steps to transform itself into a forceful articulator of student demands, the Party strenuously objected. For these steps often conflicted with the UEC's "duty" to unquestioningly justify the Party line.

The students were continually thwarted in their efforts to improve their organization. Piel was unable to forge an alliance with UNEF; the *italiens* were denied autonomy; the leftists were condemned for creating the FAU; and the Maoists were discouraged from carrying out their theoretical and ideological work.

One of the major causes of the rebels' discontent was their frustration at being assigned secondary roles. Consequently, the students expressed their displeasure by attacking the primary group, namely, those responsible for their continued subjugation. Both the revisionists and the leftists among the students began by denying the theoretical competence of the PCF leaders. According to the right, Thorez was hopelessly caught up in Stalinist dogma; as a result he was incapable of carrying out the reforms initiated by Khrushchev. According to the left, Thorez and Rochet had sold out to Khrushchev: the PCF had succumbed to Moscovite revisionism and had lost its revolutionary character.

In both cases, the student dissidents were not only following the initiative of prominent intellectuals, but they were also echoing their specific criticisms. The *italiens* of the UEC repeated the position of

Sartre: they spoke of the "déformation dogmatiste et mécaniste subie à l'époque de Staline." The *chinoises* repeated the criticisms of Althusser. They spoke of the "dégénerescence idéologique" of the PCF and attacked the "idéologies électiques, humanistes, et révisionistes."

The intellectuals affirmed their theoretical superiority by setting forth counter-theories and counter-strategies. While Gorz revised Hervé's theory of "reform communism," the Maoists attacked the "voie parliamentaire" and substituted a policy of guerrilla warfare. Frank, Mandel, and their fellow Trotskyists clung to the old-fashioned concept of a massive, spontaneous working-class uprising.

Each of the so-called groupuscules was designed to carry out one of these strategic alternatives. The FER, JCR, UJC(ML), and ESU were all action-oriented—but, at the same time, they were all guided by certain definite ideological convictions. The oppositionist students therefore established organizations intended to translate the intellectual's theories into concrete political practice.

5 The Party's Response to Its Critics

The Party leadership's traditional response to internal dissidence is perhaps best illustrated by its struggle against the *chinoises.*

Althusser and his followers are only the most recent of a long series of bourgeois intellectual critics who have periodically stepped forward to challenge the hegemony of the Party's proletarian leadership. Like their predecessors, the pro-Chinese students have failed to create serious dissension in the ranks of the PCF. They remain a small and relatively isolated groupuscule. If the Party viewed the threat posed by the UJC(ML) in an objective manner, it would probably dismiss this tiny cabal without comment. But the Party does not look at any political entity objectively; it views all social phenomena through the perceptual structure provided by Marxism-Leninism.

When Rochet perceives his Althusserian opponents, he does not see a numerically insignificant clique of fanatics; he sees a dangerous faction capable of formulating serious theoretical challenges and, thus, capable of articulately challenging the legitimacy of his authority.

In 1966 Rochet was so disturbed by the Althusserian position that he published a short book in which he attempted to refute it. In *Le Marxisme et les chemins de l'avenir* he concentrates his attack on the elitism which he and Garaudy argue is implicit in Althusser's theory.

> In his work *Lire Le Capital* Comrade Althusser explains that in order to be scientific, a theory must be verified by purely internal criteria, such as those that are applied in a mathematical demonstration, so as to be beyond all ideology.
>
> It seems that according to this conception, Marxist theory must be elaborated and developed by specialists in philosophy, well trained in abstract reasoning, but without any real ties with social practice.[1]

According to Althusser, only the rigorously trained theorist can manipulate the intricacies of Marxism. Since Communists base practice on theory, this would seem to imply that only a highly educated intellectual elite is capable of making strategic decisions for the working class. But according to Rochet, this consequence of Althusser's logic immediately invalidates his theory, for elitism is clearly contrary to the egalitarian and democratic basis of socialism. Hence, Rochet uses the Socratic dialectic to disprove Althusser's argument.

To strengthen his stand, Rochet turns to Garaudy's political empiricism. Theoretical hypotheses, he argues, must be validated through revolutionary practice. The competence of an empiricist depends largely on his skill as an experimenter. If his concepts have been subjected to extensive and exacting tests, they are apt to be sound and practicable. It is obvious that Waldeck Rochet—a professional revolutionary for thirty years—has conducted far more "experiments" than Louis Althusser, who has rarely ventured beyond the Rue d'ulm. By clinging to Garaudy's notion of *praxis,* the proletarian revolutionary is trying to vindicate his right to rule.

Althusser tries to avoid the accusation of "interfering in politics" by drawing sharp distinctions between theoretical, ideological, and political practice. Each, he argues, involves the transformation of qualitatively different objects or raw materials into distinct finished products. In each case, the tools or elements through which the actual process of transformation occurs arrange themselves into distinct, qualitatively different structures.[2]

The theorist, for example, works upon ideological notions of society; by using the scientific structure of his methodology, he transforms them into concepts, which permit us to grasp the objective reality of social existence (the "real-concrete"). Political practice, on the other hand, works upon the existing relationships among social classes; it creates new relationships by leading a particular class in its struggle to achieve hegemony within the political, ideological, and economic regions of society.

Althusser admits that the various forms of transformation are related to one another. For example, *one* of the tools employed by the vanguard party is Marxist-Leninist theory. The Communist party directs the class struggle in accord with the scientific principles of its doctrine; the latter guides the leaders of the proletariat in their efforts to destroy old social structures and create new ones. But although they are related, these forms of practice are said to be relatively autonomous. Each works upon distinct objects, each uses distinct tools, and each produces a distinct type of finished product. In addition, the different structures within which the various forms of practice occur all posit their own criteria—upon whose basis the finished products are judged and evaluated. In short, the politician has no right to use the criteria of political practice to judge the products of intellectual practice; likewise, the theorist has no right to employ the criteria of pure, scientific practice to evaluate the strategy and tactics of the vanguard party.

By creating a relatively autonomous realm of activity called "theoretical practice," Althusser tried to bring into existence a sphere of action in which the student and intellectual members of the PCF could freely and creatively expend their intellectual energies without arousing the hostility of the political apparatus. The leaders of the Party, however, refused to accept this compromise. Althusser was forced to criticize himself for failing to recognize the "intimate connection of theory and practice."[3] Within the Communist movement, theory and ideology are—and always have been—the formal and traditional foundations of political legitimacy. Consequently, Althusser's claims to scientific expertise in the field of Marxist-Leninist theory were perceived by the PCF leaders as a serious threat and challenge.

Until this conviction is overcome, until the apparatchiki construct new bases for their legitimacy as a ruling elite, the activity of the Communist intellectual will continue to be subjected to close scrutiny. Since the death of Thorez in 1964, the Party has engaged in a partial liberalization process; it is significant that neither Garaudy nor Althusser was immediately expelled for his heresies. But within the ideological sphere, this liberalization will be contained within definite limits until the close psychological association between theory and authority is broken.

Within the PCF, this association is complicated by the leaders' apparent sense of inferiority—a sense which seems to emerge from their lack of formal education, their working-class roots, and the assertiveness and articulateness of their bourgeois intellectual opponents.

This innate feeling of cultural inferiority is disguised through the dogma of the proletarian ideology. For example, when the Party set out to discredit Althusser, it immediately resorted to a crude theory of sociological determinism. Rochet demonstrated the "unreliability" of his opponent by examining Althusser's social origins.

In his *Chemins de l'avenir* (1966), Rochet questions Althusser's bifurcation of science and ideology by introducing the distinction between bourgeois and proletarian ideology. The first, he argues, is invariably unscientific. By virtue of his social and economic role, the bourgeois ideologue lives in a world of illusion and mystification. His consciousness is necessarily false. But since the scientific principles of Marxism-Leninism have thoroughly permeated the working-class movement in France, an antithetical state of consciousness has arisen: the scientific proletarian ideology. The Communist worker—fully conscious of the realities of both his situation and his historical mission—has achieved true consciousness. Rochet concludes: "If all ideology has a class character, this does not mean that all ideology is false. The essential thing is to know what role the class in question plays in the development of society."[4]

In the last analysis, one's world outlook depends upon his class background; hence, although Althusser's theories are clever, they are nevertheless suspect. Rochet's theories, on the other hand, although simplistic, are fundamentally reliable. Althusser, in a thinly veiled self-criticism, was forced to accept this position. In the April 1968 issue of *La Pensée* he admitted:

> It is not easy to be a Marxist-Leninist philosopher. A professor is a "petit-bourgeois," as is any intellectual. When he opens his mouth, it is the petit-bourgeois ideology which he speaks; his resources and tricks are infinite.[5]

RITUALISTIC RESPONSES

The Party's treatment of Althusser can be viewed as a ritualistic response produced by the dogmatization of Marxist theory. The proletarian who is usually unaccustomed to operating on a high level of abstraction, tends to reduce Marxism-Leninism to a set of concrete, often simplistic formulas.

This is not to imply that the process of simplification is inevitably bad, or that it always leads to distortions. But to the bourgeois intellectual and to the academic Marxist, the process almost invariably appears as a brutal vulgarization.

However, it could be argued that the radical reduction of ideology is a necessary product of the movement's growth. The French Communist party, for example, has constructed an immense apparatus, staffed primarily by what Fejto calls "administrative types of working-class origin." The concepts of Marxism have had to be adjusted to the needs and the capacities of those who man it. The average functionary, recruited from the mines and factories of France, is rarely theory-oriented. In all probability, he finds the illusive abstractions of *Capital* far less appealing than the clear, pedagogic formulas of Stalin's *Short Course.* Consequently, the development of the Party's organization is accompanied by the simplification— or, if one prefers, the dogmatization—of its theory.

Marx said that ideas become powerful social forces once they have permeated the minds of the masses. It is difficult, however, to permeate mass consciousness with three 600-page volumes of obtuse observations about nineteenth-century British capitalism.

Hence, the Bolsheviks drew the pragmatic distinction between theory, propaganda, and agitation. One of the primary tasks of the professional revolutionary, according to Lenin, was to translate the scientific insights of Marxism (theory) into readable pamphlets (propaganda) and inspiring slogans (agitation), which could be used to gradually raise the level of mass consciousness.

Over time, however, this threefold distinction was swallowed up by the all-inclusive term "ideology." One of the reasons for this has already been repeatedly stressed: the proletarian apparatchik's reluctance to accept the identity of a mere propagandist or agitator, whose task it is to actualize the high-powered theoretical discoveries of the bourgeois intelligentsia.

But the triumph of "ideology" can also be attributed to its new organizational functions. Within a hierarchical bureaucracy characterized by an intricate division of labor, doctrine fulfills many useful roles. First, it maintains the morale of the functionaries and militants, who spend virtually "the whole of their lives" working on dull, routine tasks. It transforms these tasks into essential elements of a sacred mission. Second, its schemas and paradigms provide the decision maker with a tremendous sense of self-confidence. When confronted with a confusing welter of social "data," the ideologically initiated Communist feels he is on top of the situation; he can employ his doctrine as cognitive map to chart a path through the complex economic and political problems.

Third, ideology helps maintain the unity and cohesion of the Party's far-flung organizational empire. Upon the diverse tactical objectives of its various subsystems, ideology imposes a clear and distinct set of overriding strategic imperatives. Fourth, the simplistic formulas of ideology provide an organizational code that facilitates communication among the various levels and branches of the Party's hierarchy. When the politburo publishes a declaration on page 1 of *l'Humanité* calling for vigilance against "adventurist provocations," Communist cadres all over France immediately know what sort of activities they should initiate. This terse statement is, in effect, an instruction to (1) begin an intensive campaign in all cells and mass organizations directed against prevailing non-Communist ideological notions; (2) cease contacts with outside groups; and (3) "clean house," that is, restore internal unity and discipline.

Within the PCF the "reduction" of Marxist-Leninist theory has meant the creation of a limited number of simple, dichotomous constructs endowed with strong, unequivocal value signs: $A(+)$/ non-$A(-)$. Constructs of this sort have many advantages. They are easy to comprehend and internalize; they generate a clear, crisp picture of the world of experience; and they provide the believer with a precise and unambiguous identity concept.

For the French Communists, Marx's and Lenin's complex and highly sophisticated concepts of class, consciousness, and ideology have all been reduced to a single, clear-cut formula. The bourgeoisie is a reactionary class; the proletariat is a progressive one; consciousness reflects the material conditions and the social roles of the classes,[6] hence, the bourgeois ideology is false and the proletarian ideology scientific. "Bourgeois ideology (bad)/proletarian ideology (good)."

The acceptance of this formula has obviously been encouraged by power-struggle patterns within the Party. It permits the proletarian apparatchik to immediately discredit challenges put forth by the bourgeois intelligentsia. One need only look at the manner in which the Party responded to the criticisms of the *italiens*. After the Sixth Congress of the UEC, Roland Leroy published an article in *l'Humanité* in which he pointed out that "only about thirty sons and daughters of workers were delegates to the last congress."[7] In light of their social origins, Leroy argued, it was thus hardly surprising that the delegates adopted positions contrary to the interests of the working class. In their open letter (see previous chapter) the *italiens* expressed great displeasure over this antibourgeois prejudice. They decried the concept "whose aim is to present the intellectual, the militant, as the unconscious plaything of his origins, of his ideological past; which results in reintroducing into Marxism the concept of original sin."

It is also interesting to note that the PCF leaders who denounced the *italiens* seemed to automatically assume that attacks on the specific policies of the Party leadership were simultaneously attacks on the PCF as a whole *and* the working class. According to Roger Garaudy, the program of the UEC's Sixth Congress "departs deliberately from the positions of the working class, the Party and of Marxism-Leninism."[8] This instant identification of the Party and the proletariat is made possible by the reduction and simplification of a second paradigm posited by Marxist-Leninist theory: the theses used to justify democratic centralism.

Originally, this Leninist concept was the dialectical resolution of a complex matrix of contradictions which plagued the revolutionary socialists in early twentieth-century Russia. Democratic centralism was designed to resolve the contradictions between the democratic aims of the socialist movement and the autocratic nature of Russian society; between the need to create a mass movement and the need for secrecy created by Tsarist police methods; and between the revolutionary potential of the proletariat and its "primitive state" in Russia. After the revolution, the Bolsheviks no longer faced this particular set of contradictions. Nor were these contradictions necessarily relevant to the Communists of Germany, France, or America. Nevertheless, democratic centralism was proclaimed a universal principle of revolutionary practice. For Party leaders found certain aspects of this doctrine extremely useful in silencing criticism—particularly that emanating from the troublesome bourgeois intelligentsia.

By radically simplifying Lenin's original analyses, his successors justified this universalization and apparent "deformation" of democratic centralism. In his *Short Course* and his *Foundations of Leninism*,[9] Stalin argues that the strength of the proletariat ultimately lies in its sheer numerical superiority. He points out, however, that this superiority can be utilized only if the proletariat maintains its monolithic unity. The Bolshevik party is viewed as the guardian of this unity. Oppositional activity fragments the group and consequently negates the essential unity, and strength, of the working class. Hence, factionalism has to be unequivocally forbidden.

The vulgar Marxism of Stalin banishes complexity and in its place posits a neat, rigid causal pattern: oppositional activity fragments the party, weakens the working class and objectively strengthens the bourgeoisie. This simple paradigm provides the working-class Communist leader with an ideal excuse to mercilessly stifle the criticism of the dissident intellectual. It is not even necessary to refute his frequently clever and attractive arguments. The very fact that he is voicing these arguments is sufficient proof that he represents a malicious, devisive force.

"Unity (strength)/faction (weakness)." This construct is easily fused with the "bourgeois (bad)/proletarian (good)" formula. Since the middle class is internally heterogeneous, it naturally produces a wide variety of ideological notions. Since it is balanced uneasily between the ruling class and the proletariat, its political consciousness vacillates in a corresponding manner. Hence, the petit-bourgeois intellectual is particularly prone to engage in debilitating factional activity because the stratum from which he springs lacks the unity, discipline, and homogeneity of the proletariat.

By developing sets of clear-cut, dichotomous categories and by radically simplifying their evaluative and affective dimensions, the Communist movement has provided itself with certain automatic response patterns. When one's perceptual equipment allows one to see the world in totally unambiguous, black-and-white terms, reflection and conscious choice become superfluous processes. They can be safely superseded by spontaneous reaction.

When Communist leaders are confronted with internal challenges, they automatically respond by accusing their opponents of giving aid and comfort to the enemies of the working class. Trotsky and Bukharin were said to be allies of Hitler. Beria was unmasked as a "British agent." The Hungarian revolutionaries were called Fascists, CIA men, and agents of the Vatican. Likewise, Sartre was a "servile executor" of a mission entrusted to him by Wall Street. Hervé was, in effect, a spokesman for John Foster Dulles.

One cannot simply dismiss this response pattern as evidence of Stalinist paranoia or as a manifestation of Communist deceit and dishonesty. When the Party accuses its internal critics of aiding the enemy, it is merely expressing the truth *as it sees it*. If several individuals simultaneously criticize the Party leadership, they are engaged in factional activity, and hence, undermining the strength of the working class and "objectively" helping the capitalist system. If they are of bourgeois origin, then their oppositionism reflects bourgeois interests and is therefore likely to be particularly pernicious.

Granted, there is a difference between "objectively" and "subjectively" aiding the enemies of the working class. But in the eyes of the Party the end result is the same. Consequently, when the Party accuses Sartre of being "in the pay of the American ambassador," it is not really lying; it is merely exaggerating for effect.

When the Party leadership found itself confronted by the *italiens* of the UEC, it resorted to this same formula. In March 1963 Paul Laurent began the offensive by accusing the students of succumbing to the "opportunist deviation."

> That which basically characterizes their position is the replacement of a firm ideological and political struggle with the spirit of compromise.[10]

In April, Roland Leroy escalated the attack. Instead of arguing that the students had made mistakes and deviations, he accused them of more serious crimes.

> Currently the leaders of the UEC have passed from the attitude of duplicity, which caused them to pretend that they were in agreement with our policy, to an open attack against communist principles.[11]

Finally, Roger Garaudy announced in *France Nouvelle* that the UEC had passed over to the enemy camp. "Their program deliberately abandons the positions of the working-class, of the Party and of Marxism-Leninism."[12]

The Party's response to internal critics almost invariably follows this formula. If the critic refuses to recognize his sins and engage in self-criticism, he is confronted with the ultimate threat of expulsion. This sanction is utilized for two reasons. First, it is the logical response to the threat *as it is perceived* through the categories of Marxism-Leninism. Organized dissent fragments the Party, weakens the working class, and helps the forces of reaction. Consequently, the "faction" must be silenced or eliminated in order that the unity and strength of the proletariat can be restored. Second, the Party apparently feels that the threat of expulsion has certain distinct psychological effects on the accused. The leadership seems to assume that its followers share its Stalinist world outlook. This view posits a mystical identification between the Party and the working class. The proletariat is seen as an organic unity led by a single monolithic movement and guided by a universally valid line. In addition, the Party and its program have a sacred character. He who opposes them opposes the proletariat, progress, and the will of history.

For those who have accepted these attitudes, the threat of expulsion is terrifying. There is no salvation outside the Party; it is the one organization through which the forces of goodness and justice manifest themselves. Consequently, when accused of class treason and threatened with expulsion, the passionate believer usually hastens to repent.

The leaders of the Party are perfectly aware of this phenomenon. For evidence, one need only examine a warning that a central committee member recently directed toward a pro-Chinese faction within one of the PCF's federations. After threatening expulsion, the official proceeded to outline the implications of this step.

> Finally, comrades, think it over. Without the Party, without the true line of the Party, which is never mistaken, you will be nothing, nothing at all. Finished, finished, you will be finished. It's

like a raindrop which falls from the roof. It is detached, it slides, it hits the edge, then it shatters.[13]

In the eyes of the convinced Communist, the individual is *nothing* outside the Party.

MODIFIED RESPONSES

By 1963 this Stalinist world outlook was beginning to weaken. Many Party members, especially the intellectuals, no longer shared the perceptual equipment of their working-class leaders. The revelation of Stalin's crimes, the invasion of Hungary, the opportunism of the PCF, and the philosophy of radical existentialism all contributed to the demystification of the Party. Sartre, Hervé, and others were attempting to construct an independent Marxist perspective—one that would legitimatize the role of the non-Party intellectual.

In addition, expulsion from the Party did not necessarily mean that one was excluded from the working-class movement per se. The *exclus* were no longer reduced to impotent isolation. Mao on the left and Togliatti on the right could provide them with material and ideological support. After the PCF cut off *Clarté*'s funds, the journal began to receive a subsidy from the Italian Communist party.[14] On March 20, 1964, *l'Unità*, the PCI's newspaper, published an interview with Pierre Kahn, one of the leaders of the UEC rebels.

As a result, the Party was compelled to modify its traditional, automatic response. The harsh line voiced by Laurent, Leroy, and Garaudy ended in May 1963. The student dissidents had not been intimidated by charges of "bourgeois opportunism," "duplicity," and "abandoning the positions of the working-class." Their oppositionism continued unabated.

From May 8 to 10, the central committee held a special session to discuss "the Communist student facing the great problems of our epoch."[15] As usual, the Party mobilized its chief intellectual spokesmen—Lucien Sève, Guy Besse, Leo Figuères, Roger Garaudy, and Aragon—to discredit the theses of the opposition. But the tone of the speeches was mild and conciliatory. Maurice Thorez expressed the hope that "this discussion [can] be carried out in a fraternal and comprehensive manner."[16] He stressed that the Party leadership must patiently respond to all the questions and arguments of the students; it must show respect for the youth—while at the same time demanding that "the young people, in exchange, have respect for their older comrades."[17]

Roland Leroy asserted that the Party had no desire to "attack this or that comrade"; instead, he claimed, "we want to aid the UEC as a whole to rediscover a proper orientation and a proper field of activities."[18] The rest of his speech, however, cast doubt on the sincerity of this declaration. He proceeded to concentrate his anger on the "errors" of a few leaders of the UEC, emphasizing in particular the "responsibilities of comrade Fourner," who, as secretary-general of the UEC, shared the leadership of the *italiens* with Pierre Kahn.

It was no longer a question of the petit-bourgeois students expressing the reactionary ideology of their class; instead, the problem was said to concern a handful of troublemakers. "We do not confuse the majority of our student comrades," Leroy asserted, "with the nest of politicians who dream of exploiting the hesitations and uncertainties of the students against the best wishes of the Party."[19]

When the Seventh Congress of the UEC convened in January 1964, it was apparent that this new approach had not been entirely successful. The "great mass of the student comrades" overwhelmingly supported the positions of Kahn and Fourner.[20] As one group of students stated in April 1964: "We are not going back to the methods of Stalinism, nor to the refusal to grant the UEC a part in the working-out of the political line of the Communist movement."[21]

In response to this student intransigence, the Party resorted to intrigue and organizational manipulation. Since most of the revisionists were Parisians the leadership began to search for allies at the fringe of the movement—particularly in the less sophisticated sections of Lille, Orsay, Caen, and Nancy.[22] By mobilizing loyal "Thorezians" in the provinces and by exploiting the divisions between the *italiens* and the new left, the Party regained control of the UEC at the Eighth UEC Congress in March 1965. The rightists were purged from the National Bureau and proposals for an autonomous line and the toleration of divergent tendencies were defeated. A new coordinating council for the Mouvement de la jeunesse communiste (MJCF) was set up; this placed the UEC under the firm control of Party-appointed functionaries.[23]

Nevertheless, the Party made certain concessions. The new leadership introduced a motion which criticized *l'Humanité* for its "distorted, one-sided interpretation" of the Congress' debates; the motion passed and *l'Humanité* subsequently printed an apology.

Why, it might be asked, did the PCF tolerate vocal oppositionism in its student organization for more than two years? Why did it abandon its ritualistic response; and why, after its final victory, did it accept a mild rebuke from its opponents?

This modified response seems to have been shaped by three principal factors. First, the Party was faced with a new breed of internal critics who did not respond in the anticipated manner to the accusations of "bourgeois deviationism" and the once awesome threat of expulsion. Second, it would have been difficult to carry out an effective purge of the UEC. In the aftermath of the Algerian war, the French students seemed to have become "de-politicized." They were generally disillusioned with established parties and organizations. The PCF would have had many problems filling its student ranks with new recruits.

The situation was further complicated by the beginnings of the Sino-Soviet dispute. Apparently, there were fears that Peking would exploit a UEC purge to precipitate a general crisis within the Party's ranks. The Chinese had already succeeded in detaching factions from the central committees of the Swiss and Belgian Communist parties. It has therefore been suggested that the CPSU ordered Thorez to go slow in ridding the PCF of oppositionists.[24]

Although the PCF made minor concessions, it refused to alter its conception of the "proper function" of the UEC. In 1965 it reiterated its demand that the Union continue to play its traditional educational role.

> For all students who want to draw closer to the Communists, but who do not feel ready to join the Party, the UEC must be the school where they will find the teachings of the French Communist Party. The UEC, like the Communist Youth Movement as a whole, turns to the Party for the correct orientation of its work.[25]

Almost as soon as the Party had silenced its rightist critics, it was forced to confront a new challenge from the left. In 1964 Professor Althusser began his Marxist-Leninist discussion group at the Ecole Normale; likewise, crypto-Trotskyist Alain Krivine assumed the leadership of the UEC's Sorbonne-Lettres section. The opposition-ism of both groups came to the surface during the 1965 presidential campaign.

When faced with the critics on the left, the Party leadership abandoned its patience, its sympathetic demeanor, and its slow, cautious, manipulative tactics. In January 1966 the UEC summarily dissolved the Sorbonne-Lettres section—even though that section constituted almost 40 percent of its Parisian membership.[26] In November it expelled the Althusserites and the pro-Chinese.[27] In two swift blows, almost half of the organization was dismantled.

This reversion to hard-line tactics appears somewhat paradoxical. After the death of Thorez, the new leadership attempted to assume a more liberal image. In 1966 it intervened in the Garaudy-Althus-ser debate; but it did so cautiously, with a decidedly gentle hand. Yet, when it came to dealing with the new student opposition, Rochet and Marchais reacted even more decisively and brutally than had the Stalinist Thorez.

Several factors underlay the sharp contrast in the Party's treat-ment of the left and the right. First, the new leadership no doubt wished to consolidate its position by demonstrating its determina-tion to maintain organizational discipline and unity. Second, the left seemed to pose a far greater threat than the right. The alterna-tive strategy proposed by the revisionists was not particularly danger-ous; it differed from the Party's only in degree. By 1965 the PCF was following an essentially reformist, social democratic line. Con-sequently, the criticisms of the UEC dissidents were annoying but not scandalous or unsettlingly heretical.

However, by moving this far to the right, the Party had become extremely vulnerable to attacks from the left. The PCF's proletarian rank and file generally ignored revisionist criticisms. Working-class cells have never been particularly interested in the issue of internal Party democracy. But both the ex-resistance fighters of the maquis and the unreconstructed Stalinists tended to cast a dubious eye on the Party's new reformist posture. The PCF found itself extremely vulnerable to *gauchiste* criticism.

The crisis of the international Communist movement complicated the situation. By the summer of 1965, Peking was giving financial assistance to the ultra-leftist Fédération des cercles marxistes-léninistes. This organization was energetically trying to seduce disgruntled revolutionaries from the official Communist party. It appears that the apparatus felt seriously threatened. It is not surprising, then, that it took drastic measures to quell an incipient Trotskyist or Maoist revolt.

It is important to keep in mind this vacillation between harshness and mercy when examining the Party's response to the student revolt of May–June 1968. Its initial—perhaps spontaneous—response was the traditional, ritualistic act of unequivocal condemnation. But when intimidation and innuendo failed, it turned to flattery, coaxing, and manipulation.

On May 3, the first day of serious rioting, it appealed to its usual formulas. It issued a statement calling the rebels "bourgeois adventurists" and accusing them of acting as tools for the Gaullists. Georges Marchais argued that "in developing anti-Communism, the groupuscules serve the interests of the bourgeoisie and of monopoly capital."[28]

Again, these charges seem to have been part of an automatic reaction. Since the logic of Stalinism had been fully internalized by both the leaders of the Party apparatus and the functionaries who staff it, the perceptions of the Communist bureaucracy were framed by certain categories and paradigms. In May 1968 the students were perceived as factional critics of bourgeois origin. This meant that their activity reflected the interests of the ruling class and served to undermine the strength of the proletariat. The student revolt therefore provided the stimulus which triggered a ritualistic response. The Party was ideologically conditioned to accuse the rebels of "class treason" and "collaboration with the enemy."

Unfortunately, this response seems to have caused more problems than it solved. The student rebellion continued and gradually assumed a progressively stronger anti-Communist character. In addition, many young workers began to imitate the tactics of the students. They occupied factories and initiated wildcat strikes. Late in May, a group of prominent Communist intellectuals marched on Party headquarters and demanded that the antistudent line be modified.[29]

It became obvious that a sizable segment of the Party's rank and file no longer perceived reality in Stalinist terms and, as a result, no longer responded in a positive manner to traditional Stalinist reaction patterns. Consequently, Rochet fell back on the Party's alternative response. He tried to flatter, divide, and manipulate the students. He drew a distinction between the great mass of the students, who were a "progressive force," and the handful of troublemakers, who were trying to lead their comrades astray.

As in 1965, the Party leaders tried to isolate the student leaders and woo their followers. In the words of Georges Séguy: "The students lack the leaders they deserve."

> By their adventuristic slogans, by their concept of violent action by small groups, they offer no concrete perspective, and they impede the mass mobilization of the students, which alone will allow them to stand up to the powers that be.[30]

Although attacking the *gauchistes,* Séguy complimented the majority of the students. Their demands, he said, were perfectly justified, and the Party would do all it could to see that they were met.

> The Communist Party of France . . . calls on you to struggle for your true, immediate demands, and it supports you in this struggle.[31]

In a sense, the Party was trying to buy off the students. It tried to coax them into abandoning their "troublesome leaders." The students were advised to reject "pseudo-revolutionary endeavors," and pursue, instead, "immediate demands." If they did so, the Party promised to place the strength of the working class at their disposal.

Given the traditional political attitudes of the radical intelligentsia, this response pattern appears skillfully devised. The intellectual tends to view himself as a manipulator of words and ideas, while the proletariat is seen as a concrete social force that can translate intellect into action. Consequently, the Party confronted the students with both a promise and a threat. If they fulfilled their proper roles, the PCF would use the might of the working class to help them achieve their objectives; but if they turned on the Party, then it would respond by isolating them. And having lost the support of the proletariat, they would remain impotent intellectuals, helplessly trapped in the margins of the French political arena.

The Party's goal, in turn, was to isolate its *gauchiste* critics. It hoped to cut them off from the student mass, whose activities could lend a measure of practical substance of their oppositionist verbiage.

STUDENTS AS IDEOLOGUES

In the past, these ritualistic responses have been generally reserved for the Party's internal critics. But the student revolutionaries were operating outside the Party. The UEC—emasculated by a series of massive purges—proved almost totally submissive.* The radical dissidents were all non-Communists. Yet they were treated in almost the same manner as Hervé, Casanova, the Althusserites, and the Trotskyists had been treated. They were apparently regarded as "factional, bourgeois critics." This seems to stem from the fact that many of the student radicals were disciples of bourgeois dissidents within the Party. As has been pointed out, the students were putting into practice theories and strategies already set forth by members of the French intelligentsia.

On the surface, the opposite would appear to have been the case. As always, student rebellion was closely linked to the activities of the Party's intellectuals; but during May and June the latter appeared to be a response to the former, rather than vice versa. In the midst of the crisis, one of the Party's leading intellectuals, André Barjonet, resigned. He did so for classical reasons. In his *Révolution trahie de 1968,* he explained how, in his view, the PCF leadership had "betrayed" certain sacred Marxist-Leninist principles. He attributed this largely to the fact that the intellectuals had been systematically

---

*The latest "cleansing" of the UEC occurred after the Middle Eastern war of 1967. At the insistence of the Party, the UEC took a firm pro-Arab position. As a result, many students with Israeli sympathies left the organization.

excluded from the Party's decision-making process. Instead of being allowed to fulfill the creative tasks of the true Marxist scholar,
he argued, the intellectual had been forced to merely dress up the
dogmatic pronouncements of the theoretically inept Party leaders.

Barjonet's complaints were strikingly similar to those of Sartre,
Hervé, Lefebvre, and Althusser. But, where their criticisms stimu-
lated student dissidence, his was a *response* to such dissidence.
On the surface, it appeared that the students had become the vanguard element of the bourgeois intelligentsia.

At first glance, the student revolt seemed to represent a blanket
repudiation of the radicalism of the entire adult generation. While
the old UEC rebels had recognized certain tutors and guides, the
students of May and June recognized none. They seemed to form
an independent, self-directed vanguard—partially because the cur-
rently fashionable intellectual cliques made no serious efforts to
forge links with the young revolutionaries. Throughout the revolt
the structuralist Marxists were silent. Neither Lévi-Strauss nor
Maurice Godalier offered the students support or assistance. In fact,
Lévi-Strauss viewed the uprising as an unqualified disaster. Its only
success, he argued, was that it revealed the total bankruptcy of the
modern French university. The technocrats were openly hostile.
Michel Crozier publicly proclaimed his support for de Gaulle.

Several heroes of the past tried to reassert their influence. But
when Aragon and Althusser appeared in the Latin Quarter, they
were booed for refusing to break with the Party. Likewise, Sartre
was booed for insisting that the revolution must be "not only *for*
the workers, but also *by* the workers." The students seemed to have
completely severed all ties with the old radicals. However, when one
examines the actual strategic goals and tactical choices of the revolutionaries, one sees that the intellectual dissidents of the past still
exercised a significant influence. The political perceptions of many
of the students were obviously guided by the ideological categories
posited by Togliatti and Sartre, Mandel and Trotsky, Althusser and
Mao.

"Student power" and "worker power," for example, can hardly
be viewed as original contributions of the new generation. When
stripped of the verbiage of a Cohn-Bendit or a Jacques Sauvageot,

these notions reveal themselves as variations on the ancient theme of autogestion. One is reminded of the goals of the old anarcho-syndicalists and of the factory councils called for by the Italian Communist Antonio Gramsci in 1919. But the contemporary configurations of these concepts have found their clearest expression in the works of Trentin, Jeanson, Gorz, and other members of Sartre's *Temps Modernes* group.

In May 1968 Sartre selected Cohn-Bendit as his "existentialist man of the year," much as he had selected Castro for a similar honor in the early sixties. He interviewed Coh-Bendit for a special "revolution issue" of *Le Nouvel Observateur*. Throughout the interview, Sartre maintained a curiously passive posture; as was the case with Castro, it was as if the great thinker had decided to play the straight man for the man of action. One has the impression that these performances were staged to demonstrate that the acts of the men of action are merely concrete, existential proofs of the words of the great thinker.

Before examining the theories of Cohn-Bendit, it might be useful to glance briefly at the doctrine of his immediate predecessors, the so-called situationists. The situationists directed one of the first French student uprisings, the revolts at the University of Strasbourg in 1966 and 1967.

Although their concepts were formulated by former disciples of Sartre, the situationists claimed to have broken decisively with both the theory and the practice of the existentialists. Nevertheless, an analysis of their manifestos reveals that they were still very much preoccupied with the fundamental Sartrian problematic.[32] Both they and Cohn-Bendit were acutely aware of the classical dilemmas of the alienated bourgeois intellectual. But neither accepted Sartre's solutions; instead, they set out to create new, "improved" ones. Their innovations, however, were not at all novel; on the contrary, they were disconcertingly traditional. Cohn-Bendit and the situationists ultimately reverted to the ancient formulas of European anarchist and socialist thought.

Like the early existentialist thinkers, they began with a total rejection of the bourgeois order. They condemned capitalism, not because it produced poverty and exploitation, but because it was a gigantic "spectacle" that spiritually enslaved its population, who were both its actors and its audience. The bourgeoisie were passive; they were "other-directed voyeurs" who were fascinated and cretinized by the commodities and spectacles that the capitalist market offered. Instead of engaging in free, conscious activity, capitalist man "readily accept[ed] an alienated spectacular participation."[33]

The situationists, like the existentialists, basically objected to the *style* of bourgeois life: "the boredom of everyday existence, the dead life which is still the essential product of modern capitalism, in spite of its modernizations."[34] Their identity as revolutionary intellectuals was defined in terms of their opposition to the nature of bourgeois existence. They wanted to grasp their "situation" clearly, without illusions. They wanted to tear aside the veil of ideology and reveal capitalism in all its naked banality. Instead of surrendering to a passive, other-directed mode of being, they wanted to act, to consciously supersede the limits of their present oppressive condition.

They recognized, however, that this rejection of bourgeois existence produced certain perplexing dilemmas. Negative freedom discovered in the initial act of revolt had to be supplemented by a theory which justified positive action and provided the intellectual guidance necessary to make this action effective.

The situationists admired the juvenile delinquents (the *blousons-noirs*) who terrified and disrupted bourgeois society in the fifties. But the nihilistic, totally negative character of their revolt, it was argued, ultimately resulted in their co-optation. "The 'young thugs' despise work but accept goods. They want what the spectacle offers them—but now, with no down payment." In addition, the non-critical nature of the delinquents' revolt inevitably resulted in the unconscious reproduction of the basic structures of bourgeois society. "On the fringe of society, where poverty reigns, the gang develops its own hierarchy, which can fulfill itself only in a war with other gangs, isolating each group and each individual within the group."[35]

In the situationist view, the nihilistic beatniks of the "degenerate world of art" suffered the same co-optation. Lacking a theory to support a movement beyond capitalist society, they invariably become mere spectacles to entertain and amuse the bourgeoisie.

At the same time, the situationists rejected the possibility of becoming foot soldiers for the adult intellectual opposition. Getting entangled in the debates of the intelligentsia was just another way of passively participating in the bourgeois "game."

> In the cultural spectacle (the student) is allotted his habitual role of the dutiful disciple. . . . Impervious to real passions, he seeks titillations in the battle of his anaemic gods, the stars of a vacuous heaven: Althusser—Garaudy—Lévi-Strauss . . . and between their rival theologies, which are designed, like all theologies, to mask the real problems by creating false ones: humanism—existentialism—scientism—structuralism . . . etc.[36]

All prepackaged theoretical systems were rejected as oppressive negations of the freedom the situationists discovered through their initial act of revolt. But they simultaneously realized the need for a theory—a coherent vision of what is and what ought to be. Hence, the existential anguish of the late forties was again reproduced and rephrased.

Like Sartre and Merleau-Ponty, the situationists were profoundly troubled by the dilemma of powerlessness. They rejected the "pallid anarchism" of the Dutch Provos and the "abstract opposition" of the American leftists. If the alienated intellectual was to concretize his revolutionary ambitions, he had no choice but to ally with the proletariat. "The proletariat is the motor of capitalist society, and thus its mortal enemy: everything is designed for its suppression (parties, trade union bureaucracies, the police, the colonization of all aspects of everyday life) because it is the only really menacing force."[37] However, while they wished to ally with the workers, they refused to accept the workers' established political representatives. The Communists and their "so-called socialist bureaucracies" were unequivocally rejected. The China of Chairman Mao was dismissed as "the most elephantine bureaucracy of modern times."[38]

The manifesto published by the Strasbourg students did little more than restate the troubling dilemmas already examined by the radical existentialists. Its content was not particularly original—except, perhaps, in its interpretation of the capitalist system as a vast, cretinizing spectacle. The *form,* however, was new and entertaining. The text was printed in the "balloons" of a long comic-book made up of old photographs, film stills, and cartoons.

When all was said and done, the "theory" of the situationists was rather uninspiring. It accepted the Marxist assertion that the proletariat is the only revolutionary class; but it explained its apathy by appealing to sociological notions about the "society of mass consumption."

The situationists described their "situation" but presented no real, strategic perspective for its transformation. The task of forging concrete solutions was left to Daniel Cohn-Bendit, the principal ideologue of the May revolt.

In his discussion with Sartre, Cohn-Bendit again restated the essence of the Sartrian problematic. First, how does one develop a practical theory, which allows him to gain lucid insights into his condition, without letting this theory degenerate into a rigid, confining ideology? And second, how does one develop organizational structures, which facilitate revolutionary action, without setting the groundwork for oppressive bureaucratic hierarchies?

"The power of our movement," Cohn-Bendit said, "rests precisely on its 'uncontrollable spontaneity'—which gives it an élan, without seeking to canalize it, without utilizing it for some purpose beyond itself."[39] Since one naturally wants to control and understand his situation, there is a tendency for revolutionaries to immediately create an organization and define a program. But initiatives of this sort "inevitably become paralyzing."[40] "The only chance which the movement has lies precisely in its disorder, for it permits the people to speak freely and it generates a form of self-organization."[41]

One is immediately reminded of the *Critique de la raison dialectique,* in which Sartre rigorously described the self-destructive dynamic of the revolutionary project. Since the revolutionary must transform a "seriality" of isolated individuals into a coherent, self-conscious group, he creates a radical ideology and a structured organization. At first, these serve as tools, which permit the members of the group to collectively pursue their immediate objectives—namely, to cooperate in their efforts to understand and negate the limits of their oppressive situation. But after the overthrow of the old order, a "thermidorian reaction" sets in as the organization degenerates into an "institution" and as ideology becomes embedded in this institution and thus transforms itself into a rigid, dogmatic doctrine. The revolutionary subjects become passive, manipulated objects. An institutional elite emerges and initiates new forms of oppression. Ideology is used to disguise the reality of this situation, and it hides opportunities for further revolutionary action. The individual becomes enslaved in the drift of the apparatus and succumbs to its natural inertia.[42]

Cohn-Bendit sought to escape this fate by refusing the temptation to evolve either a coherent ideology or an intricate organization. He argued that the masses should be mobilized not with a hierarchical structure but by *the force of example.* The collectivity should be unified not by a set of ideas but by *a shared experience.*

The notion of a vanguard party was totally rejected. Instead, Cohn-Bendit proposed the theory of the "minorité agissante" (the active minority). "The latter can, because it is theoretically the most conscious and the best prepared, light the detonator and plunge into the breach. But that is all. The others can follow or not follow."[43] When, as in May 1968, the others do follow, the goal of a spontaneous uprising is achieved.

For Cohn-Bendit, the radical youth is the active minority of the present; their exemplary actions inspire the masses and thus set off an explosion, that is, they create a "contestation globale"—a struggle at all levels of society. There is, consequently, no need for the student or the intellectual to formally ally with the working class. The different forms of the spontaneous revolt occur in separate but parallel ways. Hence, one overcomes the dilemma of powerlessness without compromising his freedom as an intellectual in revolt. One merely sets an example; one inspires the proletariat but remains independent of it. One does not try to impose one's own leadership—but neither does he submit to the leadership of the "other."

Through his act of violent revolt, the student presents the rest of society—and particularly the proletariat—with a possibility:

But what is important is not to elaborate a program for the reform of capitalist society, it is to throw forth *the experience* of a complete rupture with it; an experience which may not last, but which leaves behind *a possibility:* one perceives something which is transient and which dies. But it suffices to prove that such a thing *can* exist.[44]

In a sense, Cohn-Bendit has become more Sartrian than Sartre. In his system, one does not communicate with the "other" through a stereotyped ideological discourse; and one does not cooperate with him by enslaving him in a hierarchical organization. One cooperates and communicates through the force of one's own concrete choices. One enlightens and mobilizes the "other" through the actual consequences of one's own actions. In addition, Cohn-Bendit's normative goal is essentially an existentialist one. "We do not want to have a destiny imposed upon us, we want to chose it ourselves."[45] Freedom is affirmed through choice—through the conscious creation of one's own essence.

According to Cohn-Bendit, the only institution in which this vision can be actualized is the small, self-governing collectivity. The latter must be structured so that each individual can function as a free, decision-making subject. Hence, he calls for the creation of "action committees" in every faculty, neighborhood, and factory. Above all else, there must be no superior and potentially oppressive "coordinating committee."[46]

The ultimate social utopia envisioned by Cohn-Bendit is hardly novel. It is lifted directly from Marx's *German Ideology* (1845). Cohn-Bendit dreams of the abolition of the alienating division of labor of modern industrial society. In the future socialist community, the distinction between "mental" and "physical" labor will be abolished once and for all.

> One can imagine another system, in which everyone will work at productive tasks—reduced to a minimum thanks to the progress of technology—and in which everyone retains the possibility of pursuing, at the same time, continuing studies. It will be a system of simultaneous work and study.[47]

One will work in the morning and study in the afternoon—thus actualizing both one's physical and intellectual capacities. Thus, in the future utopia, the gap between student and worker will finally be overcome.

COMMITTEES

Almost all the radical activists of May shared Cohn-Bendit's interest in local action committees. In these *comités d'action* and *comités d'occupation,* the themes of the right and the left opposition were fused. In this respect, the May revolt bore a strong resemblance to the Algerian crisis.

These committees had a two-fold function. First, they were administrative bodies, designed to manage "liberated areas." Second, they were revolutionary organs, designed to mobilize the masses.

The ethical desirability of such autogestive bodies rests on a Sartrian commitment to the ideal of individual freedom. But their strategic feasibility rests on an equally rightist or revisionist assumption: the belief—shared by Gorz and Trentin—that the transition to socialism can be effected by transforming each basic social unit into an autonomous, self-governing cooperative of workers.

This belief is utterly foreign to Maoists, Trotskyists and other left-oppositionists. Yet the most ardent supporters of the *comités d'action* were the ultra-leftists of the JCR. This seems to be due to the fact that the creation of "self-governing collectives" could be easily reconciled with the Trotskyist strategy of "dual power."[48] The committees could be viewed as "soviets," designed to destroy the legitimacy of the prevailing authority structures by assuming the day-to-day tasks normally performed by the agents of the capitalist state. By successfully running the universities, the *comités d'action* hoped to demonstrate that the Ministry of Education bureaucracy was superfluous and, hence, illegitimate. Factory soviets would demonstrate that the capitalist boss was equally unnecessary.

To the left-oppositionist, however, "student power" and "worker power" were not ends in themselves; they were merely means for radicalizing the masses and transforming their attitudes toward the existing authority relationships. Once they destroyed the capitalist system and seized control of state power, the Trotskyists undoubtedly planned to institute a centralized dictatorship of the proletariat. The ultra-leftists had no intention of letting autogestion persist.

The fusion of oppositionist themes of both the right and the left therefore created an unstable alliance. What some radicals regarded as ultimate ends, others viewed only as functional instruments. For a brief period, both Trotskyists and neo-Sartrians rallied to the support of the *comités,* but the unity they created was illusory. Ultimately, their alliance disintegrated, for they were guided by fundamentally irreconcilable theoretical outlooks. The tactical behavior of the student revolutionaries was structured by the theories posed by several sets of oppositionist leaders. As a result, the students eventually began fighting among themselves—just as Althusser had once fought Sartre and Mao had attacked Togliatti.

At times, the theories of the dissident intellectuals had a negative effect on the way in which the student disciples reacted to the May uprising. For example, the most striking characteristic of Althusserism is the inordinate stress it places on ideological work. According to the professor, the prime duty of the vanguard party is to create *a mass base endowed with revolutionary consciousness.* The Communist militant must continually teach the masses the essence of Marxist-Leninist theory so that they will come to understand the logical necessity of revolution. If a revolutionary mass base does not exist, a revolutionary initiative will inevitably fail. Consequently, the UJC(ML) initially opposed the demonstrations in the Latin Quarter.

A revolutionary upheaval was inconceivable for the students had not yet been politically educated. Only a tiny minority were Maoists. Consequently, the riots and confrontations served no positive purpose for the rioters were not conscious of the political and economic significance of their actions. They lacked a theoretical awareness of the consequences of their behavior. Hence, the riots were merely manifestations of petit-bourgeois adventurism. The UJC(ML) wanted no part in them.

Throughout May and June the Maoists continually stressed the necessity of "going to the people." Instead of rioting in the Latin Quarter, they went into the factories to ideologically educate the workers. Hence, initial student-worker contacts were made, contacts which some feel played a significant role in bringing about the "grève générale illimitée." Althusser's theoretical guidance thus inhibited the Maoists' efforts to organize the student movement. At the same time, however, it encouraged them to look toward a student-worker alliance.

The zigzag course taken by the May revolution was largely a reflection of the often contradictory, often poorly digested teachings of the dissident Communist intelligentsia. The students of May were acting out the ideas and schemes of the dissident intellectuals. Through the *comités d'action* the revisionist students of the "Etudiants socialistes unifiés (ESU) and 22 Mars were putting into practice the existentialist's dream of a democratic, decentralized, revolutionary organization.* Through their efforts to "serve the people," the Maoists were putting into practice Althusser's and Mao's notions of ideological education. Through its soviets, the JCR was attempting to utilize Trotsky's and Mandel's strategy of revolutionary transformation.

Hence, the students were viewed by the Party in the same manner as the "bourgeois intellectual critics." They were perceived as posing the same essential threat. But the student challenge was viewed as far more serious than the challenge posed by the intellectual critics. Intellectuals are usually isolated individuals, only capable of "spouting words." But by creating the UEC, the Party had unwittingly created a mass organization that was willing and able to translate these words into actions. The *italiens* of the UEC put Togliattism into practice; the leftists of the Sorbonne-Lettres section put Trotskyism into practice; and the ultra-leftists of the "cercle d'ulm" put Althusserism into practice. The Party seems to have viewed the 1968 revolution as a repetition of these events—but in monumental pro-

---

*The ESU is the student branch of the PSU—the Parti socialist unifié. The latter is a small splinter party made up of Socialist and Communist dissidents. It contains an extremely diverse membership, ranging from the social democrat Mendès-France to the left-Marxist Michel Rocard. From a Communist perspective, it provides a perfect example of petit-bourgeois revisionism. The PSU swings erratically from electoral opportunism to revolutionary "adventurism." It thus mirrors the instability of the petit-bourgeois political personality.

portions. Almost all the Party's theoretical opponents tried to exploit the May uprising; Maoists, Trotskyists, and anarchists simultaneously manned the barricades in an effort to put their counterstrategies into operation. The Party therefore had a definite interest in seeing that the revolution failed. For if it had succeeded—or even come close to succeeding—the countertheories of the Party's opponents would have been empirically proven.

If the ESU had achieved particular success, the Party's organizational theories would have been seriously threatened—particularly the concept of democratic centralism. If the Maoists had been successful, the Party's method of agitation and propaganda would have been called into question. If the revolutionary soviets of the Trotskyists had achieved significant results, strong doubts would have been raised vis-à-vis the concept of a peaceful transition to socialism through existing political structures.

Student dissidence was additionally dangerous because it managed to spark dissent and rebellion among Party rank and file. The elegant phrases and the subtle polemics of the intellectuals usually fell on deaf ears. Few workers could understand the obscure complexities of an Althusser or a Sartre. But the proletariat could understand the actions of the students. There is nothing esoteric or incomprehensible about building a barricade, standing up to the police, or taking over one's place of work. Theory becomes far more easy to grasp when translated into concrete political practice.

Qualitatively, the students posed the same essential threat as the intellectuals. They questioned the validity of the Party's ideology and, hence, challenged its ability to make strategic and tactical decisions for the working class. But quantitatively, the student threat was far greater—for it posed theoretical criticisms in practical terms.

Consequently, the *form* of the Party's response pattern was based on its ritualistic formula. The students were treated like any other group of bourgeois intellectual critics. But the *intensity* of the attack was unusually high. To deal with the UEC rebels and their adult gurus, the Party ordinarily employed obedient Communist intellectuals. Lefebvre was used to attack Sartre, and Besse to discredit Hervé. But the students were verbally assaulted by officials from all levels of the PCF hierarchy.

THE PCF COUNTEROFFENSIVE

Among the first to attack the students was Georges Marchais, second in command of the PCF and heir apparent to Waldeck Rochet. On May 3 Marchais wrote an article for *l'Humanité*: "De faux révolutionnaires à démasquer." This polemic provides us with a classic example of the Party's response pattern. Like previous attacks on dissident intellectuals, it was a direct reflection of the essential logic underlying the PCF's ideology.

Marchais began with the "theory of reflection." Because of the objective conditions of its existence, the working class was said to be the only revolutionary class in modern society.

> It is so because the working class never possesses any means of production; and because it is the most exploited class, and consequently, the only class which is really totally revolutionary. It is so because due to the conditions of development of the forces of production, the working class is the best organized, the most disciplined and the most self-conscious.[49]

He proceeded to point out that the French Communist party "bases its action above all on the working class, which is the decisive social force of our epoch." He therefore concluded: "These elementary truths prove that the French Communist Party is in France . . . the only revolutionary party."

As usual, the Party and the working class were wrapped in an indissoluble, somewhat mystical unity. As a result, Marchais could argue that an attack on one was automatically an attack on the other. By challenging the PCF's ideology and strategy, the students entered "into the ranks of the anti-Communist campaign of the Gaullists and other reactionary forces."[50] By trying to weaken the Party, the students weakened the working class and therefore aided the bourgeoisie. They became allies of the class enemies. "In developing anti-Communism, the groupuscules of the left serve[d] the bourgeoisie and the reactionary forces of big capital."[51]

Subsequent articles continued to emphasize the "treason" of the *gauchistes*. The Party's polemicists often utilized the "theory of reflection"; since the students were predominantly bourgeois, they argued, it was quite natural that their ideas and behavior "reflected" the interests of the bourgeoisie.

The PCF mobilized its still loyal intellectuals to justify its stand. They were given the task of translating the leadership's crude, anti-bourgeois prejudice into somewhat more sophisticated theoretical language.

The tone was set by Léo Figuères, editor of the Party's official theoretical journal, *Cahiers du Communisme.* Figuères modified the initial attack of Marchais. Instead of portraying the students as "sons and daughters of the big bourgeoisie," he categorized them as typical petit-bourgeois radicals. In "Le 'gauchisme': hier et aujourd'hui," he pointed out that as capitalism develops, progressively larger segments of the bourgeoisie find themselves *déclassés* and proletarianized. "As a result, the petit-bourgeois strat[um] submits and submits more and more to monopoly capital's policy of elimination."[52] Consequently, this stratum is radicalized; the "objective condition" to which it is subjected compels it to seek revolutionary solutions. Nevertheless, it cannot entirely shed its middle-class background. Subjectively, the petit-bourgeois group still identifies with the ruling class. As a result, its political activity is confused and unstable. "It remains vacillating by nature, but becomes violent by necessity."[53]

Figuères proceeded to examine student behavior in the light of traditional, petit-bourgeois *gauchisme.* He concluded that the anarchism of Bakunin, the ultra-leftism of Trotsky, and the adventurism of the students all share the same essential traits: brief outbursts of desperate violence that soon give way to "submission, apathy, and vain fantasy." Bakuninist violence soon becomes social democratic passivity: in the last analysis, *gauchisme* reveals itself as merely a passing phase of bourgeois opportunism.

In contrast, the logic of the proletariat's "objective situation" compels it to become a firm, decisive, unified force. The middle class, however, subjects its members to environmental factors which produce only fickle, inconstant radicals. "The petit-bourgeoisie lacks the discipline, the perseverance and the firmness which the proletariat by the force of circumstances acquires."[54]

Claude Prévost expanded upon these themes in an article in *La Nouvelle Critique* called "Les bases de l'idéologie gauchiste." He argued that students and intellectuals cannot play a "directing role" in the revolutionary struggle for the simple reason that they do not constitute a homogeneous class. Part of the intelligentsia is solidly implanted in the managerial stratum, while part has entered the white-collar working class: the *salariat*. Yet another segment—the lawyers, doctors, writers, and artists—constitutes a marginal non-salaried stratum. The student population reproduces and, in a sense, magnifies this heterogeneity. Some students know they are destined for the managerial or professional elite, while others know that they will end up as salaried technicians. But most remain insecure and uncertain. They teeter uneasily between a bourgeois family background and a semi-proletarianized future. The instability of the student manifests itself in his political behavior. "A non-homogeneous social strat[um], the students produce very different forms of action: heterogeneous, even contradictory, in which adventurism often plays a large part."[55]

In his July 9 report to the central committee, Waldeck Rochet officially sanctioned these themes. He justified the Party's hostility to the students by arguing that they were false revolutionaries. Since they did not come from a homogeneous social class, they lacked "a clear consciousness of the goals and means of revolutionary action." In addition, "neither their social origin nor their upbringing predisposes them to recognize the decisive role of the working class."[56]

6 Conflict within the Party

Figuères and Prévost assumed the roles of "good" bourgeois intellectuals. They used their theoretical expertise to reveal the essential theoretical correctness of the manner in which the proletarian apparatchiki responded to the bourgeois students. They dressed up the automatic and ritualistic responses of Rochet and Marchais.

This concept of the "ritualistic response" rests on the assumption that the Party can be viewed as a bureaucratic organism, which has been ideologically conditioned to respond to certain stimuli with set reaction patterns. This model provides only a partial explanation; it obviously cannot capture the full richness and subtlety of Party behavior.

The notion of the bureaucratic organism stresses the unifying function of ideology. The Party is viewed as an organizational hierarchy, permeated at every level by the Marxist-Leninist outlook. This total ideological permeation facilitates communication and promotes bureaucratic regularity and predictability. All members of the Party organization perceive and react to specific stimuli in a similar manner. To a certain extent, the Party can therefore be treated as a unified entity.

But the cohesive force of ideology is offset by the divisive forces generated by organizational structure. The PCF, like most modern bureaucracies, is structured on a division-of-labor principle. The Party is broken down into numerous functional subunits—journals, reviews, unions, associations, and clubs. All have specific roles and duties whose coordinated fulfillment will theoretically lead to the Party's seizure of state power.

As we have seen, the functions of secondary organizations are two-fold: ostensible and real. The real goal of the UEC is to train loyal and obedient Marxist-Leninist intellectuals. Its ostensible goal is to canalize and articulate student protest. It has been hypothesized that over time a member of a secondary organization tends to identify himself with his organization's ostensible goals. Thus, the Communist student becomes convinced of the prime importance of mobilizing student protest.

Most crucial Party decisions now seem to be made in the politburo, which is composed primarily of the leaders of the PCF's most
important subsections. Consequently, each politburo member has
a unique organizational perspective. But this is not to say that the
politburo is simply an aggregating mechanism that reconciles conflicting organizational interests. Each leader may, to a certain extent, be concerned with particularistic concerns, but he perceives
and articulates these concerns through the universal language of
Marxism-Leninism. In all Party bodies the legitimate mode of communication is ideological discourse.

The unifying force of ideology reasserts itself. But in doing so,
ideology becomes subject to partial determinations. Garaudy adapts
theory to his purposes, and Séguy to his. Different versions of
Marxism appear. This becomes clear when one examines the manner in which particular politburo members interpreted the student
revolt of 1968. Each had a distinct Marxist-Leninist perspective.
Each related the students to the total social matrix in a unique
fashion.

Since Georges Marchais was the PCF politburo member in charge
of organizational matters, he was primarily concerned with the
preservation of the Party's organizational empire. Consequently,
during the crisis situation the focus of his attention was on threats
to this empire. The most salient of these was the militant anticommunism adopted by de Gaulle.

In the middle of the crisis, the general went on television and
solemnly swore to save the French nation from "totalitarian enterprises" *by any means necessary.* This appeared to be a thinly veiled
threat to the PCF: further agitation would be used as a pretext to
take militant action against the Party structure.

Mindful of the possibilities of reprisals and repression, Marchais
remained faithful to the traditional, ritualistic response. The violent
tactics of the *gauchistes,* he argued, were manifestations of a secret
government conspiracy.

> But it is evident, and life has since confirmed what we said at
> the time, that the leftist groups, which have been manipulated
> in a manner favorable to the Gaullists . . . have been a party to

violent excesses in Paris and the Latin Quarter. This violence
was encouraged and facilitated by police provocation.[1]

The students were "tools" that the Gaullists intended to use to cripple
the Party.

The pronouncements of the politburo's union men differed somewhat in emphasis. For Georges Séguy, the May revolution contained
not a threat but a promise. If the Confédération générale du travail
(CGT) could win significant gains for the workers, its influence and
power would be greatly strengthened. For Séguy the political verbiage of the students was at best a distraction. At worst, the JCR and
the UJC(ML) represented potential competitors—and thus a possible
challenge to the traditional union structure.

As a result, Séguy's primary interest was to segregate the students
from the workers. This was partially achieved by playing on old
antibourgeois prejudices.

> The movements of the French working class, as it now exists,
> endowed with a long experience of class struggle, which has
> contributed to its maturity, has no need of petit-bourgeois
> leadership.[2]

In addition, he stressed the difference between the "political verbiage" of the students and the "concrete material gains" with which
the workers were preoccupied. He emphasized that the CGT was
primarily interested in the latter.

> The time has not come yet for babbling about profound social
> changes, in which everyone sets forth whatever comes into his
> mind. . . . We will not permit our concrete objectives to be rele-
> gated to the background in favor of vague formulas; co-ad-
> ministration, the reform of structures, etc.[3]

The strike movement was viewed almost as an end in itself. Séguy's
pronouncements represented a clear rejection of the instrumental
view of trade union activity. It would therefore appear that Séguy,
no less than the UEC rebels, was mistaking the ostensible functions
of the CGT for its real ones. Incrementalism was embraced and long-
range political goals were all but ignored.

Other Party leaders put forth a distinctly different view of strike activity. According to them, the *grève générale* fulfilled a primarily tactical objective. "In bolstering the confidence of the workers," Henri Krasucki, another politburo member, argued, "it accelerates the current in favor of political changes."[4]

The strike increased the unity and confidence of the working class and therefore created the basis for a future revolution. "The ten million employees are united for goals which are the cement of their political solidarity."[5] The material demands were a means toward working-class solidarity, which was, in turn, a precondition for effective political activity.

Claude Harmel argues that a struggle developed within the politburo between the unionists (Séguy and Frachon) and the politicians (Rochet, Krasucki, etc.). He presents evidence that suggests that the latter utilized Party cells to encourage the workers to reject the accords negotiated by Séguy at Grenelle.[6]

According to Harmel, after May 19 the Party leaders decided to exploit the strike to achieve political ends. Working-class agitation was used to press for the creation of a *gouvernement populaire,* a left-wing cabinet with Communist participation. The pure instrumentalism of Séguy was decisively rejected.

GARAUDY'S OPPOSITION

A fourth perspective could be identified within the politburo: that of Roger Garaudy, the highest-ranking Party intellectual. His oppositionism was apparent in an article entitled "La Révolte et la révolution," which appeared in the April-May 1968 edition of *Démocratie Nouvelle.*

In it, Garaudy presented a firm refutation of the *ouvrièrist* position found in the articles of Prévost and Figuères. He unequivocally rejected the notion that the "nefarious" character of the student dissidents could have been automatically deduced from their social origins.

If we say: by virtue of their social origins, the students do not make up a homogeneous social group, and the dominant petit-

> bourgeoisie confer on this group the political characteristics of
> the petit-bourgeoisie, with all of their hesitations and vacillations,
> etc., then we content ourselves with a mechanistic sociology
> which has nothing to do with Marxist analysis, and the practical
> consequences of this theoretical error will be deadly.[7]

This represented an abrupt break from the traditional theory of reflection. Garaudy seemed perfectly aware of this, and he argued that
his antimechanistic position was in basic accord with the original
concepts of Marx.

> It is necessary to remember quite clearly that, from a theoretical
> point of view, it was not Marx but Hippolyte Taine who suggested
> this sort of predestination and this mechanistic link with the
> milieu of origin.[8]

Garaudy proceeded to set forth an almost classical interpretation
of the role of the bourgeois intellectual. He pointed out that Marx
and Lenin were able to achieve "true consciousness," even though
"one was the son of a petit-bourgeois and the other of a big bourgeois."
Their ideology was, according to Garaudy, not the product of their
socioeconomic milieu but of their "intelligence du mouvement historique."

Garaudy's debate with his neo-Stalinist adversaries centered not
only upon the nature of the intelligentsia's subjective consciousness
but also upon its objective importance in the class struggle. Both
Garaudy and his opponents dismissed the Marcusian notion that
the proletariat's *rôle historique* had been usurped by the students
and the intelligentsia. But their treatments of this question differed
radically. Waldeck Rochet contented himself with reasserting the
conviction that the proletariat was the most revolutionary class in
modern society.

> . . . it is the one which submits most directly to capitalist ex-
> ploitation. It is the one which is deprived of all means of pro-
> duction; it is the last exploited class in history, which does not
> exploit or aspire to exploit any other social class.[9]

This polemic amounted to little more than a rephrasing of certain
passages from the *Manifesto*.

Garaudy set forth a far less orthodox repudiation of Marcuse's thesis. In "La Révolte et la révolution," he argued that it makes no sense to draw a sharp analytical distinction between the intelligentsia and the proletariat. *For "big industry" has begun to fully integrate these two groups.* The intellectual is no longer a generalist, performing essentially managerial functions. The development of the division of labor has transformed him into a narrow specialist, a salaried technician, and a wage slave. Consequently, the modern proletarian and his intellectual counterpart share a similar state of consciousness; both are subjected to the same essential forms of alienation. Both suffer the tyranny of the "patron," and both feel unfulfilled due to the narrow, one-sided nature of their tasks.

Garaudy further declared that as big industry develops, as the forces of production become more intricate, the relationships of production become increasingly "socialized." All workers, whether they be manual or intellectual, form a single, organic, collective laborer. Garaudy argued that with the introduction of automation and cybernetics, the technical intelligentsia becomes the key element in this collective entity. The old-fashioned "workers of the hand" are rendered superfluous; all workers evolve into technicians. The proletarianized intelligentsia becomes *the* productive class.

Garaudy then set forth the rather audacious conclusion that this process leads to the supersession of the classical Marxist contradiction between labor and capital. New contradictions unforeseen by Marx appear.

> And they contribute to rendering more and more acute and unbearable the irrationality of a system which requires tremendous initiative from a worker in his technical capacity, but also his unconditional obedience to the private or collective owner of the means of production.[10]

The radically different theoretical approaches of Garaudy and Marchais produced divergent attitudes toward student revolutionaries. Marchais, an orthodox neo-Stalinist, argued that the student revolt was a marginal, relatively insignificant phenomenon.

> It has been said that the student movement has been the "detonator"; that it has played a certain role, I do not contest. But how

could one believe that it was sufficient to launch a strike movement of such dimensions? The strike expresses the discontent accumulated over years and years in the face of the refusal of management and the government to satisfy the workers' demands.[11]

The convergence of student and working-class struggles was viewed as almost accidental. In the opinion of Marchais, the Party should lend its support to the legitimate demands of the students, but it should scrupulously dissociate itself from the adventures of the *gauchistes*. For the prime task of the Party is to satisfy the needs and aspirations of the workers. It must singlemindedly pursue this task, and it must, at all costs, avoid being distracted or sidetracked by irresponsible petit-bourgeois adventurism.

Garaudy strongly disagreed. The student revolt was not tangential to the proletarian revolt. On the contrary, not only did the two struggles converge but, in essence, they were one in the same. In Garaudy's view, students should not be regarded as "fils de grands bourgeois" but as future technicians—future wage slaves. Their ideologies are not products of their family backgrounds but of the future roles which they will perform in the neocapitalist system of production. The student revolt was thus viewed as a rejection of a system of education that transforms the intellectual into a narrow specialist—a passive, uncreative, and unfulfilled tool of monopoly capital. The students "begin to realize that the contradictions of which they are victims are only one particular example of a system of dependence and alienation of which the exploitation of the working class is the most perfect and significant embodiment."[12]

Garaudy rejected Marchais's demand that the Party ally itself with "sympathetic" peasants and shopkeepers. He argued that these groups were basically conservative and would ultimately desert the Party when the essential issue of socialization emerged. He therefore advocated that the PCF turn to *la jeunesse*. For it was the youth who seemed most acutely aware of the primary contradictions of bourgeois society. It was the youth who were spontaneously rising up against the capitalist system. Most important, it was the technicians of *la jeunesse* who would form the nucleus of the new proletariat—the collective laborer of neocapitalism.

Throughout the crisis of May and June, Garaudy demanded that the Party adopt a conciliatory attitude toward the *gauchistes*. He attacked the positions taken by his fellow politburo member, Georges Marchais. He condemned the alliance-with-the-moderate-left formula, and he urged the PCF to absorb the revolutionary ultra-left.

The oppositionism of Garaudy provides us with another illustration of the way in which the zealous militant tends to transform tactical objectives into ultimate strategic goals. After the popular front strategy was adopted, Garaudy was given the task of forging an alliance with the intelligentsia, the Party's traditional bridge to the middle classes. To attract progressive, non-Communist intellectuals, Garaudy began to appropriate their themes. He strove to assimilate existentialism, structuralism, and Catholic humanism into Marxist theory.

In the process, Garaudy's formerly Stalinist ideology was transformed into an essentially revisionistic world view. Although Garaudy set about to seduce the intellectuals, he ended up being seduced by them. By 1968 his theories were regarded as unforgivably heretical by both purists like Althusser and neo-Stalinists like Étienne Fajon and Jeannette Vermeersch.

Garaudy accepted almost all the revisionists' key themes. In "La Révolution et la révolt," for example, he defended the notions of autonomy, autogestion, and economic decentralization. He argued that alienation cannot be superseded merely through the socialization of the means of production. In addition, he contended, the workers have to achieve *real freedom;* they have to regain conscious control over the work process. The Sartrian strain was undeniable. It was not surprising, then, that Garaudy ended up calling for autonomous workers' self-governing councils. He openly applauded the Italian and Czech "roads to socialism" and by implication, condemned the PCF's "voie polonnaise."[13]

Most important, Garaudy came to espouse the traditional revisionist thesis that the intellectual must play a vanguard role in the revolutionary struggle. For he adopted the Gorzian concept that neocapitalism has subjected the work process to "profound mutations." Like Gorz, he argued that the "travailleur intellectuel" has gradually become the decisive element in the "collective laborer" of modern society.

Since the student is considered the intellectual proletarian of to-morrow, Garaudy demanded that the Party abandon:

> this paternalism which regards the student movement in its en-tirety, as eternally minor, an ally which is necessarily unstable, as is the petit-bourgeoisie, from which in general the students come.[14]

This demand that the Party alter its sometimes condescending, some-times hostile attitude toward the student was, therefore, a direct outgrowth of his essentially Gorzian analysis.

Originally, Garaudy was given the task of forming a tactical alli-ance with the intellectuals, which, it was hoped, would facilitate the construction of a popular front. But by May 1968, he had trans-formed this "means" into an absolute strategic necessity. He had also rejected his original "end." In effect, Garaudy advised the Party to jettison its attempts to form a popular front; instead, he urged the PCF to invest its hopes in the revolutionary intelligentsia.

Like the *italiens* of the UEC and like Séguy, Garaudy seems to have mistaken his ostensible goal for his real one. His day-to-day tasks brought him into constant contact with non-Communist writers, professors, and students; in a sense, they became his clientele. He seems to have expended a great deal of energy attempting to win them over to the Communist cause. In the process, he gradually in-ternalized many of their attitudes and ideological theses. It appears that he developed a strong sense of personal identification with both his clientele and with his ostensible mission. Consequently, a tactical means evolved into a strategic end.

THEORETICAL STYLES

Identification with a particular subunit affects not only the content of an individual's ideology but also its style. Marchais was concerned primarily with the *preservation* of organization; consequently, his theoretical style tended to be static and analytic. Garaudy, on the other hand, was concerned with the *extension* of Communist activity into the intellectual community; therefore, his style was dynamic and dialectical.

To grasp the essential differences between the Marchais and Garaudy approaches, one must realize that the Marxist method has both a synchronic and a diachronic aspect. The first provides insight into the structures of a given society at a given moment in time. The second gives us a conception of the evolution of that society through time. The two are related through the concept of contradiction. At any particular moment, the economic structure of a given society will contain certain antagonisms. The way in which these conflicts work themselves out determines the pattern of the society's development.

Marchais, Prévost, and Figuères confronted French society as it stood in May 1968, and they proceeded to work out a purely synchronic analysis. They began by imposing certain universal deductive categories. Many of the actors were immediately categorized as petit-bourgeois. This implies a number of absolute, unvarying characteristics. The petit-bourgeoisie is inevitably "unstable" and is expected to vacillate unpredictably from the extreme left to the extreme right. As Jean-Marie Vincent says:

> The reaction of the petit-bourgeoisie and of the middle classes [was] either idealized (that is to say, conceived as very close to those of the working masses) or on the contrary, described very pessimistically (no extreme action which might throw the petit-bourgeoisie into the arms of fascism) not as a function of the dynamic relationships between classes.[15]

Garaudy followed a far different analytical procedure. He began with certain diachronic assumptions. He realized that as the nature of the technological base changes, so do the corresponding relationships of production, and so do the prevailing forms of consciousness and class ideology. The "new technology" of neocapitalism has created a new working class—a proletariat characterized by the organic unity of manual laborer and technical intellectual. Because of the similar nature of their work processes, they share almost identical forms of political and economic alienation.

While Marchais and Prévost imposed certain static, unchanging categories on the students, Garaudy tried to deduce their class character by examining the positions they occupy in the ever-changing relationships of production.

These two approaches suggested radically different practical solutions. Since Marchais was equipped with traditional and unchanging categories, he perceived a static, unchanging reality; hence, he advocated no change in PCF tactics. Garaudy, on the other hand, utilized dynamic analysis. Thus, he argued that the temporary union of students and workers was a manifestation of the gradual unification of intellectual and manual labor—which was, in turn, a product of the evolution of the means of production.

As a result, Garaudy felt that the events of May 1968 provided an essentially new situation—and therefore called for new tactical responses. The old alliance between workers and shopkeepers had to be abandoned. A new coalition—of workers, technicians, and students—had to be created.

Despite the skill of his analysis, Garaudy's oppositionist efforts were doomed to failure. The central committee, the politburo and the Party apparatus were all safely in the hands of neo-Stalinists of working-class origin. Bourgeois intellectuals—or those sympathetic with their viewpoints—had little influence.

The PCF's proletarian leadership has consistently limited the intelligentsia's access to the Party's decision-making organs. Rochet and his heir apparent, Georges Marchais, seem acutely aware of the dangers involved in letting intellectuals accumulate "excessive power." As soon as Garaudy was admitted to the politburo, he was releived of his editorship of *Cahiers du Communisme.* * He was ordered to concentrate on the relatively innocuous task of administering the Centre des études et des récherches marxistes. His principal dealings have been with the PCF's non-Communist allies; he therefore has had little chance to develop a significant following among the Party's rank and file.

In the politburo, Garaudy found himself almost totally isolated. His only support seems to have come from François Billoux. But

---

*Garaudy is the first intellectual in forty years to have been admitted to the Party's supreme policy-making organ. It is probably significant that he is not a bourgeois intellectual but a proletarian one. His father was a worker. By virtue of his social origins, he was apparently regarded as a reliable member of the generally unreliable intelligentsia.

this temporary alliance, this "micro-faction," had no firm theoretical basis: Billoux is an ex-resistance fighter and "old Bolshevik," and he invariably looks on any sort of revolutionary activity with nostalgic benevolence.*

Waldeck Rochet and the rest of the politburo seem to have supported the hardline approach formulated by Georges Marchais. Garaudy consistently found his pro-student propositions voted down by 8-2 majorities.[16] He had the same problem in the central committee. His only allies seem to have been Paul Laurent, René Piquet, and Louis Aragon.** Outside of a small coterie of Parisian intellectuals, Garaudy apparently found no supporters.[17]

The inner-sanctums of the PCF were firmly dominated by those with an essentially *ouvrierist* outlook. As a result, the Party was consistently hostile to student initiatives. The Garaudy-Marchais struggle was yet another manifestation of the ancient struggle between the PCF's proletarian leaders and its bourgeois intellectuals. But from the very beginning, Garaudy was doomed to failure. Past experience had alerted the leadership to the dangers posed by the "unstable" intelligentsia. Hence, the Party's decision-making organs were carefully stacked with loyal, working-class followers. The bourgeois intellectuals were hopelessly outnumbered.

---

*Evidence of Billoux's oppositionism can be found in the May numbers of the *Marseillaise,* a provincial Party journal which he edits. It maintained contact with the JCR and other extreme leftists whom *l'Humanité* had condemned in no uncertain terms. It expressed sympathy with the most violent of student demonstrations, and, unlike the Party itself, it openly condemned the government for dissolving the ultra-radical groupuscules.

**Aragon manifested his oppositionist sympathy with the students by turning over an entire issue of *Les Lettres Françaises* (du 15 au 21 Mai) to student dissidents—both Communist and non-Communist.

7 The Issues of Organization and Consciousness

As the PCF militant moves through his political world, one of the assumptions that guides his journey is that all that is bourgeois is bad, and all that is proletarian is good. His perceptions are also guided by another dichotomous construct: the opposition of spontaneity to consciousness. Undirected, spontaneous political action is invariably ineffective; while conscious and purposeful political action is invariably effective.

Like the bourgeois/proletarian construct, the consciousness/spontaneity formula finds its root in the original theories of Marx and Lenin. Marx forcefully condemned the anarchism of Bakunin, and Lenin polemicized endlessly against the narodniks and the ultra-leftists. The May revolution can be interpreted as another in this series of ideological confrontations. The student revolutionaries were, for the most part, champions of Luxemburgist spontaneity. The PCF, on the other hand, was a forceful advocate of conscious, directed, and, above all else, *organized* political action.

THE LOGIC OF LENINISM

In the structure of Leninist thought, the category of "consciousness" is intimately related to the category of "organization." The vanguard party is an organization of professional revolutionaries—a professional being one who engages in political activity full time and thereby acquires a firm grasp of the dynamics of the revolutionary process. He is "conscious" in the sense that he is an "expert."

Organization provides the institutional setting in which professional consciousness can develop. The Party supports and trains full-time activists. But it also provides the institutional structures through which professionalism is put into practice. Through the Party, the expert makes tactical and strategic decisions for the working class.

The development of an organization of conscious professionals was necessitated largely by the oppressive nature of the Tsarist state. The Russian police were technocrats of repression; if the Communists were to deal successfully with this enemy, they had to become technocrats of revolution. In the words of Lenin:

> One cannot help but to compare this kind of warfare (spon-
> taneous uprisings) with that conducted by a mob of peasants
> armed with clubs against modern troops.[1]

The modern troops of the Tsar could be defeated only by the modern
troops of the Bolshevik vanguard. Amateur activists invariably ended
up in Siberia. "Ten wise men," warned Lenin, "are harder to catch
than ten fools."[2]

But Lenin was careful to point out that the vanguard fulfills not
only a technocratic function but also an educational one. It awakens
true consciousness among the masses; it teaches the proletariat the
principles of scientific socialism. For "theory becomes a social
force once it is grasped by the masses."[3]

On his own, the worker develops an "instinctive combativeness"
and a "primitive awareness of the necessity for collective action."[4]
But he is unable to spontaneously achieve a comprehension of the
structure of the capitalist economy, its internal contradictions, and
its relationship with the ideological and political superstructures.
The proletariat is thus incapable of grasping the logical necessity
for a thoroughgoing revolution.

Therefore, the vanguard must make the worker conscious of both
his historical mission and the concrete realities of his present situation. The proletariat must be made aware of the fact that it is the
"universal class." It must come to understand that its particular
liberation depends upon the liberation and reconstruction of society
as a whole. The vanguard must translate this theoretical principle
into concrete terms. The best way to accomplish this is to help the
proletariat play a leading role in the struggles of all oppressed groups.
By playing such a role, the worker transcends his narrow economic
concerns and achieves a broad political consciousness.

> What does "the workers accumulating forces for the struggle"
> mean? Is it not obvious that it means the political training of
> the workers by revealing to them all aspects of our despicable
> autocracy?[5]

At this point in Lenin's argument, a tension emerges between his
strategic goals and the concrete conditions of Russian society. On

the one hand, the Party must educate the proletariat and coordinate its activities with those of all oppressed groups; the revolution must be a mass movement of vast dimensions. On the other hand, the realities of autocracy demand that the Party be an elite vanguard composed of professional actors.

The tension is resolved by fusing mass organizations to the vanguard party. All workers can join the trade unions; and all students can join the youth movement. But only full-time experts can staff the Party itself.

The mass organizations are placed in a position of complete subordination to the Party. For "broad democracy in the Party organization amidst the gloom of autocracy and the domination of the gendarmes is nothing more than a useless and harmful toy."[6] In Lenin's view, "a handful of revolutionaries (should) appoint bodies of leaders for each town district, for each factory district, and for each educational district."[7]

The organizations become transmission belts for the commands of the elite. By manipulating these belts, the vanguard engages the masses in political action that (1) weakens and demoralizes the ruling class; and (2) raises the level of proletarian consciousness.

Lenin's logic is, therefore, an attempt to adapt the universal strategic precepts of Marxism to a particular national setting. Again and again, Lenin stresses the exigencies generated by the Russian autocracy. Professionalism, hierarchy, and the subordination of lower bodies to higher ones—all these Bolshevik principles are responses to the specific conditions of a single context.

Rosa Luxemburg saw this quite clearly. "What is in order," she said, "is to distinguish the essential from the accidental excrescences in the politics of the Bolsheviks."[8] She argued that the Leninists err when they try to raise the particular to the level of the universal.

> . . . The danger begins only when they make a virtue of necessity and want to freeze into a complete theoretical system all the tactics forced upon them by these fatal circumstances and want to recommend them to the international proletariat as a model of socialist tactics.[9]

THE CULT OF ORGANIZATION

It could be argued that the PCF has, in the words of Luxemburg, mistaken the "excrescences" of Leninism for its "essence." The ideology of Leninism attaches strong, positive, affective dimensions to centralized organization, hierarchical discipline, and professional consciousness; yet it seems incapable of justifying its commitment to these qualities with Leninist logic.

The Party's condemnation of spontaneity and democracy cannot rest on the threat of autocratic repression. Even France under de Gaulle cannot be seriously compared to Tsarist Russia. Nor does a truly Leninist relationship exist between the PCF and its mass organizations. It is impossible to describe the Party as an elite vanguard. On the contrary, almost anyone can join; by its own admission, only a quarter of its 400,000 members can be classified as cadres.[10]

Moreover, the Party cannot claim to fulfill the same educational function as Lenin's vanguard. Unlike the Russian working class of the late nineteenth century, the French proletariat is not a minority group composed primarily of displaced peasants. As has been pointed out, Waldeck Rochet, in *Chemins de l'avenir,* claims that the French worker has internalized the teachings of Marx and Lenin and that, consequently, the ideology of the proletariat is now scientific. In light of this assertion, the Party's condemnation of spontaneous consciousness seems contradictory.

It would therefore appear that the Party has retained the affective structure of Lenin's theory but has abandoned its evaluative or logical structure. When Rochet defends the organizational forms of the PCF, he does not employ the dialectical reasoning of *What Is To Be Done?* but instead appeals to simple doctrinal formulas. "The organization of our Party is based on democratic centralism which . . . assures the conditions for unity and effectiveness."[11] Discipline and hierarchy are said to be the necessary prerequisites of proletarian unity, which, in turn, is the necessary prerequisite of proletarian strength.

As far as we're concerned it has been demonstrated that a party which claims to be proletarian, but which has no unity of action

> and in which everyone, on his own, does everything he pleases, cannot direct the working class or the popular masses and lead them to victory.[12]

The Party's centralism is no longer a resolution of contradictions between the universal and the particular or between strategic imperatives and national conditions. Instead, it is stated as a basic postulate—as an a priori, deductive principle. The PCF has universalized Lenin's position. As Gorz, Togliatti, and others have suggested, it has taken an organizational structure designed for an underdeveloped, despotic state and imposed it upon a Western industrial democracy.[13]

This universalization is often blamed on the Communist International (Comintern). In 1921 each party had to pledge to observe twenty-one "conditions" before it could be granted admission. The fourth condition demanded that foreign parties emulate the internal organizational structure of the CPSU(b).

> Parties belonging to the Communist International must be built up on the principle of democratic centralism. At the present time of acute civil war, the Communist Party will only be able to fully do its duty when it is organized in the most centralized manner, if it has an iron discipline, bordering on military discipline, and if the Party center is a powerful, authoritative organ with wide powers, possessing the general trust of the Party membership.[14]

During the first several years of the Comintern's existence, however, this condition was often ignored or, at most, was generally enforced with flexibility. Only with the rise of Stalin did the tendency to universalize bolshevism become absolute. Then, an attempt was made to make all Communist parties follow the conditions to the letter.

This development can be partially traced to the interactions between the bureaucratization of the Soviet party and the power struggle at its summit. After the revolution, the CPSU(b) had to transform itself from a small, compact detachment of revolutionary intellectuals into an army of administrative functionaries. The apparatchiki became Russia's new ruling class and, hence, the principal power base in Soviet politics.

Stalin set about to capture this base. Consequently, the interpretation of Marxism-Leninism which he set forth was designed to appeal primarily to the bureaucratic mentality of the new elite. As Isaac Deutscher and others have pointed out, Stalinism became the ideology of the emerging state and party apparatuses.[15] Those aspects of Marxism-Leninism that conformed with the attitudes and interests of the bureaucracies were retained and emphasized; and those which conflicted were ignored.

Many of the latter were championed by Leon Trotsky. Trotsky tried to use ideological weapons to discredit the apparatus and thus undermine the basis of his opponents' power. Consequently, his polemics were full of violent attacks on the abuses of bureaucratization. The principal theme of a series of articles and pamphlets published in 1923, later collected in the *New Course,* was the necessity to find some means of checking the growing power of the new administrative organizations.[16]

Stalin responded by promoting a cult of organization. While the Trotskyists condemned "bureaucratism," the Stalinists tirelessly preached its virtues. The *Short Course in the History of the Communist Party of the Soviet Union (Bolshevik)* (1938) eventually became the bible of this cult. In it the glories of organization are repeated ad infinitum.

The Party is not only the vanguard, the class consciousness detachment of the working class, but also an *organized* detachment of the working class, with its own discipline, which is binding on its members. Hence Party members must be members of some *organization* of the Party. If the Party were not an *organized* detachment of the class, not a system of *organization,* but a mere agglommeration of persons who declare themselves to be party members, but do not belong to any party *organization,* and therefore are not *organized,* hence not obliged to obey Party decisions, the Party would never have a united will, it could never achieve the united action of its members, and consequently it would be unable to direct the struggle of the working class. The Party can lead the practical struggle of the working class and direct it towards one aim only if all its members are *organized* in

> one common detachment, welded together by unity of will,
> unity of action and unity of discipline.[17]

Like the cult of organization, the theory of building socialism in one country seems to have been designed to win the hearts and minds of the functionaries and apparatchiki. By 1925 most regional Party secretaries probably had little interest in the prospect of world revolution. For eight years the Communist leaders had been confidently predicting imminent upheavals in the West, but their prophecies had remained unfulfilled. Trotsky's internationalism must have appeared wishful and utopian to the provincial bureaucrat. Socialism in one country, on the other hand, had a reassuringly practical and hard-headed sound. In addition, Stalin's theory appealed to the administrator's immediate concerns, his narrow, localistic outlook, and his latent sense of national pride.

Acceptance of the "one country" concept had profound implications on the Communist parties abroad. In 1924 Stalin declared that world capitalism was experiencing a period of "temporary stabilization." During this phase, revolutionary projects would prove futile. Hence, the Communist parties of the West should strive to consolidate their organizational strength. "The process of the definitive crystalization of the true Bolshevik parties in the West has begun; it constitutes the basis for the future revolution in Europe."[18]

As a result the PCF was ordered to "bolshevize" its organization. The French Party eagerly embraced certain aspects of this program. It seemed to find the principle of bureaucratic centralism particularly appealing. The "center" immediately began to set down intricate operational codes to govern the behavior of the "base." On December 31, 1924, the leadership of the PCF issued a detailed statement which prescribed the structure, composition, duties, and procedure of each cell. According to Gérard Walter, "The instructions furnished by this text offer a perfect model of bureaucratic minutiae, such as the most far-sighted, the most experienced administration could not surpass."[19]

Even the Comintern was disconcerted by the PCF's extreme predilection for bureaucratic uniformity. Giorgio Rovida reports that the executive committee attacked the "sectarian mentality of the leadership, for whom bolshevization meant, in short, the mechanical initiation of executive orders."[20]

Nevertheless, this organizational rigidity persisted. In 1940 the PCF central committee issued a "Plan d'organisation et de travail d'un cellule." The leadership told the cells how to occupy literally every minute of their meetings.*

A number of factors seem to have contributed to the French Party's enthusiasm for the cult of organization. First, the power struggle in the Soviet Union was accompanied by parallel struggles in the PCF. While Stalin fought Trotsky, Thorez and his colleagues fought Alfred Rosmer and Boris Souvarine. A new generation of working-class organization men struggled against both the bourgeois intellectuals and the old revolutionaries who had founded the Party. The former advocated the Stalinist virtues of organization and centralism; the latter defended the principles of Trotskyism, party democracy, and anarcho-syndicalism.

The cult emerged in the course of these early leadership battles, and it took root as the new organizational elite established itself. It is now the core of the Party's ideology. At the present time, the PCF has an extensive permanent staff. Marchais and Rochet preside over a veritable empire of organizations. They administer trade unions; numerous clubs and associations; newspapers, reviews, and journals; travel agencies; municipal governments; summer camps; and import-export companies. The Party has a reported income of 23,295,000 francs and thousands of full-time, paid employees.[21]

According to the PCF, the working class is the "heart of the nation"; one might extend this statement to read: "The functionariat is the heart of the Party." The present leaders have almost all been career apparatchiki. Annie Kriegel argues that the growing Party apparatus has gradually transformed itself from a tool into an end in itself: "Thus weighted down, the Party machine, while functioning very correctly, risks functioning increasingly for its own sake."[22]

By sanctifying the concepts of organization and professionalism the PCF sanctifies its massive functionariat; its bureaucratic routines

---

*See the excerpt from the "Plan d'organisation" in the appendix to this chapter.

are transformed into holy *rites*. This process also strengthens the legitimacy of the present leaders, most of whom are organization men.

This zealous commitment to the concepts of hierarchy and centralism can also be accounted for by an understanding of the French national character as it has been described by Blancard, Wylie, Pitts, Crozier, and others.[23] The French are said to have a tendency to convert authority into sets of impersonal rules. Whenever possible, the need for personal leadership is eliminated through the creation of rigid operational codes. Organizations are structured so that residual authority is allocated in such a manner that it is kept at a safe distance from those affected. As Crozier says:

> Face-to-face dependence relationships are, indeed, perceived as difficult to bear in the French cultural setting. Yet the prevailing view of authority is still that of universalism and absolutism; it continues to retain something of the seventeenth-century's political theory, with its mixture of rationality and *bon plaisir*. The two attitudes are contradictory. However, they can be reconciled in a *bureaucratic* system, since *impersonal rules* and *centralization* make it possible to reconcile an absolutist conception of authority and the elimination of most direct dependence relationships.[24]

A number of social mechanisms serve to perpetuate and reinforce these traditional attitudes. According to Jesse Pitts, the source of the problem lies in the "child's" relationship to his "parents."

> Within the nuclear family the parents try to be omnipresent and undisputed. The child is allowed little initiative—officially. The proper forms of behavior, the *principles,* exist once and for all, and the parents require perfect performance before the child is allowed to make his own decisions.[25]

The effects of the family socialization experience are two-fold. First, the child develops both a dread of authority and a yearning for independence. Second, he identifies "proper conduct" with certain set, absolute principles.

If the analyses of Métraux and Mead are correct, the French school system probably reinforces these attitudes. French education, they argue, is "characterized by a tight control and a repression of movement and physical aggression; a great pressure of the outside world with shaming and nagging and a reliance on oral aggression as a way of relief."[26] In both the primary school and the lycée, personal dependence relationships are restrictive and often unpleasant. Pitts agrees: "In school the French child gets more of what he has gotten at home."[27] Crozier also points out that French education puts an inordinate stress on universal norms and values.

> The emphasis of French education on principles and on the deductive aspects of science, the place it gives to subject matters requiring precision and clarity, and the reluctance it shows for controversial or ambiguous problems have been noticed by many French and foreign observers.[28]

We might tentatively conclude that the PCF ardently embraced the Bolshevik organizational structure because it was culturally predisposed to do so. The impact of both primary and secondary socialization mechanisms lead many French Communists to passively accept a position in a stratified hierarchy in which power is concentrated in a distant center and operations are guided by clear and precise principles, regulations, and directives. It could therefore be argued that the organizational patterns of the PCF are as French as the Code Napoléon.*

When Lenin accepted centralism and organizational hierarchy, he was consciously and creatively responding to environmental demands; when the French Party accepted them, it was unconsciously submitting to an environmental demand—that is, the force of "national culture."

In summary, the ideology of the PCF contains two central dichotomies: "organization/anarchy" and "consciousness/spontaneity." The first term in each of these dichotomies is endowed with strong,

---

*Any generalization about "national culture" must remain tentative until formulated into workable hypotheses and subjected to empirical tests. The theories of Pitts and Crozier have not yet been, in any sense, "proven." Consequently, what has been outlined above is no more than a *possible* relationship between organizational ideology and national attitudes.

positive affective dimensions. This development seems to have been the product of a number of factors: the forces of Leninist tradition, cultural predispositions of the French people, and, last but not least, the particularistic interests of the "functionariat"—the hegemonic faction within the Party.

THE CULT OF SPONTANEITY

When Cohn-Bendit attacked the bureaucratization of the PCF, Rochet responded by saying: "In fact, it is a question of old theories from the beginning of the century, which the revolutionary workers' movement has been combatting and defeating for a long time."[29] Rochet was correct. Cohn-Bendit was essentially a "Luxemburgist." His debate with the Party was in many respects a repeat of the Lenin-Luxemburg debate which was carried out in the pages of *Iskra* in 1903.*

In *Obsolete Communism* (1968), Cohn-Bendit quotes Luxemburg approvingly. "The reason why spontaneity is important for the struggle of the Russian masses is not that the Russian proletariat is 'uneducated,' but rather that the revolution cannot be run by schoolmasters."[30] The student radicals had no intention of letting PCF schoolmasters lead them in their struggle against their university schoolmasters.

Cohn-Bendit continually stressed that vanguards and hierarchies are incompatible with the phenomenon of revolution. In the middle of May he told Sartre that "our action has proven that spontaneity retains its place in the social movement. . . . No vanguard, not the UEC, the JCR or the M-L, has succeeded in assuming the leadership of the movement."[31]

This argument rests on the assumption that organization naturally nurtures conservatism. Centralized structures imply the existence of an elite; elites tend to assiduously protect whatever power they have managed to accumulate. Since the PCF has succeeded in inserting itself into the French parliamentary system, its elite now tries to preserve the power and influence the Party has thereby gained.

---

*See Helmut Gruber, *International Communism in the Era of Lenin* (Greenwich, 1957), for the relevant documents and a cogent commentary on the 1903 controversy.

As a result, the PCF is reluctant to abandon electoral tactics—even when new conditions seem to call for new approaches. As Luxemburg puts it: "The tendency is for the directing organs of the socialist party to play a conservative role."[32] As the Party gains strength, "the leaders transform it at the same time into a kind of bastion which holds up advance on a wider scale." The Party adjusts to life in a parliamentary regime, and, consequently, "electoral tactics come to be regarded as the immutable and specific tactics of socialist activity."[33]

The position of Cohn-Bendit is almost identical to Luxemburg's. The PCF, he argues, is a traditional bureaucratic hierarchy. It has managed to accumulate a share of the power in the existing social system. It has deputies in parliament, its mayors administer cities, and it is now in the process of "trying to wrest a seat on the very centers of economic power, on the boards of the increasingly important state industries."[34] As a result, the PCF no longer wants to revolutionize the system. On the contrary, its elite desires to preserve the system so that it might increase Party power *within* it. The PCF's revolutionary verbiage is therefore belied by its electoral opportunism, thus creating "an unsavory mixture of theoretical rectitude and electoral compromise."[35]

Luxemburg and Cohn-Bendit also present another argument against Leninism. They contend that the unorganized masses tend to be far more creative than the organizational elites. According to Luxemburg, "the ultra-centralism asked by Lenin is full of the sterile spirit of the overseer. It is not a positive and creative spirit." The masses are the source of true, revolutionary creativity. "But what has been the experience of the Russian socialist movement up to now? . . . The most important and most fruitful changes in its tactics during the last years . . . have been the spontaneous products of the movement in ferment."[36] In 1898, for example, workers "spontaneously" invented the general strike. And in 1901 students "spontaneously" invented the massive street demonstration.

Bolshevism stifles this innate "creativity." Lenin points out that factory workers often make the best Communists since they have been subjected to the iron discipline of the industrial plant. The worker knows how to obey; he knows how to unquestioningly carry out orders. Instead of trying to overcome this submissive attitude,

Lenin exploits it for it facilitates the vanguard's manipulative projects.

But Luxemburg argues that a strategy based on manipulation is fundamentally unsound. All Marxists realize that tactics must be adjusted to prevailing conditions. Luxemburg therefore argues that tactics are best selected by the workers in each factory and the students at each university. They possess an intimate and intuitive grasp of the nature of their own environments. The center is too remote. When a paramilitary command lays down universal regulations, it usually ends up imposing inappropriate solutions on unfamiliar terrains. The masses must be allowed to creatively respond to the particular conditions of their own milieus.

It is clear that Cohn-Bendit shares this belief in the spontaneous creativity of the masses. He argues that the preconceived theories of the professionals are invariably inferior to the dynamic theories that emerge from the political action of the masses. Ideas do not precede practice; practice produces ideas.[37]

Cohn-Bendit constantly emphasizes that control and direction are totally hostile to mass creativity. In his interview with Sartre, Cohn-Bendit asserted: "The strength of our movement is precisely that it rests on an uncontrollable spontaneity."[38] In *Obsolete Communism* he states that "if a revolution is to succeed, *no form of organization whatsoever* must be allowed to dam its spontaneous flow."[39] The masses can attain power only through free, unorganized, and unplanned collective action.

When the PCF viewed Cohn-Bendit's criticism, they saw heresy and scandal. In the words of Rochet, they heard "old themes from the beginning of the century," which the proletariat had "struggled against and vanquished." Cohn-Bendit's polemics were viewed as heretical attacks on Lenin's sacred texts—texts whose "holy" character was reinforced by national character and bureaucratic interests.

The reaction of the Party might have been considerably less hostile had Cohn-Bendit been merely an isolated intellectual. But "Danny the Red" (as he was called) was unquestionably the dominant personality of the May revolution. Despite his attacks on leadership and hero worship, he had innumerable disciples. His anarchism apparently struck a responsive chord among the great mass of the students.

UNIVERSITY STRUCTURE

To understand why the students were attracted to the Luxemburgist attitudes, one must examine the structure of the university community.

By way of introduction to this topic, we know that Lenin recognized that factory conditions prepare the worker for the iron discipline of the Bolshevik party. The Leninist model seems perfectly adapted to the psychological terrain of the industrial plant. It fully exploits the proletarian's submissive mentality.

At first glance, there appear to be certain similarities between the factory and the college campus. As Seymour Martin Lipset points out, both aggregate and socialize a great mass of individuals.

> There are factors inherent in the ecological structure of universities that facilitate collective action. Like a vast factory, a large campus brings together great numbers of people in similar life situations, in close proximity to one another, who can acquire a sense of solidarity and wield real power.[40]

But Lipset's analogy is somewhat misleading. The lecture hall and the assembly line tend to create radically different attitudes toward organization and discipline. Industrial labor is *social activity*. It is invariably a cooperative venture. The individual proletarian produces nothing; the finished commodity is the product of a *collective laborer*. But study is purely an *egoistic activity*. The university in itself produces nothing; it is merely a collection of disparate individuals, each of whom is engaged in an attempt to educate himself.

The two environments produce antithetical life-rhythms. The workers all arrive at the factory at eight; they work until noon; they lunch together; they work for four more hours; then they all go home. The nature of the work process imposes a uniform routine. But each student is free to establish his own schedule and his own rhythm. The Parisian student may or may not attend one or two hours of lectures each day at the Sorbonne. Aside from that, he is totally free. He can study in the library from eight to twelve in the morning, or in a café from eight to twelve at night. As Bourdieu and Passeron point out: "To experience life as a student, is first and perhaps foremost, to feel free to go to the movies whenever one wants to and consequently, never on Sunday, like everyone else."[41]

Studying in itself need never be a cooperative endeavor. Nevertheless, a "community of scholars" can be artificially created, as at Harvard, Oxford, or Cambridge. But Paris possesses few such communities. Only a small minority live in official university dwellings (see Table 1).

Table 1: *Type of Living Quarters of Parisian Students* (42)

	With parents	Independent lodgings	University dormitories
Boys	34%	52%	14%
Girls	45%	43%	11%

There is no campus. Laboratories, lecture halls, and student restaurants are dispersed throughout the city. The university itself provides the student with few opportunities to meet his comrades. Most student interaction occurs on a random and informal basis—in the Latin Quarter's numerous cafés, bookstores, and restaurants.

The heterogeneous nature of the student community also contributes to its atomization. Students come from a wide variety of backgrounds. As the PCF points out, they form a highly differentiated strata—in contrast to the relatively homogeneous proletariat (see Table 2).

Table 2. *Social Origins of French Students* (43)

Salaried farm workers	1,208	.6%
Farmers	11,791	5.6%
Service personnel	1,854	.9%
Blue-collar workers	13,661	6.4%
White-collar workers	16,669	7.9%
Industrial and commercial executives	37,535	17.7%
Middle-level management	37,921	17.8%
Liberal professions and upper-level management	60,374	28.5%

Table 2 (*cont.*)

Property owners, without professions	14,769	7.6%
Others	16,097	7.6%
Total	211,879	100%

Not only are the students' backgrounds varied and dissimilar, but their fields of concentration vary widely. And in Paris, law, medical, history, and literature students have little formal interaction. One's liberal education is obtained at the lycée; the university student immediately specializes. Thus, sociology students rarely take history of art courses. In addition, there is no sense of common destiny among Parisian students. The undergraduates at Harvard or Oxford all have a reasonably good chance of gaining admission to the ruling strata. Many will become leading figures in the worlds of business, government, and the arts. But French students face widely dissimilar futures. Members of the Grandes Ecoles will no doubt enter the power elite, but many law students will end up as government clerks. Likewise, students in the science faculties are likely to spend the rest of their lives as salaried technicians.

In short, neither the social roots of the students, nor their present routines, nor their future possibilities provide them with any concrete basis for a sense of collective identity.

It would be a mistake to characterize the French university as a totally atomized mass society. Over one-third of the students live with their parents and are, to a greater or lesser extent, still integrated in the primary family group. The rest are saved from isolation and anomie by a proliferation of formal and informal secondary groups. Fifty-seven percent of the students under twenty-one are members of a student union; 15 percent are members of political organizations.[44]

Nevertheless, there are indications that the university community—like French society as a whole—is relatively resistant to the formation of stable, cohesive secondary associations. Sociometric studies indicate that, in any given classroom, personal exchanges outside the lecture hall—and even the simple knowledge of names—are likely to be extremely rare.[45]

In addition, those who attempt to organize collective activities invariably encounter stubborn obstacles. The authors of *Les Héritiers* mention that:

> Each year philosophy students from the liberal arts colleges in the provinces try to organize collective activities; they fail regularly, doubtless because they come up against the aristocratic individualism of the "philosopher."[46]

Since similar difficulties also occur in other university departments, however, it would probably be a mistake to place inordinate stress on the aristocratic individualism of philosophy students.

One would conclude that Leninism does not provide particularly useful guidelines to campus mobilization; in the absence of a collective consciousness and in light of a general resistance to discipline, strategies based on *control, organization,* and *manipulation* are difficult to implement.

THE DELINQUENT COMMUNITY

It has been argued that the authoritarian structure of the French family tends to produce an individualistic reaction and a subsequent dislike of collective activities.

If this thesis is valid, it would seem to bear particular relevance to the members of the university community. For the Parisian student, who lives either in a dormitory or on his own, has finally managed to escape the despotism of parental authority. After 18 years of stifling, face-to-face, dependence relationships, he is finally free. It is perfectly natural that he should be somewhat jealous of his newly won independence; it is understandable that he might be reluctant to join a highly organized secondary group, for fear that the radical freedom of student life might thereby be compromised.

The theories of Jesse Pitts and Michel Crozier can also be used to provide additional explanations for the generally unstable character of student groups. According to Pitts, both the French family and the French school tend to foster a distinct type of peer-group interaction, which he calls the "delinquent community." This community is characterized by transience, instability, and a general aura of ille-

gitimacy. Within the nuclear family the parents try to be omni-
present and undisputed. But the child learns that he can gain
"evasion and relief" through covert relationships with members
of the extended family. "These relatives offer the child preferen-
tial treatment [in which] he can find oases of relaxation and security from the exacting pressures, particularly those of his father."
But these liaisons are illegitimate because they bypass the "doc-
trinaire-hierarchical values upon which parental authority is based."[47]

In the primary school and in the lycée, peer-group interaction
tends to assume a similar character. The teacher's authority is
equally "doctrinaire" and "hierarchical." As a general rule, he is
aloof, impartial, and exacting—"an Olympian diety." Pitts contends
that the students resist the teacher's tyranny by forming semi-
clandestine alliances.

> Every student as a student has to recognize the legitimacy of
> the teacher's demands in homework and formal instruction. On
> the other hand, the teacher's classroom administrative author-
> ity will not be taken for granted. On the contrary, the teachers
> will find the peer group engaging in a continual battle against
> him, a battle in which the best he can get is a truce; and he
> gets it by his capacity to punish—without pity and without
> argument.[48]

These mischievous alliances strive to subvert the teacher's authority. The administration is perfectly aware of this situation and "attempts to exercise the most rigid supervision of student groups at
all times." Consequently, the group is neither stable nor enduring.
The loyalty of its members is tenuous; for the group operates above
all else as an organization which promotes the pleasure and liberty
of the individual. As a result, "the peer group understands that the
member cannot prejudice his interest position for the sake of the
group, since the raison d'être of the group is to protect his interest
position."[49] In addition, since the group systematically debunks
all official morality, it is hardly in a position to uphold the "moral
necessity" of suffering in the group's interest. Competition provides
another disintegrative force. As a general rule, only the top 50-60
percent of a lycée class wins their baccalaureates. A tendency there-

fore arises to view "the other" as a threat to one's own success. This hardly encourages the development of group solidarity.

The autocratic teacher faces an essentially atomized student community. The formation of stable cliques is thwarted by both external and internal pressures. The students can evade this situation only through collective rebellion. As Crozier says: "The children can resist the strong pressures of the system only by resorting to an implicit negative solidarity and occasional revolts—the famous *chahuts.*"[50]

From time to time, classes are disrupted by spontaneous uproars. Discipline is temporarily shattered and the teacher completely loses control. As Victor Brombert describes it, "classes are interrupted by the launching of paper airplanes, the explosion of stink bombs, or the anonymous, collective humming which drowns [the teacher's] voice under the weight of Russian choir effects."[51] But soon the revolt is suppressed and order is restored. The chief culprits are mercilessly punished, and the solidarity of the group disintegrates.

Thus, when revolt occurs in the lycée, it is definitely not of a Leninist variety. On the contrary, it is decidedly Luxemburgian— that is, spontaneous, anarchic, and undirected.

THE UNIVERSITY: STRUCTURE AND STRAINS

Habits and attitudes formed in the family and the lycée seem to be carried over into the university setting. Secondary groups retain the illegitimate aura of the delinquent community. And as a result of numerous factors, the community remains atomized. Having liberated himself from the despostism of parental and school authorities, the student is reluctant to yield to the despotism of the tightly organized association. The development of a uniform group consciousness is hampered by the students' radically different backgrounds, studies, and future orientations—and by intense competition. Finally, the egotistic nature of the study process encourages radical individualism and fails to imbue the student with a submissive Leninist mentality.

The *chahut* therefore remains the most effective means of transcending mass atomization. When pressures build up during exam time, the Latin Quarter invariably explodes into violent *monômes,* which often have to be suppressed by the police.

The May revolution began as a series of lycée-like *chahuts*. At Nantes, students pelted their psychology professors with tomatoes to protest against the "repressive ideological content" of their lectures.[52] At Nanterre, Cohn-Bendit disrupted Crozier's lectures on American sociological problems by shouting, "What does all this have to do with Vietnam?" Anarchic debates would follow.[53]

At the university as in the lycée, the student community is highly individualized. As Sartre would say, it is *sérialité*. Authority patterns are also similar. Again we have the absence of intimate, face-to-face relationships between subordinates (the students) and a distant authority (the teacher). In fact, the university teacher tends to be even more unapproachable and autocratic than his counterpart at the lycée. The number of professors is very small, and in many faculties there are no lower-level instructors, assistants, or tutors. Rigid, one-way authority relationships predominate with no opportunity provided for feedback.

When dissatisfaction develops, the violent uproar remains the only feasible means of expression. And when this discontent reaches mass proportions, the *chahut* naturally develops into the riot.

The social structure of the university is conducive to anomic collective behavior. But authority and peer-group relationships merely provide the possibility for spontaneous violence. Before behavior of this sort actually develops, the social structure must be subjected to serious strains.

Since the end of World War II, a major source of structural tension has been the student population explosion. In 1946 there were 123,000 students; in 1961, 202,000; and in 1968, 514,000.[54] Libraries and laboratories have been overrun. Lecture halls are so crowded that students sometimes have to arrive an hour early and sit through the previous lecture in order to get a seat. Student-teacher relationships have completely collapsed. Competition has become increasingly intense. Only 55-60 percent of each class actually take their degrees.

The dissatisfied student who feels that his situation is intolerable has a number of alternatives. First, he can approach the authorities and personally register a complaint. This is apt to be an unsatisfying strategy because, on an academic level, the professor is an almost totally inaccessible figure; communication is one-way: from the top down. On an administrative level, complaining has been equally ineffectual. As Seale and McConville point out:

> A French university is like a factory in Russia: it works to norms
> ordained by the center. In 1968, all twenty-three universities in
> the country were state-run; they were administered on rigidly
> standardized lines, like a government department. The local
> administrative staff was impotent, the students resentful, and
> their mutual relations hostile.[55]

Even if they were so inclined, the university administrators could
not respond to student demands. "Correct" procedure was explicitly
prescribed by the Ministry of Education in Paris. Discontented students had little recourse but to write a letter to the minister.*

The alternative to individual complaint is collective action. But,
as has been shown, stable and enduring pressure groups are difficult
to maintain. In addition, the governments of the Fifth Republic
have been singularly unresponsive to demands set forth by student
unions. In 1962, the Gaullists discontinued UNEF's state subsidy.
The same year they set up the Fédération nationale des étudiants
de France (FNEF)—a "company union"—in order to seduce UNEF's
following. Unable to negotiate with the state and starved of revenue,
UNEF has stagnated. While in 1961 it had 100,000 members, it now
has less than half that number. At the same time, the total student
population has risen from 250,000 to half a million.

On one hand, then, the student community, prior to May 1968,
had been subjected to increasingly severe strains; on the other hand,
its pressure groups had become increasingly ineffectual. Certain
structural strains had created massive student dissatisfaction. Since
the university social structure is composed of an atomized peer-
group facing remote, unresponsive authorities, dissatisfaction can
be effectively expressed only through outbursts of violent and
spontaneous collective behavior. The riot temporarily transforms

---

*This overcentralization has, to a large extent, been negated by the extensive
reforms which followed the events of May. For a survey of this reform see
discussions of Edgar Faure's "Loi d'orientation de l'enseignement supérieur"
in the 8 January 1969 issue of Le Monde, pp. 1, 8-9.

the student seriality into a cohesive group; it also places direct pressure on usually aloof and indifferent authorities.

Unfortunately, the Communist party has failed to come to grips with these realities. Guided by Leninist ideological principles, it has forcibly condemned student spontaneity. It has tried to channel student discontent by mobilizing the university community into the UEC—an "organization communiste de masse." This is a self-defeating endeavor. Strong psycho-cultural factors militate against organizational discipline; and the development of group identity and collective consciousness is inevitably thwarted by the radical heterogeneity of the student milieu.

In addition, the Bolshevik organizational model is irreconcilable with the essential features of the student revolt. To achieve their goals, the students have to negate certain aspects of the university social structure. They have to destroy the basic aspects of what Crozier calls the "bureauractic phenomenon." They have to overcome the profound distance which isolates those in command positions from those in subordinate positions. They have to transcend student atomization—student inability to unite for constructive purposes.

In 1968, therefore, the students rebelled against the bureaucratic structure of the university community. To exploit this rebellion, the Party tried to induce the students to accept an almost *identical bureaucratic structure.* Within the Party authority is distant and unresponsive; the policies of the Union des étudiants communistes are decided by the politburo of the PCF. No deviations are tolerated. In addition, democractic centralism and the interdiction of factions atomize the rank-and-file membership. Within the movement, Communists are not allowed to "unite for constructive purposes"—namely, to formulate and support alternative policies and strategies. As the experience of *les italiens* and *les chinoises* shows, cliques and tendencies are strenuously discouraged.

If they had joined the UEC, the students would have been forced to accept the very structural characteristics they had set out to negate. In short, Leninism posits an organizational model totally inappropriate to the university community.

Appendix: "Plan d'Organisation"

(This set of instructions, issued when the Party was forced to go underground after the outbreak of World War II, is taken from Angelo Rossi, *A Communist Party in Action,* New Haven, 1949.)

The cell is the Party's basic organizational unit. It is therefore imperative that each cell obey the following instructions to the letter:

A. The cell should have a maximum of six members. The resulting decentralization facilitates the holding of meetings. It also makes for improved division of labor and enables the Party to maintain a close check on each militant's performance.

B. Each cell is required to hold weekly meetings. The time and place of these meetings will be changed each week, and those who are to attend will be notified at the latest possible moment. Each meeting will adjourn at the end of 60 or at the most 90 minutes.

C. The agenda for each of these meetings will be as follows: (1) questions relating to finances; (2) questions relating to the cell's operations; (3) questions relating to training and policy.

The secretary of the cell will work out a detailed agenda based on this outline, and will explain it to the comrades present at the meeting in clear and precise language.

Example: questions relating to finances (15 minutes). This will be the first item on the agenda. The treasurer must not fail to explain how important funds are to the Party, or to remind the comrades of their duty both to contribute to these funds and to collect contributions from the Party's numerous sympathizers. Everything relating to money should be taken up under this item.

Questions relating to operations (20-30 minutes). During this important phase of the meeting the cell leader, bearing in mind the Party's security regulations, should assign the members their respective tasks, and make all necessary explanations. Pamphlets; posters; slogans on walls and sidewalks. Display of map of surrounding neighborhoods; assignment of stations and streets to each member. Decision on the most favorable hour for performing each mission, *to be based on recommendations by the comrades.*

Questions relating to training and to Party policies (30 minutes). We must never forget that the cell is the Party's classroom, and that the comrades are expected to make a genuine intellectual effort to understand Party policy and Party tactics. The meeting should, to this end, discuss the Party's circulars, pamphlets, and newspapers. One of the comrades will offer a brief talk on current problems. Continuous study of the *History of the Communist Party of the Soviet Union (Bolshevik)* and *Left-wing Communism: An Infantile Disorder.*

Comrades, the present situation—beyond any in the Party's history—calls for order, discipline, courage, caution. You must seek these qualities in yourselves.

Forward, comrades—to become the true élite of the people and the guarantors of the final victory.

8 The Issue of Violence

THE STYLE OF COMMUNIST VIOLENCE

The Party condemned the student riots, calling them "provocative" and "irresponsible." The vehemence of these protests might lead the naive viewer to conclude that the French Communists have become ardent pacifists. But an examination of the PCF's history and ideology indicates that the Communists have nothing against violence per se. They do, however, believe that *correct* political violence has a definite style, function, and goal.

First, violence must always be controlled from above. According to Eugene Methvin, the Communist's insistence on this control leads to an intricate division of labor among riot cadres. In his study of the Iraqi riots of 1947-48, Methvin identifies seven types of agitators. First, there is an external command, safely removed from the field of battle. Second, there is an internal command within the crowd, protected by a third group—the "bravados" or body guards. Special messengers, the fourth group, carry instructions from the external to the internal commands. Armed shock guards accompany the demonstrators and charge into the crowd in case of police attack—thereby providing for an orderly retreat of the main body of Communist participants. Banner carriers and cheering sections complete the list and are deployed at specific locations throughout the crowd. "By assigning key men to stay near specified banners, the command knows their location at all times and can dispatch messengers to them with instructions for stepping up the tempo, shifting slogans or inciting violence."[1] Methvin notes that Communist riots follow an almost ritualistic scenario: first, preconditioning; second, the selection of proper revolutionary slogans; third, the creation of a crowd nucleus; fourth, on-the-scene agitation; and fifth, the manufacture of martyrs.[2]

The French Party has staged a number of controlled and directed riots, which have followed a program very similar to the one described by Methvin. In November 1948 the Communists used a rise in tramfares to mobilize angry crowds in Marseilles. As the Sixth

Comintern Congress, held in 1928, had instructed: "The task is to utilize minor, everyday needs of the working class as a starting-point from which to lead the working class."[3] Communist conductors refused to apply the new rate; there was a lockout and then a demonstration before the town hall. Four demonstrators were arrested; the Communists tried to "liberate" them, and one man was shot.

The Party then had a martyr. His funeral march turned into an attempt to storm the town hall. The city administration was forced to call in the army; and from November 17 to November 20, Marseilles was in a state of civil war.

The Party used the incident to provoke similar uprisings in other parts of France. Soon, the initial precipitating events were forgotten, and the PCF utilized the agitation to put forth "correct" political slogans. The 1948-52 outbursts became protests against the Communists' expulsion from the government and against the Marshall Plan and the Atlantic Pact.

On May 28, 1952, the Party staged a full-dress battle in the Place de Stalingrad to protest the arrival in Paris of General Matthew Ridgeway. As Fauvet describes it: "The Party, which has never relied on the spontaneity of the masses, carefully organized the day of the 28th." Several thousand militants were mobilized, "with well-trained and experienced men to lead them, armed with iron signs." In the course of the riot, a barricade was built and one participant was killed.[4]

By making sure to maintain control of mass violence, the PCF can use that means to achieve desired tactical ends. In the late forties, for example, mass violence was a useful tool in the struggle against American aid and expansion. In addition, the Party can also use violence of this sort to "raise the level of mass consciousness." Thus, by instigating demonstrations against General Ridgeway and against the electrocution of Julius and Ethel Rosenberg, two alleged Soviet spies, the PCF helped spread an "anti-imperialist ideology."

But the Communist is always careful to regulate the scope and intensity of mass outbursts. He is careful to make sure that the level of violence is appropriate to the existing period of the revolutionary struggle.

Lenin and Stalin break the process of revolution into three "stages." Each stage represents the struggle for a major socialist objective: first, the creation of an equilibrium of forces, that is the destruction of the hegemony of the ruling class; second, the upsetting of this equilibrium, that is, the seizure of state power; third, the establishment of a new disequilibrium, that is, the consolidation of the dictatorship of the proletariat.[5]

Violence serves a specific function in each stage. During the first, it is used to weaken and demoralize the ruling class. During the second, it is used for insurrectionary purposes. Both Lenin and Stalin stress that it is absolutely impermissible to engage in insurrectionary violence unless an equilibrium has been established. One cannot use "stage two" violence unless "stage one" violence has completely fulfilled its function.

Thus, the violence of the 1948-50 period was strictly limited in scope. No attempt was made to seize state power. Instead, the PCF tried only to disorganize and confuse the ruling class. In the words of Jules Moch, Minister of the Interior:

> Were the strikes a sign of an insurrectionary movement? I for one do not think so. The documents in our possession show that Communist tactics were much more subtle. They had orders to cause trouble . . . in all areas benefitting from American aid, but not to prepare for a revolution.[6]

The PCF invariably responds in a negative manner to violence which is not (1) initiated from above; (2) directed toward correct political goals; and (3) appropriate in intensity and scope to the existing period of the revolutionary process. In 1947, for example, a series of wildcat strikes broke out at the Renault plants. Christian and Socialist unions supported the strikes, but the Party did all it could to encourage the men to return to work. A similar situation developed in 1953 when, after several years of union inactivity, a series of spontaneous strikes broke out all over France. Again, the Party did everything it could to liquidate them. In both cases, spontaneous forms of social protest proved incompatible with the ritualistic pattern of Communist violence.

It is not surprising, then, that the PCF condemned student behavior in 1968. Far from being directed and controlled, the student riots

were spontaneous and anomic. It was therefore impossible for the
Party to use these uprisings to develop "correct mass consciousness." The undirected students had irresponsible and utopian goals
such as autogestion and autonomy. By approving of the riots, the
PCF would have been giving tacit approval to those ideologically
unsound aims. In addition, the scope and purpose of the violence
were—from the Party's viewpoint—totally unrealistic. The JCR
wanted to seize state power, and the 22 Mars group wanted to destroy it. The *enragés* wanted to skip "stage one" and engage in
"stage two" violence. From the perspective of PCF ideology, this
was hopelessly adventuristic. The Communists, therefore, found
the overall style of the student's political action extremely uncon-
genial.

STRATEGIC PERSPECTIVES

The antagonistic views of violence held by the students and the Party
can be partially traced to the fact that the students were, for the
most part, operating within the subjectivist revolutionary tradition,
while the PCF was caught within the confines of an antithetical objectivist tradition.

Sartre and Luxemburg, two of the students' guides, clearly belong
to the subjectivist camp. For Luxemburg, the revolution ultimately
occurs as a result of the proletariat's "will to power" and its "strength
to act." According to Sartre, the revolution is a project embarked
upon by the free and conscious individual. Both thinkers begin
with the mind of man. Revolution is viewed as a process whereby
man radically restructures the external world in order to bring it
into accord with some sort of internal scheme, desire, or "will."*

Lenin's life belies an undeniable voluntarist tendency. But his
writings, especially as they were codified by Stalin, are dominated

---

*This is not to say that either Sartre or Luxemburg ignores objective con-
ditions. Luxemburg has produced a number of excellent "objective analyses"
of the political and economic situation in Germany. And in his later work,
Sartre has placed an important stress on "conditioning." But in both cases,
the ultimate emphasis is placed on the subjective, voluntarist moment.

by strong antisubjectivist attitudes. He treats revolution as an event that occurs once certain specific objective conditions have developed. These concrete conditions define a "revolutionary situation." It is the height of political irresponsibility to take revolutionary action without first having made certain that such a situation in fact exists. For the Bolsheviks the immediate configuration of the external world determines, or at least radically limits, the internal attitudes and decisions of revolutionary men.

The orthodox Communist takes subjective feelings into account, but he views them as the outgrowth of objective factors. The states of mind of the masses are conditioned by the material bases of society. In addition, attitudes are viewed as "social facts" that exist outside and independent of the observer. The typical Bolshevik is primarily concerned with an objective evaluation of the attitudes of "the other." He is rarely preoccupied with the condition of his own will to power or strength to act.*

The Communist measures and evaluates subjective "facts." He cannot determine their nature, but he can accentuate it. His primary tools are organizations. Cells, journals, election meetings, clubs, and strikes all serve to raise the level of mass consciousness.

The subjectivists, on the other hand, view organization as a continual danger to revolution. Luxemburg tells us that regulations, hierarchy, and central directives stifle the proletariat's will to power. Sartre's survey of recent Russian and French history suggests that bureaucratic institutionalization invariably compromises the success of the revolutionary project.

Most of the students seem to have been acting on the basis of subjectivist assumptions. This is evident in their fierce hostility to *les appareils* and *les bureaucraties.* It is also revealed in their notorious slogan, "imagination au pouvoir." It found what was perhaps its most unsettling expression in the assertion that utopia would occur when the last bureaucrat was strangled with the guts of the last political scientist.†

---

*The Chinese Communist, who in theory continually engages in self-criticism, might prove the introspective exception to this generalization.

†Political scientists (particularly American political scientists) are characterized by their insistence on objectivity and empiricism. The passions and de-

In addition, a subjectivist bias pervades the popular student conception of the manner in which the events of May developed. The students tended to view themselves as the "detonators" of revolution. They felt their barricades in the Latin Quarter had inspired the proletariat. By standing up to the *flics,* they had taught the workers a lesson.

For the subjectivist, violence plays a crucial role. It is not only an expression of the "esprit révolutionnaire" but also a method of nurturing and strengthening it—and of awakening it in others. This position is, of course, carried to the extreme by Franz Fanon, who argues that terrorism is "therapy" which can be used to free the colonial subject from his slave mentality.[7]

In the eyes of the students, the revolution would come once the "exemplary violence" in the Latin Quarter caught on and spread to the factories, offices, and farms of France.

The PCF regarded such theories as the height of political naiveté. Revolutionary consciousness, they argued, does not spread from group to group, as if it were the measles or the chicken pox. On the contrary, each class in society has a distinctive set of political attitudes, conditioned by both its social roles and the objective conditions to which it is subjected.

The PCF has made a serious attempt to gain a clear picture of mass consciousness. In 1966 it commissioned the Société d'études et des récherches en sciences sociales to carry out an extensive attitude survey of the French voting public. The results were printed in the December 1967 and January 1968 issues of the Party's theoretical journal, *Cahiers du Communisme.* Great attention was paid to the variations between social classes and "catégories socio-professionelles."*

---

sires of the masses are "facts" to be measured and calculated. This detachment is viewed as repressive and reactionary.

*In engaging in what the students viewed as "bourgeois empiricism," the PCF was following sound Bolshevik precedents. Wolfe informs us that Lenin used detailed questionnaires and sample surveys to assist him in making up pamphlets. *Three Who Made a Revolution* (New York, 1948).

But the empirical investigations of the PCF are guided by certain definite theoretical preconceptions. One's political ideology is thought to be determined by the position he occupies within the existing economic structure. As a result, when the Communist sets about to predict the behavior of a certain segment of the population, he begins by examining its current economic status.

In the eyes of the PCF, the status of *all* socio-economic groups in French society is primarily determined by the fact that capitalism is now in "the epoch of its general crisis."[8] Advances in technology (or changes in the "organic composition of capital") have had two consequences: capital has become concentrated in the hands of a clique of monopolies; and the rate of profit has steadily declined. As a result of these two intimately related developments, the state is no longer simply a tool used to maintain bourgeois order. It has now become an economic agent which directly serves the monopolies. The dominant political fact of the present period is "capitalisme monopole d'état (CME)."[9] De Gaulle, for example, was a faithful servant of the massive enterprises.

The monopolies use the state to try to counteract the effects of the decline in the rate of profit. Government acts to check the power of the trade unions in order to facilitate the *surexploitation* of the proletariat. It also assists the monopolies in their efforts to exploit colonial areas. The state becomes an *état imperialiste;* hence, de Gaulle's stress on national grandeur.[10]

Finally, the state helps the monopolies in their attempt to exploit the nonmonopolistic segments of the bourgeoisie. The technocratic pretentions of Gaullism are no more than simple excuses to use governmental power to rapidly eliminate small and "inefficient" enterprises. Hence, the "Commissariat du plan" has made numerous enemies among the small businessman, the farmer, and the shopkeeper.

In a sense, the state becomes a focus of contradictions within capitalist society.* The monopolies rely on the state more and more

---

*The notions of "accumulation of contradictions" and the "displacement of contradictions" from the economic to the political structure are basically Althusserian (see *Pour Marx,* Paris, Maspero 1968). However, Rochet often borrows these concepts in outlining PCF strategy. See, for example, *La Marche de France au socialisme* (Paris, 1967).

to maintain economic and political stability. But to assist business, the state has to progressively increase its control over business. As regulatory agencies grow in power, the sacred rights of private property are negated. In the words of Claude Vernay, a leading Party economist:

> On the one hand, the role of the state will doubtless be strengthened, The growing domination of the monopolies will increase the pursuit of immediate profits. But this, in turn, increases the necessity for state control, which alone is capable of instilling the necessary impetus for technological progress, and at the same time, keeping expansion within certain limits, which is the only way to give a momentary respite to capital. However, this increase in the role of the state contributes to the exacerbation of the contradictions within State Monopoly Capitalism.[11]

The main losers in this process are the small businessmen. For the state is manipulated by their enemy, the monopoly clique.

The Party draws a number of strategic conclusions from this analysis. First, the main force of the revolution remains the proletariat—since it directly experiences the *surexploitation* of monopoly capital. But the working class has two potential allies—the petit-bourgeois and the nonmonopolistic segments of the bourgeoisie itself. The latter also suffer at the hands of state monopoly capitalism. As a result, the PCF has formed a proliferation of pressure groups to protect these dislocated capitalists; the Society for the Protection of Family Farms is such a group.

Following the guidelines set down by Khrushchev at the Twentieth Congress of the CPSU, the PCF has tried to consummate this alliance in parliament. It has tried to overthrow the Gaullists by allying with the lower-middle-class parties—the SFIO and the Radical Socialists.

The Communists justify this use of parliament by arguing that the economic contradiction between monopoly and nonmonopoly capital has been displaced into the political structure. It appears as a contradiction between the executive of the state and the legislature. The monopolists and their Gaullist servants have consolidated their control over the state administration; they therefore seek to expand its power at the expense of the National Assembly which still contains representatives of the lower- and middle-class parties.[12]

Consequently, the PCF can pose as the guardian of parliamentary democracy. It dramatizes this role by projecting two future possibilities. If the Gaullists succeed in their project, CME will be transformed into fascism—as happened in Germany in the thirties. If this is to be averted, the bourgeois democrats must unite with the Party to form a "gouvernement démocratique et populaire."[13]

The Communists thus insist upon placing de Gaulle and his successors in the antiparliamentary tradition of Bonaparte, Louis-Napoleon, Boulanger, and Pétain. This places the Party in the National Assembly tradition—of 1789, of the Paris Commune, and of the Second, Third, and Fourth Republics.

The strategy of the PCF is therefore based on an "objective analysis of the social totality.[11] This analysis reveals the weakest point within the French capitalist system: the contradiction within the state between the executive and the legislature—which, in turn, reflects the economic contradiction between monopoly capital and the middle classes.

The analysis also reveals the manner in which the weakest point must be attacked. The executive must be assaulted through a parliamentary alliance between the PCF and the bourgeois democratic parties. Hence, the Party must project a definite image. It must pose as the protector of traditional democratic and parliamentary traditions.

It is essential to take this total analysis into account when one examines the manner in which the Party reacted to the student uprising. First, the rebellion was viewed as a contradiction *within* the ranks of monopoly capital.* According to *l'Humanité*, the rebels were "composés en générale de fils de grande bourgeoisie."[14] Claude Lecompte, editor of the Communist youth magazine, explains it in the following manner. Since the end of World War II bourgeois culture has gone through a process of steady degeneration. There has been a general crisis in bourgeois art, literature, philosophy, morality, and values. This was dramatically illustrated by the prophets of nihilistic despair, the existentialists, and the glorifiers of the absurd.[15]

---

*This particular interpretation seems to conflict with that of Prévost and Figuères, who argued that *gauchisme* was a manifestation of "petit-bourgeois political consciousness."

The rebellion of May represents a climax to this process. The sons and daughters of the bourgeoisie were refusing to accept the "hypocritical values and morals" of their parents. They manifested their refusal by demanding the radical alteration of the university, which is the heart of degenerate bourgeois culture. The ruling class was therefore experiencing a profound, internal ideological crisis.

Consequently, the Party viewed the events of May as contradictions within the enemy camp. As such, they could be used and exploited by the Party. But in traditional Leninist-Stalinist terms, these contradictions were the proletariat's *secondary reserves.* [16] Its *main reserves* were the segments of the population with which it can immediately and directly unite—in this case the middle class.*

If the Party had given support to the students, the proletariat might have lost its most promising allies. For the attitude surveys carried out by the PCF indicated that the middle classes still harbored deep suspicions of the Party's goals and motives.† It was difficult for the PCF to pose as the defender of parliamentary traditions while, at the same time, fulsomely praising the USSR and outlawing dissent within its own ranks.

It was thus of utmost importance that the Party convince its potential allies that it was a sincere supporter of traditional constitutional processes. This objective was totally irreconcilable with either support for the student riots or Communist participation in anti-system behavior. Allying with the students would have meant sacrificing the proletariat's main reserves for its indirect reserves—a policy which would have made no strategic sense.

Since the PCF was operating within the objectivist tradition, it had a broad strategic perspective. It viewed the university community as one unit in the social totality. Within this single unit, the arguments of Luxemburg, Sartre, and the Fanonistes undoubtedly had

---

*In *Foundations of Leninism,* Stalin described the proletariat's "main reserves" as including the "peasantry and the intermediate strata of the population within the country." Within the secondary or *indirect* reserves, he includes: "the contradictions and conflicts within the non-proletarian classes within the country." One never sacrifices one's *direct* for one's *indirect* reserves.
† See *Cahiers du Communism,* December 1967, January 1968.

a certain amount of validity. Given the structure of the university environment, spontaneous violence fulfilled a functional role. It fused the atomized student mass, gave it a sense of solidarity, and allowed it to place direct pressure on remote and unresponsive authorities. But if the Party had adapted itself to the needs of this single social unit, it would have lost the support of other units. Its total strategy would have been disrupted.

THE RALLY AND THE RIOT

The radically different strategic and tactical perspectives of the Party and the student revolutionaries can be easily discerned in the actions of each group on the evening of June 10, 1968.

The Rally

The PCF began its election campaign on that night with a massive rally in a sports arena on the outskirts of Paris. It was a well-controlled and carefully staged event. It began precisely at 8:30 with a singing of the "Marseillaise" and ended precisely at 10:30 with the "Internationale." The seating arrangements mirrored the Party's hierarchical structure. The Parisian candidates for the National Assembly occupied the stage; in the first row sat the politburo and, in the center, the secretary-general, Waldeck Rochet. Behind them ten red flags were interspersed with ten tricolors. The floor of the arena was occupied primarily by members of working-class cells. Delegations from the UEC sat in the balconies. This was only fitting for the working class is the main force of the revolution; the students are merely an auxiliary force.

There were approximately 8,000 persons in the hall; outside, some 3,000-4,000 more listened to the speeches on loudspeakers. Many sat in adjoining cafés and sipped beer or *café crème.*

Fajon, Aragon, Vaillant-Couturier, Ballanger, and Rochet all read brief, carefully prepared speeches. As *France Soir* put it: "One does not improvise at a Communist meeting. Waldeck Rochet is not an orat His speeches roll on, imperturbably, like a slow river without twists or turns."[17]

The audience was docile; "spontaneous" crowd reactions were perfectly predictable. Whenever a government official was mentioned there were hisses. Quotes from de Gaulle and Pompidou were greeted with sarcastic laughter. References to the Party's role in the Liberation, its steadfast defense of the proletariat, and its general heroism and responsibility—all brought stormy and prolonged applause.

The rally bore absolutely no resemblance to the student meetings at the Sorbonne, the Mutualité and the Odéon. No speakers were interrupted; no one from the audience demanded to speak; and there was no critical feedback. Perfect order was maintained. In a sense, the authority structure of the meeting reproduced the authority structure of the lecture hall. An unchallenged elite faced a totally submissive mass.

It was precisely this sort of relationship which had sparked the student revolt. As one of the first Nanterre manifestos declared: "The dynamic between teacher and taught must be permanently saved from retrogressing into the old hierarchical relation of master and disciple."[18] At the PCF meeting Rochet clearly set himself up as a master. The audience, on the other hand, was expected to comport itself as an assembly of obedient disciples.

Communist ideology prescribed the form and tone of the meeting. It was structured on the Leninist norms of hierarchy, control, and discipline; a sophisticated vanguard imposed "correct consciousness" on the untutored mass.

But a Blanquist element was also apparent. An elite used and manipulated its popular following in order to seize power at the summit. One of the primary purposes of this grand rally was to demonstrate the magnitude of the PCF's mass base. Rochet had to prove to the Federation of the Left that a sizable segment of the electorate *demanded* that the Communists be included in any popular government. The Party had to use its electoral strength to destroy the possible formation of a non-Communist, center-left coalition. This desire is clearly—if somewhat circumlocutiously—expressed in Rochet's speech to the rally.

> The workers and democrats wish neither a patched-up Gaullist regime, nor some sort of a "third force." We are for a popular government and a democratic union based on support from all parties on the left and on the will of the people—a government in which we, the Communists, will have the role due to us.[19]

If the PCF was to retain and expand its electoral following, it had to improve its image. De Gaulle was doing his best to associate the Party with the violence and anarchy of May. He hoped to thus seduce the more conservative elements of the petit-bourgeoisie and proletariat, many of whom usually voted for leftist candidates.

Rochet had to destroy the notion that the Communists were enemies of order. Consequently, he firmly denounced the *gauchistes*. "By their methods, their recourse to violence, these groups have done everything to discredit the great popular movement which opposes the Gaullist power. We Communists are not adventurers."[20]

The style and tone of the grand rally were intended to reinforce this verbal declaration. The Communists were not rioters and barricade-builders; on the contrary, they were responsible citizens who held orderly, decorous meetings. The PCF had no intention of violently destroying the Republic. It decorated its meetings with a profusion of tricolors, and it began its rally with a rousing rendition of the "Marseillaise." In short: Communists are orderly, peace-loving patriots.

THE STUDENT RIOT

Just as the meeting was ending, a group of fifty students was leaving the Sorbonne and marching down the Boulevard St. Michel chanting "Ils ont tué un camarade." That afternoon a boy named Giles Tautin had accidentally drowned when he fell into a river while running from the CRS, the national riot police. He was a seventeen-year-old lycéen who belonged to the Union des jeunesses communistes (marxistes-léninistes). At the time of his death he was in a Parisian suburb trying to "serve" the striking workers at a Renault factory.

Fifteen minutes after the Communist rally ended, a crowd of angry demonstrators had gathered in the Place St. Michel. By 12:30 A.M., the original group of fifty had grown to several thousand. They faced a cordon of CRS agents who were blocking the entrance to the Pont Neuf. Directly across the Seine was the Prefecture of Police—the Paris headquarters of the "forces of order."

Within an hour the violence had begun. Police and students exchanged tear gas and molotov cocktails. A police van was burned down, and numerous barricades were constructed. All available evidence indicates that the riot was totally spontaneous. An analysis of this "hostile outburst" will provide some useful insights into the natural political tendencies of the student mass. In the course of this analysis, it should become obvious that the ideology of Marxism-Leninism-Stalinism keeps the PCF from adapting itself to these tendencies.

BACKGROUND AND ANALYSIS

In his *Theory of Collective Behavior* (1962), Smelser points out that most hostile outbursts are touched off by precipitating incidents. To act as an effective catalyst, these incidents must reinforce the generalized beliefs of the hostile subjects.[21]

Throughout the months of May and June, stories of police brutality had been circulating in the Latin Quarter. The newspapers and magazines were full of atrocity stories. Early in June UNEF and SNEsup published the *Livre noir,* an anthology of such incidents, which remained at the top of the best-seller list for several weeks.

Animosity toward the CRS was widespread. Its brutality and sadism were universally recognized. Consequently, many found it easy to believe that the police had "murdered" Giles Tautin. When I arrived in the Place St. Michel, I asked a bystander why the crowd had gathered. He informed me that the police had "drowned" a young lycéen. When I expressed surprise, another assured me that this indeed had been the case. CRS agents had captured the boy, thrown him into the icy river, and stood by and gleefully watched him drown. There were a number of other variations. Some said that the police had first knocked the boy down, beat him unconscious, and then tossed him in the water. In short, the CRS then were "generally believed" to be capable of anything. The death of Giles Tautin was an ideal precipitating incident.

Communist agitators are often unable to use exciting, ready-at-hand precipitants; for they must consciously select events which illustrate—or at very least are congruent with—the prevailing party line. The death of Giles Tautin obviously could not have been exploited. He was a Maoist, and the elimination of an irresponsible left adventurist is hardly a valid reason for a mass uprising. (On the contrary, it is a cause for discreet celebration.)

When the PCF starts riots, it chooses "principled" issues, or it puts "unprincipled" issues (i.e., high tram fares) into principled terms. In the early fifties, for example, it utilized the implementation of the Marshall Plan, the arrival of General Ridgeway in Paris, and the arrest of Jacques Duclos as excuses for rioting.

At times, such events are genuinely inspiring. The deaths of the French workers in the 1947-48 strikes are a good example. But frequently, as was the case with the American aid issues, the party line has little to do with generalized beliefs and predispositions. Hence, the PCF's ability to mobilize the masses by provoking hostile outbursts is seriously circumscribed by ideology.

The Leninist would argue that this is as it should be. In theory, the main purpose of riots and demonstrations is to raise the level of mass consciousness. One strengthens the individual's grasp of ideology by letting him translate certain aspects of it into concrete activity. There is no value in rioting for rioting's sake; rioting is simply *one* method of political enlightenment.

But the "leftist" would argue that participating in collective and violent action is in itself educational. Revolutionary personalities emerge from revolutionary action. By building barricades and tossing paving stones, one develops "un esprit révolutionnaire."

The first step in the mobilization process entails spreading word of the precipitating incident. Modes of communication must obviously be adjusted to the nature of the milieu in which one is operating. The labor agitator has all his potential hostile subjects aggregated in the factory. He can call a meeting, confront the workers, and explain to them the purpose, goals, tactics, and location of the proposed demonstration. Parisian students, on the other hand, are dispersed throughout the Latin Quarter. The only places where sizable crowds congregate are lecture halls and the university restaurants—where agitation is officially forbidden. Nevertheless, there are ways in which messages can be circulated. Rumors travel rapidly through informal communications networks.

Bourdieu and Passeron point out that although the student community lacks stable secondary groups:

The sporadic contacts and chance conversations are sufficient
for the propagation of rumors, often of the panic type about
professors, their requirements and their manias. Although the
circulation of the information about the subject and organization of examinations is slow and uncertain, the propagation of
the most extravagant rumors is fast and widespread.[22]

There are a number of areas in the Latin Quarter where students
customarily congregate: cafés, bookstores, movie houses, etc. The
news of a precipitating incident can be rapidly circulated in these
places. As Kaplan points out, "When . . . circumstances for collective behavior provide an opportunity for crowd behavior, the social
situation of students makes it likely that they will hear of it, have
associates in it, and have time to join themselves.[23]

There are a number of tactical advantages to be obtained from
this method of mobilization. First, rumors are extremely malleable.
When one hears a vague and hurriedly repeated story, he tends to
select those elements which are congruent with his preestablished
beliefs, prejudices, and preferences. When one passes a rumor on to
another, he emphasizes and omits on the basis of his perceptions
of the other's preestablished system of beliefs.

The story of Giles Tautin's death passed rapidly from café to café,
and from book stall to book stall. On the way, it adapted itself to
the generalized beliefs of the student mass. In addition, as it passed
from student to student, it was also adjusted to the individual outlooks of those who heard it.

When a Communist agitator confronts a crowd and speaks to it
directly, this sort of flexibility is impossible to obtain. If the party
line has been formulated in such a way that it conflicts with the
basic predispositions of the audience, the demonstration will probably be a failure. The possibility of adaptation is severly limited.
There will be slight variations in understanding and interpretation,
but all will hear essentially the same message.

Consequently, clear communication often inhibits the effectiveness of a hostile outburst. The PCF agitator tells the potential hostile
subjects the causes, goals, style and tactics of the demonstration.
Some subjects may disagree with the goals, others with the tactics.

As a result, many may stay home. But when one is told that "the CRS have killed a lycéen and a crowd has gathered in the Place St. Michel," one can make of it what he will. Flexibility of this sort obviously has its advantages in a radically heterogeneous milieu.

For example, the day after the June 10 demonstration, I recorded interviews with fifty riot participants encountered on a random basis in the courtyard of the Sorbonne. Since this sample was limited and unscientifically chosen, it is impossible to draw definitive conclusions about student motivations. These interviews do, however, reveal that students participated for a wide variety of reasons. Some expressed explicitly *political* motives.

> The demonstration showed that the young people of the extreme left have succeeded, through the force, the effectiveness, and the firmness of their principles, in spreading throughout the whole country their basic demands—that is to say, an increase in worker's wages and the overthrow of the present regime. Although the original cause of the demonstration was the bludgeoning of a young lycéen and his subsequent death in the Seine, the demonstration also shows a continuity with our basic demands.

A Maoist informed me that he had demonstrated because the murder of Giles Tautin was:

> a new act of the Gaullist powers against the young students and intellectuals who wish to place themselves at the service of the workers in their struggle against the capitalist state.

Although both subjects were highly politicized, they expressed significantly different ideological outlooks. The first envisioned the students in vanguardist terms—as an elite which spread certain demands throughout the nation. The second spoke in orthodox Maoist terms. He saw the petit-bourgeois student as placing himself at the service of the proletariat.

Many of those interviewed spoke in nonpolitical terms. The following subject, for example, emphasized that he was not a member of any political organization.

It (participating in the riot) was the logical thing to do after
what happened yesterday at Flins. It is inevitable that there
be violence after a man is killed like that.

The June 10 crowd was definitely not a "uniform, undifferentiated
mob." Each individual seems to have been motivated by a unique
set of factors; and each appears to have sought a unique set of psychic
satisfactions.

The Communist demonstration, on the other hand, is not designed
to provide disparate individuals with disparate satisfactions. The
PCF agitator attempts to impose uniform goals and a uniform sense
of purpose. However, while his mode of organization might very
well be suited to the homogenous factory, it seems ill-adapted to
the varied and heterogeneous university milieu.

Each individual participates in the hostile outburst for particular
reasons. Nevertheless, the *form* of the riot is produced by the underlying structural characteristics of the community as a whole. The
rioters are members of an atomized community, which feels itself
oppressed by a distant and unresponsive state. The students' collective behavior in May 1968, therefore, had to fulfill certain functions. It had to negate the individuated, disunified nature of the
community; and it also had to strike a direct blow at the authorities.

Atomization can be overcome only if a sense of group consciousness can be created. Thus to transcend their heterogeneity, the students had to find themselves in a situation in which common beliefs,
attitudes, and emotions could develop. The Communist rally and
the riot both formed "collectivities." Both aggregated a mass of disparate individuals, subjected them to common experiences, and
aroused with them similar ideas and emotional responses.

But before a true "group" can emerge, the individuals must become aware of their similarity. *The "one" must see his "self" in the
other.*" One can sense the feelings of the anonymous "other" only
if he translates them into activity of some sort. At the rally, common activity was limited to the singing of two songs, sporadic applause, and occasional hissing. During the riot, on the other hand,
common emotion tended to express itself in dramatically explicit
terms. For example, the students were united in their common hatred

of the CRS. One immediately became aware of the "other's" hatred, for he expressed it by hurling paving stones, setting police cars on fire, and tossing molotov cocktails.

In Sartrian terms, the student seriality was transformed into a *group-en-fusion* as its members realized that they were confronted by a common threat and subsequently reacted with a collective response.

> When the outside group [in this case the CRS] totalizes the multiplicity [the students] the latter totalizes itself. . . . Each individual knows himself to be unified with all the others by a common exigency. His danger is my danger and vice-versa.[24]

The rioters joined the demonstration for many different reasons But in doing so, all took the same risks, broke the same laws, and courted the same danger. When one looked into "the other's" face, he saw his own fear. When one saw a comrade being clubbed by a policeman, he saw his own "future possibility."

Consequently, the individual student made a decision to both protect *himself* and protect the *group*. He cooperated in the building of the barricades. Whatever their subsequent symbolic value, the barricades were initially constructed as a method of self-defense. They were simply a means of interposing a protective barrier between the advancing CRS and the students who were "under attack."

At the same time, the building of the barricades was a manifestation of—and a major contribution to—the emergence of a firm sense of group consciousness. If the individual had been interested in merely protecting himself, he would have fled. Instead, he strove to protect himself *as a member of a group.* He tried to defend the integrity and cohesiveness of the collectivity by constructing a protective fortress.

Sartre's analysis of the storming of the Bastille is relevant in this regard.

> The apparent contradiction between me as an insider of a passive seriality and me as an outsider who totalizes the series under menace finds its solution in *action.* The Parisians storm into the streets and *through their act* overcome the psychological malaise.

> Through *action* one is practically integrated. The third man [the individual student] emerges both as human organizer of a unity and as human part of that unity, but in the very act of free participation, whether as unifier or unified, he dissolves the seriality.[25]

At the Palais de Sport, this phenomenon did not develop. Collective admiration for Rochet was periodically expressed through applause. But on the whole, possibilities for cooperation and collective endeavor were few. By virtue of the individual's absolute submission to the Party leadership, he remained a passive object rather than becoming an active subject. He was not allowed to become the Sartrian third man, who through his free, individual action totalized the group.

Some may infer from this analysis that many students found riots to be more satisfying than mass meetings. And, indeed, given the structure of the university community, we can safely assume that certain psychological states were widespread. The atomized nature of the community probably generated a certain sense of isolation and anomie. The oppressive, unresponsive authorities probably aroused feelings of anger, resentment, and frustration.

At the riot, atomization was overcome; for several hours an intense mood of solidarity and unity was created. The participant developed a strong sense of group consciousness. The meeting, on the other hand, provided only a vague sense of belonging. On the whole, both "oneself" and "the other" remained passive and anonymous entities.

In addition, the rioters—by virtue of their group membership—felt they could strike a direct blow at the authorities. For once they could leap the gulf that usually separates those in command positions from those who must obey. The student could express his hostility and resentment toward the "they." He could displace his aggression toward the overbearing parent, the aloof teacher, the unresponsive administration, or the all-powerful state. The uniformed police were perfect symbols of authority; they provided an ideal target for long repressed aggressions.

The psychic satisfactions of the rally were meager in comparison. One was able, on a number of occasions, to boo and hiss at de Gaulle.

However, while some might obtain a certain vicarious pleasure from such activities, they really do not compare with being able to hurl molotov cocktails at riot police. At the rally, one's direct relationship to authority (i.e. Rochet and company) was one of submission—not rebellion or revenge.

While the rally provided only a limited sense of solidarity and only a modest opportunity for indirect aggression, it nevertheless demanded significant concessions from the individual. The PCF line was imposed on an obedient and uncritical audience. If a member wished to submerge himself in the Communist community, he had to abandon his personal beliefs and attitudes. For the duration of the meeting, at least, he had to accept the PCF's ideology. He had to clap for the Party's conception of "good" and hiss the Party's conception of "evil."

The riot demanded no such psychic surrender. Some rioted to protest injustice; others rioted to weaken the capitalist state; still others rioted for the sheer pleasure of rioting—"parce que la révolution, c'est un fête." Participation in the riot did not imply the acceptance of any line, doctrine, program, or ideology.

LUXEMBURG, THE STUDENTS, AND THE PCF

The Parisian student community—like all communities—contains its own characteristic contradictions. In May 1968 the PCF imposed its universal Leninist-Stalinist solutions and, as a result, found itself unable to cope with the particularity of these contradictions.

As Luxemburg points out, the members of a given community have an immediate, intuitive grasp of the tactical problems posed by their milieu. As a result, they can spontaneously develop creative solutions to these problems. Central apparatuses, on the other hand, tend to impose inappropriate policies on unfamiliar terrains.

The university community in France is troubled by a combination of structural and psychological contradictions. Since students are "oppressed" by distant and unresponsive authorities, they must unite and bring their collective power to bear. But this structural pressure for unity is counteracted by a number of factors—notably the extreme heterogeneity of the students and the radically free, unstructured nature of their life styles.

Presumably, this combination of atomization and radical freedom produces a certain amount of loneliness and anomie. Nevertheless, "nurturent needs" for group-belonging are counteracted by a cultural and psychological bias against collectivism. There remains a general scarcity of stable, enduring secondary groups.

The students have managed to spontaneously resolve these contradictions. They have discovered that the solution lies in the hostile outburts, that is, the chahut, the monôme, and, ultimately, the full-scale political riot. The outburst places direct pressure on the authorities. In addition, it provides an outlet for aggressions and repressed hostility. The anomic crowd temporarily provides an intense feeling of solidarity and belonging, yet it does not compromise the participant's long-range freedom. It overcomes the extreme heterogeneity of the student community but does not destroy this heterogeneity.

As Luxemburg predicted, the students have intuitively grasped their unique problems and have spontaneously evolved unique solutions—*periodic explosions of violent and anomic collective behavior.*

9 The Inhibiting Role of Ideology

For the followers of Cohn-Bendit, *les appareils* were objects of constant scorn and derision. The assumption underlying this attitude was that pyramidal organizational forms were absolutely incompatible with radical political action. "Internally," Cohn-Bendit tells us, "the PCF is organized very much like the capitalist system. It has a hierarchical structure in which the top becomes increasingly remote from the bottom"[1] After separating itself from the masses, the organizational elite attempts to accumulate power; if it succeeds in doing so, it becomes extremely reluctant to risk losing what it has gained. Consequently, its revolutionary ideology becomes empty verbiage. It looses the will to act.

When leftist critics try to interpret the PCF's inaction during May 1968, they frequently turn to this concept of organizational determinism. The *Monthly Review* in its postmortem stressed "bureaucratism" and the subsequent development of "opportunism." It argued, however, that the fundamental cause of the PCF's deradicalization was its initial decision to utilize the tactics of legal parliamentary politics.

> No mass party which is organized to work within the system of bourgeois institutions can also be revolutionary. *If it accepts these institutions and adapts itself to them*—even if it thinks it is doing so only provisionally and temporarily—*it is bound to acquire vested interests in the existing social order* which would not merely be jeopardized but wiped out by a genuine revolution. . . . In every city and town a mass party of this kind spawns a collection of bureaucrats, petty officials and functionaries, whose livelihood and security are as much bound up with the existing order as are those of their opposite number in the bourgeois parties, trade associations, chambers of commerce, etc. [my italics] .[2]

The article suggests that bureaucratized Marxist movements which utilize parliamentary and trade union tactics inevitably succumb to strategic inflexibility. Having inserted themselves into the system, they are compelled by self-interest to help sustain and perpetuate the system. As Rosa Luxemburg said: "Having adjusted to parliamentary tactics there is a tendency to regard parliamentary tactics as the immutable and specific tactics of socialist activity."[3]

Critics of the left are not the only ones who equate bureaucratization with deradicalization. In *Political Parties* (1915) Michels applies a similar thesis in his study of social democratic movements; and Robert Tucker has recently tried to use the Michels' thesis to interpret Communist party development. In *The Marxian Revolutionary Idea* (1969) Tucker argues that as the Leninist vanguard becomes larger and more powerful, it is invariably transformed into a traditional bureaucratic hierarchy. Deradicalization follows, for:

> . . . there seems to be an inverse relationship between a radical movement's *organizational strength* and the preservation of its radicalism. . . . When a radical movement grows and becomes strong, acquires a big organizational structure and a mass social constituency and a recognized place in society, *this very worldly success fosters de-radicalization* [my italics] .[4]

As a party becomes organizationally strong, its influence within the system grows, and it acquires increasing power and prestige. As a result, individuals with opportunistic motives are drawn into its ranks. Eventually they rise to positions of leadership.

> The radical tendency of mind . . . is likely to be dominant among the original generation of the movement's leaders. In the normal course of events, however, this situation will eventually change. . . . Younger persons who rise through the movement into leadership positions are less likely than the original leaders to be radical types. Ambition, organizing ability and concern for the interests of the organization and its social constituency are likely to be their predominant characteristics.[5]

When these opportunists are confronted with the choice between (1) acting in accord with traditional ideological convictions; and (2) acting in accord with personal or organizational interests, they invariably choose the latter. Ideology becomes mere window dressing, then it disappears completely.

It is tempting to use theories of this sort to explain the recent evolution of the French Communist party. But the overall history of the PCF casts doubt on the notion that "insertion" and "bureaucratization" automatically lead to political rigidity and conservatism. On the contrary, the Party's history suggests that ultracentralized bureaucratic hierarchies are capable of extreme strategic and tactical flexibility.

From its inception, the French Communist party has engaged in electoral activity. In the "popular front" period, the Party even entered into an electoral coalition led by bourgeois politicians. Yet, biting the forbidden fruit of system politics did not lead to an inevitable fall. Nor did the development of organizational strength. On numerous occasions the Party has repudiated bourgeois politics and has engaged wholeheartedly in antisystem behavior.

The Bolshevik authority structure has allowed the politburo of the PCF to effect changes in the Party's entire range of activities in a matter of days. In April 1934 the Party was engaged in an uncompromising struggle with the "social fascists"—the SFIO. In *l'Humanité,* Thorez warned that "all gossip about the marriage between Communists and Socialists is alien to the spirit of Bolshevism."[6] But in May, the Party abruptly agreed to join with both the Socialists and the Radicals in a popular front alliance. The purpose of the front was to hold the line against fascism, but in August 1939 the Party suddenly decided that Hitler was not such a bad fellow after all. After the Nazi-Soviet Pact, Party propagandists urged Frenchmen not to participate in the "phony war." As a result, the PCF was forced underground. It became a clandestine, illegal, antisystem movement.

When the occupation began, the Communists tried to reach a modus vivendi with the Germans, and the Party prepared to return to legality.[7] But in June 1941, World War II suddenly became a sacred democratic crusade. From 1941 to 1945 the PCF fought a guerrilla-like struggle for national liberation against both Vichy and the Nazis. The Party apparatus was successfully transformed into an instrument of terror, subversion, and sabotage.

Revolutionary activity ended in 1945. Thorez disbanded the Party's paramilitary organizations and declared that the PCF was prepared to participate in a National Front government under the leadership of de Gaulle. For the next three years, parliamentary regularity was scrupulously observed. But in the fall of 1947 the Communists abruptly repudiated bourgeois politics. A semi-insurrectionary general strike was launched, and throughout France, Communist militants sparked riots and violent demonstrations.

Admittedly, these strategic reversals were hardly reactions to indigenous conditions. Without exception, they were responses to similar shifts in the foreign policy of the Soviet Union. The theory of building socialism in one country demanded that each Communist party do all that it could to defend the interests of the USSR—the homeland of the proletariat.

Nevertheless, the behavior of the PCF between 1934 and the present is hardly compatible with the models set forth by Luxemburg, Cohn-Bendit, Sweezey, and Tucker. These theorists postulate the following general tendencies: after its initial decision to engage in legal forms of political participation, the organizational growth of a radical movement will produce (1) *inflexibility*, an unwillingness to abandon system tactics; (2) an *unresponsiveness* to changing conditions and the opportunities for tactical innovation which they present; and (3) *deradicalization* and a *decline in ideology*—that is, the commitment to system goals and organizational interests will replace the revolutionary objectives of the official ideology. Most of these theorists also argue that these tendencies will be particularly strong if organizational growth occurs within the context of a highly centralized, hierarchical bureaucracy.

One notes, however, that the organizational strength of the PCF reached its zenith in 1945; yet, several years later the Party risked its gains by embarking on a prolonged campaign of riot and rebellion.[8] In 1934 the Party integrated itself into a bourgeois alliance, and in 1945 it even entered a bourgeois government. Yet, each of these popular front phases was followed by sustained periods of illegal, antisystem activities.

The deradicalization hypotheses fail to account for these behavior patterns. This is partly due to the fact that the gradual growth of a hierarchical organization has not led to the decline in the impact of ideology; instead, it has led to the alteration of its function and structure. Ideology is no longer a theory, used by the leadership to analyze changing conditions and deduce appropriate strategies and tactics; rather, it has become a doctrine, used to (1) preserve the unity and the cohesion of the organization; (2) strengthen the morale of those who staff it; and (3) facilitate communication among the various levels of its hierarchy.

The structure of ideology has changed in response to the nature of its new functions. It has been reduced to a set of simple formulas, usually based on a number of clear and distinct dichotomies. Bureaucratization has reduced theory to stereotyped ideological discourse—a form of thought and communication compatible with the mentality and outlook of the average functionary. Within the French Communist party, this tendency seems to have been strengthened by the working-class origins of its members and also, perhaps, by their psychocultural predispositions.

This development has, indeed, led to inflexibility in the sense that it has produced a general unresponsiveness to changing conditions in the political arena. The apparatchik interprets his world in terms of his doctrinal formulas. He views social reality through the sharp dichotomies that structure his ideology; consequently, the dichotomies act as blinders. Rigid modes of perception keep the decision maker from recognizing possibilities for innovative action; and, in addition, the simplified formulas posit a number of automatic, ritualistic responses.

In the case of the PCF, organizational ideology has made the apparatus relatively unresponsive to changing conditions at the base, but it has made the Party extremely responsive to orders from the summit. Cohn-Bendit and Luxemburg not withstanding, the history of the Party is definitely not one of rigidity or inflexibility. The frequent zigs and zags of the PCF's policies have been due, in the last analysis, to an ideological factor: a profound, almost mystical, attachment to the CPSU and its leaders. The ultracentralized Bolshevik structure has provided the organizational preconditions for radical and rapid changes in tactics, while ideological convictions have conditioned the membership to accept these torturous twists and turns.

It is difficult to argue that organizational growth is effectively undermining this particular aspect of Communist doctrine. There

are admittedly indications that elements within the PCF leadership
wish to modify the Party's relationship with the Soviets.[9] But their
efforts to do so have been blocked by important organizational considerations. For example, in August 1968 the politburo of the PCF
issued a statement strongly condemning the Russian invasion of
Czechoslovakia. The following day the central committee issued
a new declaration significantly softening both the tone and the
substance of the original politburo statement.[10]

Several forces seem to have influenced this reversal. First, it is
known that both apparatchiki and rank-and-file militants vigorously
protested the Party's "betrayal" of the homeland of the proletariat.[11]
This particular element of the PCF's traditional ideology seems to
be deeply and passionately held by many active Communists. Any
attempts by the leadership to introduce a more pragmatic and autonomous line are strongly resisted by unreconstructed ideologues at all
levels of the organizational hierarchy.

Second, the Soviet Union can still apply powerful sanctions when
nonruling parties move to revise their ideological commitments.
The massive apparatus of the PCF—with its numerous publications
and ancillary bodies—is sustained in part by Soviet aid, which probably takes the form of both direct subsidies and commissions from
various trade arrangements. Consequently, if the Party is to maintain its access to one of the principal sources of the wealth that allows it to preserve its impressive organizational empire, it must also
maintain its basic commitment to Soviet doctrine.[12]

It is, therefore, a profound mistake to set organizational interests
in opposition to ideological faith. As the apparatus grows and becomes more complex, ideology fulfills increasingly important functions. Instead of becoming looser and more flexible, it tends to become increasingly rigid and schematic. In addition, an adherence
to ideological orthodoxy is sustained by both the practical need for
organizational revenues, and the spiritual need for preserving the
esprit de corps of both the militants and the functionaries.

IDEOLOGY AND RADICAL ACTION

The theorists of bureaucratic deradicalization tend to endow the
ideologue and the "organization man" with antithetical psycho-

logical characteristics. A firm commitment to radical theory supposedly leads to decisive or impulsive action, while identification
with an established organization supposedly leads to caution, prag-
matism, and a preference for bureaucratic routines.[13] The pure
ideologue is eager to engage in violence and insurrection; the apparatchik, however, prefers to maintain the status quo.*

The history of the Marxist movement calls these caricatures into
question, for it indicates that ideology has often played as equally
inhibiting and conserving a role as organization. Marx himself
strongly opposed the Paris Commune on strictly theoretical grounds.
He argued that the objective conditions for social revolution did not
yet exist. Likewise, Kamenev, Zinoviev, and Stalin initially opposed
the October Revolution. They apparently felt that a Bolshevik
seizure of power would have violated the traditional Marxist scenario
for historical progress; for orthodox theorists argued that it was impossible for a proletarian revolution to occur until the bourgeois
mode of production had fully exhausted its possibilities.

In neither case can the reluctance to act be traced to strong organizational interests. Marx's International Workingmen's Association had virtually no bureaucracy, nor did the Bolshevik party of
Lenin and Zinoviev. The prime restraining force seems to have been
ideology.

If one wishes to view ideological and organizational factors as two
distinct sets of variables, each of which can inhibit Marxist parties
from engaging in radical action, then in the French case the ideological factors seem to have played a key role. This assertion can be
supported by an examination of the events of May, particularly by

---

*It is interesting to note that the functionariat of the Italian Socialist party
(PSI) has consistently supported the antisystem left against the reformist
right; it has been among the Party's most vocal opponents of reconciliation
with the Social Democrats and has been a strong advocate of unity of action
with the Communists. In this case, bureaucratic "personality types" have
continued to retain their commitment to the orthodox interpretation of
their radical ideology, partially, no doubt, because of the patronage gained
from local PCI-PSI coalition governments. (See Robert Zariski, "The Italian
Socialist Party: A Case Study in Factional Conflict," *American Political
Science Review,* June 1962.)

a comparison between the activities of the PCF apparatus and those of France's nonbureaucratized and noninserted Marxist-Leninist movements.

The Maoists

Like the PCF, the Maoist groups refused to look upon the students as a unique social group. They failed to see the university milieu as a unique community with its own particular contradictions. Instead, they assumed that the students were merely a segment of the petit-bourgeoisie. Student activities were viewed through the categories posited by Marxist-Leninists to deal with the middle classes.

Since the students were considered bourgeois, their political consciousness was also bourgeois, consequently, their goals were non-revolutionary—for the proletariat is the only true revolutionary class in modern society.* Any movement oriented to the specific needs and aspirations of the students was, necessarily, bourgeois and nonrevolutionary. The UJC(ML) therefore made no effort to organize the student movement. Its activities in the occupied faculties were limited to the sale of Maoist pamphlets.

Student demands were labeled "bourgeois demands." The call for student power was said to be no more than a demand that control of the universities be shifted from one segment of the capitalist class to another. On May 9, the UJC(ML) issued a declaration denouncing the slogan "the Sorbonne for the students" and substituted the call "the Sorbonne for the workers."[14]

This deterministic view of political consciousness is reflected in the strategic outlook of the Maoists. Since the students could not fight for truly revolutionary objectives, all they could do was place themselves at the service of those who could. "The students must go to the factories and they must place themselves at the disposal of the working class." From a strict Marxist-Leninist viewpoint, the student movement had no right to exist. The student radicals were

---

*"The dangers that menace us: (the students) want to transform the working-class into a supporting force. It is the working-class which is the true vanguard of the struggles; the true revolutionary is he who allies himself, today, with the workers." *Analyses et Documents,* no. 155, May 1968, p. 3.

told to leave their faculties, abandon the struggle for university reform, and assist the striking proletarians.

> Let us sweep away the words of the purely university type of
> reformer, and the small revisionist and social democratic groups
> who are in league with them, and who are trying to bar the way
> of the popular masses, the way of the revolution. . . . Let us
> leave the bourgeois neighborhoods where there is nothing for
> us to do. . . . Let us go to the factories and to the popular quar-
> ters where we will unite with the workers.[15]

The strategy of the Maoist students consisted of (1) mingling with
the workers; (2) overcoming their own "antiproletarian prejudices";
and (3) serving the workers in their day-to-day struggles against the
capitalist class.[16]

But the Maoists shared the Marxist-Leninist belief that the working class, on it own, could not develop a revolutionary state of consciousness. A vanguard party was necessary. Since France lacked a
revolutionary party, it lacked a working class conscious of the necessity of revolution. As a result, the Maoists felt that a revolutionary
situation did not exist in May, for a successful seizure of power can
be effected only if an ideologically advanced mass base is present.
Thus, while the PCF refused to participate in a general uprising because the correct "objective conditions" were absent, the UJC(ML)
refused because the correct "subjective conditions" were absent.[17]

The Maoists therefore echoed the PCF accusation that the groupuscules were engaging in irresponsible and foolish provocations. Talk
of seizing power was premature; the construction of soviets was unrealistic; and the building of barricades in the Latin Quarter served
absolutely no useful function. Riots in the bourgeois ghettos merely
assisted de Gaulle in his efforts to isolate progressive students from
their popular allies. Consequently, the UJC(ML) firmly castigated
UNEF for encouraging student violence.

> This irresponsible gesture of the national bureau of the UNEF
> and the small trotskyist and anarchist groups which control it
> must be halted. The progressive students publicly demand that
> the national bureau of the UNEF immediately cease to play the

game of police provocateur and of small group maneuvers which
carry the student movement towards a brutal collapse, similar
to the ones which have already occurred several times in the
past.[18]

Being loyal Marxist-Leninists, the UJC(ML) felt that demonstrations
and uprisings had to be organized, controlled, and directed. Consequently, it imitated the PCF and attempted to squash the hostile
outbursts. Even on June 10, the day one of their comrades was
killed, the Maoists tried to discourage anomic violence. Soon after
the crowd had assembled in the Place St. Michel, one of the leaders
of the UJC(ML) hoisted himself up on a lamp post and delivered a
brief speech. Instead of inciting the students to revolutionary action,
he asked them to disperse.

> One of our comrades, a high school student, and a member of
> the UJC(ML) was killed by the police at Flins. He was part of
> a group which was supporting the workers and their union;
> and he was thrown into the river. Our comrade will be avenged
> tomorrow. Tonight we will go back to the Sorbonne.[19]

The crowd responded by shouting "aujourd'hui, aujourd'hui!" The
masses seem to have been in advance of their vanguard.

The official Maoist party, the PCF(ML) was equally displeased
with the spontaneous tactics of the students. They indignantly rejected the government accusation that they had directed and fomented
the "night of the barricades." They pointed out that if true Maoists
had planned the uprising, they would have followed Chinese principles of guerrilla warfare: the rebellion would have been better
organized and, consequently, more effective.

> It is necessary to return here to the government accusation ac-
> cording to which the uprisings were organized by pro-Chinese
> guerrilla commandos. . . . If the uprisings had been conducted
> according to the principles of civil war as outlined by Mao Tse-
> tung, they would certainly not have been carried out in the
> manner that they were. In fact, the principles of civil war, in a
> city like Paris with an over-equipped police force, forbid en-

circlement by the enemy; instead, small mobile forces should
be formed, which can harass the enemy by attacking it from
different sides and by thus dividing it. [20]

In short, the Maoists' response was extremely similar to that of
the PCF; both were framed by certain basic tenets of Marxist-Leninist theory. The UJC(ML) and the PCF(ML) refused to enter the student struggle because (1) petit-bourgeois revolts were inevitably
"pseudo-revolutionary"; (2) insurrectionary activity was inappropriate at that particular strategic stage; and (3) when violence is
used, it has to be conscious, controlled, and directed.

Certain Trotskyist groups also reacted in a similar fashion. The
Fédération des étudiants révolutionnaires (FER), for example, did
all it could to discourage the students from participating in the
"night of the barricades." On May 10 the organization's Parisian
militants held a meeting in the Mutualité; they discussed ideology
and strategy while a massive demonstration developed in the Latin
Quarter. It soon metamorphosed into a full-scale battle between
the students and the CRS. When FER heard the news, it dispatched
messengers who tried to circulate an order to disperse. They called
for a "grand demonstration of students *and* workers" on the following Monday: "*500,000 travailleurs lundi au Quartier Latin.*" When
the students rejected this advice, the FER militants threw up their
hands and went home.

Like the Maoists, many Trotskyists felt that exclusively student
demonstrations were purposeless. The petit-bourgeoisie could do
nothing on its own. "Isolated, the students will be defeated. More
than ever it is necessary to appeal to the UNEF and to the workers'
unions to organize a central demonstration of the working class
and the youth." [21] A controlled and directed demonstration, unit-
ing both workers and students, was thought to be far more effica-
cious than a spontaneous *chahut.*

The ultra-left initially played a conservative role. It tried to freeze
the student uprising by imposing certain preconceived limits on its
development. Consequently, its immediate response resembled that
of the French Communist party. The cause of this similarity seems
to have been common ideological convictions; the convergence can-

not possibly be attributed to insertion or organizational conservatism. None of the groupuscules had a bureaucracy. The UJC(ML) and FER were tiny revolutionary sects; neither had more than a thousand members. In addition, neither had inserted itself into the existing political system. The Trotskyists and the Maoists were totally uninterested in any sort of reformism; on the contrary, they were devout believers in the necessity of a violent and thoroughgoing revolution. But like the PCF, they wanted a revolution which obeyed the rigid schemes of their own Marxist-Leninist doctrines.

Cohn-Bendit

While the Communists, the Maoists, and the Trotskyists were either unwilling or unable to adapt their strategies to the conditions of university life, 22 Mars proved extremely successful in this regard. Cohn-Bendit was a doctrinaire anarchist. He had a doctrinaire dislike of rigid doctrines, hierarchies, and organizations. Consequently, his ideology was well-suited to the university milieu. Unlike doctrinaire Marxism-Leninism, doctrinaire anarcho-Marxism proved entirely congenial to the situational and psychocultural characteristics of the French student.

It is interesting to note that Cohn-Bendit began with the same basic assumptions as the Communists. The university, he observed, is a radically heterogeneous community; the students do not form a homogeneous social class.

> Some of us are destined to control the nation, others will become poorly paid intellectual hacks—there are 600,000 of us: the so-called "students" of the military academy at St. Cyr, the artists and the "arties," the technocrats of the Faculty of Political Science . . . and the rigid Marxist "intellectuals" of the Sorbonne, of Nanterre and elsewhere. We include readers of *l'Humanité* and "militant" journals, assiduous readers of *Le Monde* and devotees of the sporting press or the cinema, beatniks, crammers, spoilt rich kids who never graduate, girls who marry during their first year, but meanwhile study law, languages and even psychology, dunces, duds, future mathematicians and doctors.[22]

He also shared the Communist belief that the relatively unstructured nature of university life fails to endow the student with the firmness and discipline of the factory worker.

> The student, at least in the modern system of higher education, still preserves a considerable degree of personal freedom. . . . He does not have to earn his own living; he does not have a foreman on his back. . . . Now, these very factors have an inhibiting mechanism: they far too often cause his engagement to lack consistency and force.[23]

Unlike the Party, however, Cohn-Bendit did not conclude that the petit-bourgeois student was inevitably a nonrevolutionary opportunist. On the contrary, he pointed out that students have frequently conducted themselves in an extremely militant and radical manner. He noted, for example, that 25 percent of the French university population participated in militant protests against the Algerian war—while in the rest of the country "protests remained largely verbal."[24]

Although he insisted that a potential for militant behavior existed among a substantial segment of the university population, he recognized, however, that very few students were really politically conscious.[25] Only a small minority had the interest and the dedication needed to sustain a steady radical commitment. Cohn-Bendit therefore posed the essential challenge of the university organizer in the following terms. The active minority must find some means of arousing the passive majority—of inciting them to action. At the same time, it must "raise the level of their political consciousness"; it must transform their latent discontent and vague rebelliousness into a coherent revolutionary vision.

His anarchist bias immediately precluded the possibility of forming a structured movement of a Leninist vanguard; even if he had been so predisposed, he recognized that the student terrain provided a poor setting for elitist pretentions and hierarchical organizations. As a result, his active minority refused to assume a formal leadership role. "They never set themselves up as champions of the 'common interests of all students,' but simply demanded the right to express political opinions within the campus and without police interference."[26]

This ingenuous statement, of course, is totally misleading. The active minority expressed its demand for "political liberty" in the

most dramatic and provocative fashion possible. In fact, 22 Mars
continually made a spectacle of itself. When the minister of sport
came to Nanterre to dedicate a new swimming pool, Cohn-Bendit
interrupted his speech and demanded to know what his ministry
was doing to promote sexual education among the young. The
minister replied that if Cohn-Bendit had sexual problems he
could cool off in the pool. He responded by accusing the
minister of "talking like a Hitler Youth official." In a similar
fashion, Cohn-Bendit would continually disrupt the lectures of
Professor Crozier on American sociological problems by demanding to know what the professor's organizational theories had to do
with the Vietnam war.

Cohn-Bendit freely admitted that these moves were provocations.

> In reality, everything hangs on the use of provocation in the
> crystallization of thought and emotion. . . . All we did therefore
> was to "provoke" students to express their passive discontent,
> first by demonstrations for their own sake, and then by politi-
> cal actions directly challenging modern society.[27]

The elite made no effort to organize or control the masses; it merely incited them. Its disruptive demonstrations served two essential
functions. First, they forced the administration to reveal its "repressive" and "authoritarian" character; the principal contradiction of
the student community—the antagonism between the "despotic"
and "unresponsive" authorities and the impotent student mass—was
therefore accentuated. Second, the arrival of the police provided a
useful precipitating incident. By provoking the dean and the rector,
and by compelling them to commit blatantly repressive acts, the
radical elite created catalytic incidents which touched off the latent
resentment, frustration, and hostility of the student body.

There was no need to lead or mobilize the student mass; 22 Mars
simply staged spectacular provocations, which ignited a more or less
spontaneous hostile outburst among the rest of their comrades. Cohn-
Bendit therefore succeeded in overcoming the community's heterogeneity and passivity without offending its anticollectivist bias. He
did not try to discipline or organize the students, but his provocations
did provide them with the opportunity to develop a sense of solidarity
and a consciousness of their collective power.

Any pretext for inciting the students was considered useful and valid; the important thing was to overcome their passivity, to involve them in *action*. "Learning through action plays a basic part in the genesis and growth of all revolutionary movements. From analyzing what is closest at hand, we can understand society at large."[28] Even protests against visiting hours in female dormitories played a useful political role. "We show them first of all that the petty hostel regulations are impertinent infringements of their personal liberty, that learning is no substitute for the warmth of human companionship."[29]

Instead of establishing a leader-follower relationship, the elite tried to engage the masses in what might be called a demonstrative dialogue. Through its actions it revealed to them a negative and restrictive aspect of their own situation; and it also revealed how this could be combated. More important, it provided the masses with an example and an inspiration and, hence, with the will and the courage to act.

After this demonstrative dialogue had been initiated, the elite started to ideologically "enlighten" the masses. But Cohn-Bendit insisted that communication transcend the worn-out techniques and formulas of traditional Communist agitation and propaganda. Continual tactical innovations had to be introduced in order to maintain the link between ideas and action.

> Our first task is to make the students more politically conscious. In practice, this means developing new ways of communication: improvising meetings in various faculty common rooms, occupying lecture halls, interrupting lectures with denunciations of their ideological bias, boycotting the examinations, sticking up posters and slogans, taking over the public address system—in short, taking any action that openly challenges the authorities.[30]

The provocations of Cohn-Bendit acted as detonators that aroused the student community as a whole. According to the theorists of 22 Mars, the student uprising was, in turn, the detonator that touched off the proletariat's general strike.

When the police tried to pacify the Latin Quarter, the students fought back. Instead of submitting, they rebelled. They built barricades, burned police vans, and tossed molotov cocktails. As a result, many of their demands were met. Their imprisoned comrades were released; the CRS temporarily retreated to the right bank; and the faculties were reopened. Not satisfied, the students proceeded to occupy the university facilities.

The persistence and militancy of the students did, indeed, seem to inspire the workers. After May 13 the proletariat even began to copy the university tactics. They occupied their factories, and some even imprisoned their bosses in their offices and threatened not to let them out until their demands were met. A "grève genérale il-limitée" began. By May 20, ten million workers were on strike. On May 15 a million workers and students marched through Paris shouting "à bas de Gaulle" and "dix ans ça suffit." The state was intimidated and significant economic concessions followed.

As the theorists of 22 Mars reflected on this sequence of events, they developed a new strategy of mass mobilization. It was essentially a universalization of the tactics developed at Nanterre. An approach ideally suited to the university was applied to society as a whole. The role assigned by Marxism-Leninism to the vanguard party was usurped by the so-called *action exemplaire*. The latter is explained in the following manner:

> The passage from the student to the worker uprising was the fundamental point of the whole revolutionary process. What happened would have had no importance if this had not taken place. The latter occurred at the level of spontaneous and not directly political consciousness. The workers came and saw how a certain type of intervention had thrown a monkey wrench into the machinery of government, and that furthermore, there existed a situation in the Latin Quarter where there was a double power, which the bourgeois forces could not overthrow without raising the struggle to a new level. This experience, after twenty to twenty-five years of working-class defeats, after twenty-five years of partial concessions obtained within the framework of the existing system, this new experience of the transformation of power relationships was *exemplary*. [31]

Within the university community, students were extremely reluctant to let themselves be led or guided by other students; likewise, workers had no desire to be given orders by petit-bourgeois radicals. Luckily, according to 22 Mars, arrangements of this sort were totally unnecessary. More advanced segments of society could teach and inspire other segments *through the force of their exemplary action.*

In the eyes of the Communists, the conscious elite uses its knowledge of Marxism-Leninism to develop a coherent strategy, which it then uses to mobilize the masses and lead them to victory. In the eyes of Cohn-Bendit, the activities of a tiny radical elite can trigger spontaneous uprisings among the students, which can, in turn, trigger similar uprisings among the workers, peasants, and petit-bourgeoisie. The revolution is, in essence, a chain reaction of anomic hostile outbursts.

ORGANIZATION: FER AND JCR

The credit for touching off the May revolt can be given to 22 Mars. Initially, its strategy was successful. But at a certain point, it became apparent that the doctrine of spontaneity had serious limitations.

The May movement can be divided into two distinct periods: the phase of detonation and expansion; and the phase of mobilization and organization. During the first period, Cohn-Bendit's ideology seemed congruent with social reality. The beginning of the student revolt was indeed an anomic hostile outburst, and the beginning of the student-worker alliance was the outgrowth of spontaneous contagion.

To a certain point, this lack of direction was functional. The riots and occupations generated a new sense of solidarity; and the concessions from the government gave the students an exhilarating awareness of their collective power. For several weeks the movement was carried by its own momentum.

But when the state recovered from its initial shock, when it regained full use of the agencies of social control, the limitations of spontaneity began to be felt. At the same time, the students found that the spontaneous solidarity created in the streets of Paris was an extremely ephemeral phenomenon. It was an immediate emotional response to a common external threat. But when the riots were over and the bourgeois intellectuals began to reflect upon what had taken place, solidarity dissipated, and innumerable factional and ideological disagreements emerged. The student movement began to degenerate under the pressures of both internal and external forces.

A number of attempts were made to stem this degenerative process. Each of the groupuscules presented organizational solutions designed to preserve student-student and student-worker solidarity. The nature of these plans depended largely upon the traditional ideological assumptions of each group.

FER, for example, was an offshoot of Pierre Lambert's Organisation communiste internationale (OCI). Lambert left the official Trotskyist party because he objected to Pierre Frank's *entriste* policy; that is, his efforts to infiltrate existing socialist movements and reform them from within. He felt that the Stalinist bureaucracies were hopelessly deformed; totally new organizations therefore had to be constructed. By entering existing groups, one risked compromising the purity of one's Marxist-Leninist beliefs. According to Lambert, it was best to wait until objective conditions permitted the formation of a truly revolutionary party.

As a result, OCI and FER have remained isolated, sectarian groups fighting for pure Marxist-Leninist goals. They have nothing but scorn for the *corporatiste* and *dépassés* demands of other socialist organizations. Consequently, they have little to do with the great mass of student activists, most of whom have definite reformist tendencies. FER's isolation has rendered it generally unresponsive to the attitudes and opinions of its clientele. Thus, it tends to mechanistically impose its theoretical preconceptions on social reality—regardless of the probable consequences.

From the beginning of the student revolt, it sought to bring students and workers together into a new revolutionary organization. Its leaders immediately advocated the creation of a proliferation of *comités de grève* to be coordinated by a *comité central de grève*—which, in turn, would form the basis of a *front unique ouvrier.* FER attempted to introduce this structure as early as May 12 when the movement was still in its infancy—that is, in its dynamic, spontaneous phase.

The ultimate goal was to fuse student and proletarian endeavors.

But it carried out its policy in such a mechanistic fashion that, in
many cases, it seems to have accomplished the exact opposite. In
early May a committee from the Sorbonne organized a common
meeting with delegates from the strike committees of the 13th
arrondissement, which included workers from PTT, Gobelins,
and Air France. FER continually interrupted the meetings and
demanded that the various strike committees immediately feder-
ate. In the words of one observer:

> You can imagine the surprise and embarrassment of the mili-
> tants, many of whom were coming for the first time, and not
> without considerable reticence, to be suddenly confronted
> with a demand for a higher form of resistance, without its
> having been discussed in their own strike committees. This
> meeting was the first . . . and the last.[32]

During the first phase, rigid organizational patterns were premature.
Through the spontaneous hostile outbursts, the students were just
beginning to gain a sense of their collective power and solidarity.
Yet, FER did all it could to stifle these adventuristic endeavors.
Instead, it insisted that the students and workers join in orderly
street processions and submit to a new organizational hierarchy.

The rival Trotskyist group, the Jeunesse communiste révolutionnaire, had an ideological tradition that was far more suitable to
the initial period of mass spontaneity. Since the JCR was much less
sectarian than the FER, it tended to mingle with other groups and
assimilate their ideas. Following Frank's policy, the JCR had "entered" 22 Mars. Consequently, it had made numerous contacts with
the followers of the German radical Rudi Dutschke who were studying
at Nanterre. It had come to accept the Marcusian notion that the
youth formed a new revolutionary vanguard. In the eyes of the JCR
militants, this concept had been legitimized by Fidel Castro in a
recent article published in *Les Temps Modernes,* "Qui sont les
révolutionnaires aujourd'hui?" In this essay Castro proclaimed that
the young, middle-class intellectuals were in the vanguard of the
new revolutionary movement.

The JCR theorists argued that since the present generation of students had reached political consciousness after 1956, they had not

been subjected to the ideology of Stalinism. Consequently, they had no qualms about making a decisive break with the outmoded and bureaucratized Stalinist parties. As the Parti communiste internationale put it: "Contrary to 1936 and 1945, there was this time a new factor in the revolutionary forces . . . the presence of a large advance-guard of youth who were resolutely anti-capitalist."[33] Since it had fully severed all ties with the traditional Communist parties, this post-Stalinist generation constituted a possible basis for a new revolutionary party.

> The leadership of the French Communist party has lost all credit with the revolutionary youth; its prestige has been greatly impaired among the whole advanced guard of the students. This liberation of the youth from the yoke of the bureaucracy has allowed them to form a new revolutionary vanguard on a scale never before equalled in France.[34]

Since they were strongly influenced by the ideas of Rosa Luxemburg, the JCR militants felt that the students could best fulfill their vanguard role by leading the working class in direct action. They deemphasized the importance of organization and instead stressed the need for continual direct contact through common combat. Consequently, the JCR tried to integrate students and workers by engaging them in the same battles—the same hostile outbursts. "A revolutionary today," declared a JCR leaflet, "is anyone who fights against the *flics.*"

FER was bitterly denounced for suggesting that riots be replaced by street parades, which would unite established student groups with working-class unions. JCR viewed this as a surrender to the bureaucracies.

> Integration favors those for whom union with the working-class would be the liaison with the union bureaucracies. . . . For us, union with the workers does not mean sticking one's neck in the bureaucratic yoke, nor making each individual worker the representative of the working class, nor leaving in order to "serve the people." We accomplish a "union" and will in the future accomplish it *in the struggle*—we accomplished it last Monday and Tuesday . . . in the Latin Quarter.[35]

FER advocated unity at the summit through agreements between the leaders of mass organizations. JCR, on the other hand, called for unity at the base through mass participation in common struggles.

Like all good Trotskyists, JCR militants polemicized endlessly against the bureaucracy. The deradicalization of the PCF was explained almost entirely in terms of its bureaucratization. As a result, the JCR strenuously resisted all attempts to bureaucratize the student movement by channeling it through existing organizations—whether PCF or UNEF. Instead, they turned to the traditional Trotskyist solution: dual power.

> It is a question of creating dual elements of power within business enterprises and in the various sections of town, in the form of committees which assume the rights already acquired in the present struggle and which the powers that be cannot snatch from them at short notice without provoking a test of strength which will result in the enlargement of the revolutionary force.[36]

The JCR was therefore eager to infiltrate and utilize the *comités d'action,* which had been set up largely due to 22 Mars initiatives. By May 31 there were about 490 such committees in the Parisian region. These bodies were intended to be the "legitimate revolutionary governments" of the areas under student and worker control. As a result, the JCR viewed the barricades and the nightly rioting as part of a Trotskyist system of auto-defense. The students fought to protect their revolutionary gains from the government and the agents of repression.

The JCR formed a large *service d'ordre* designed to help the students organize their battles with the CRS. I was informed by one member that this group had succeeded in introducing a number of tactical innovations into the student riot. For example, as a CRS briga- advanced on its quarry, one group of militants would direct the construction of a barricade at one end of the block while another group would construct a barricade at the opposite end. Consequently, the police would be boxed in. Other militants would be stationed on the roofs of the apartments that lined the street. They would hurl paving stones and molotov cocktails on the trapped *flics.*

The JCR therefore claimed that it had managed to introduce at least a measure of consciousness into the spontaneous student revolts.

The confrontations were tactically streamlined; but more important, they were transformed from mere hostile outbursts into conscious attempts to protect the revolutionary gains of the "people's soviets."

Because of the 22 Mars' and the JCR's dread of bureaucracy, the *comités* remained extremely flexible and loosely structured. Each was totally autonomous. No ideology or common political line was imposed. They were the organizational equivalents of the anomic riots: they tried to actualize the collective power of the masses without placing inordinate collectivist demands on the individual members. There was no platform and no bureaucracy—and virtually no discipline.

Since coordination was lacking, each committee ran off in its own direction. Some supported local strikes, others carried out agitation and propaganda, and many served simply as covers—which were used by existing political parties to expand their influence. The *Comité de coordination des comités d'action* made no significant decisions; and the general assemblies of committee delegates were chaotic and unproductive. No effective force emerged to counteract the disunity and confusion.

Because of their differing ideological orientations, each of the groupuscules achieved varying degrees of success during the rebellion's successive phases. During the period of initial formation, 22 Mars played a crucial role. It acted as a restrained elite; it incited the masses but did not attempt to impose its ideas or prejudices upon them. As a result, a large and heterogeneous community was drawn into the battle.

FER and UJC(ML), on the other hand, immediately tried to introduce Bolshevik discipline and control. Their Leninist intolerance of spontaneity prompted them to deny the initial value of anomic, undirected riots. Because of their theoretical purity, their attempts to mobilize the students appeared rather crude and mechanistic; and they were almost invariably unsuccessful.

As the movement grew and developed, 22 Mars contributed less and less; for it was constitutionally unable and unwilling to give form and structure to the movement which it had set in motion. Once it became apparent that a degree of coordination and organization was necessary, Cohn-Benditism became more or less obsolete. Yet neither FER nor the UJC(ML) could fulfill the organizational function, since both groups had thoroughly discredited themselves as a result of their sectarian and dogmatic reaction to the spontaneous phase of the revolutionary process.

For a brief period, the JCR was able to lend at least a measure of direction and coherence to the student movement. Since it had assimilated both a Marcusian cult of youth and a Luxemburgist cult of spontaneity, it naturally responded in a positive manner to the student outbreak. Since its militants were conspicuously present in all the major riots, it established a firm reputation among the student mass.

As the movement entered the phase when organization became imperative, the JCR was able to make a number of useful contributions. But its dislike of bureaucracy ultimately inhibited its efforts. In addition, the Luxemburgist stress on direct action seems to have discouraged slow and patient organizational work. Consequently, the *comités d'action* remained primitive, undeveloped, and relatively unsuccessful. As a result, the movement never acquired the organizational sophistication needed to muster effective resistance to the Gaullist counterattack.

10. Contradictions on the Left

Communists claim that Marxist-Leninist theory can be used to reveal the major contradictions of capitalist society. Within the Communist movement, however, Marxist-Leninist ideology has itself become the source of significant contradictions—ones which Communist functionaries have a great deal of difficulty recognizing and resolving.

The contradictions develop on the basis of the dual function that ideology is called upon to fulfill. First, it must guide the decision maker in his efforts to analyze society and devise plans for its revolutionary transformation. Second, ideology must serve as an instrument for the maintenance of organizational cohesion within a hierarchical apparatus characterized by an intricate division of labor.

If ideology is to perform this second set of tasks successfully, it has to be adapted to the needs and capacities of the working-class Communists who staff the Communist machine. It must be reduced to a set of simple formulas based on clear, unambiguous—and therefore dichotomous—distinctions. If it is to fulfill its first role, however, it must retain its intricacy, flexibility, and complexity. There is consequently a contradiction between the "doctrinal-organizational" and "theoretical-analytical" functions of ideology.

The French Communist party has reacted to this problem by resolutely subordinating theory to doctrine. Strategic and tactical decisions are, for the most part, practical applications of the formulas posited by the Stalinist reduction of Marxism-Leninism. The task of the theorist is to employ the dialectic to illustrate, document, and otherwise dress up the strategic decisions and doctrinal pronouncements of the Party leadership.

The proletarian apparatchiki, who have ruled the Party for more than forty years, have consistently relegated the bourgeois intellectuals to secondary, supporting roles. Likewise, they have regarded the bourgeois students as potential Party intellectuals. Consequently, the Union of Communist Students has functioned primarily as a training program for loyal, obedient Party ideologues.

179

The roles assigned to the student and the intellectual have rigid boundaries, which it is impermissible to transgress. Since Marxism-Leninism posits an intimate unity of theory and practice, theoretical criticism inevitably implies criticism of practical strategy. When a bourgeois intellectual engages in innovative or creative theoretical activity, he implicitly calls into question the ideological basis of the apparatchiki's decisions and policies.

The PCF leadership therefore views intellectual dissidence as a dangerous threat to the legitimacy of its authority. The factional activity of its student members is seen as equally subversive, for the independent initiatives of the UEC or the groupuscules appear to be attempts to transform the abstract criticisms of the intellectuals into concrete political practice.

As a result, the apparatchiki and the intelligentsia have periodically engaged in bitter and vindictive conflicts. Many Marxist intellectuals refuse to accept the subordinate position assigned to them. They often justify this refusal by arguing that Thorez, Duclos, and Rochet are "incompetent theorists." Marxism, they assert, must be rescued from the dogmatism of the Party.

Arguments of this sort often rest on a refusal to recognize that a radical simplification of theory is necessary, given the Party's intricate organizational structure and mass, working-class membership. Baby, Barjonet, and Hervé failed to come to grips with the actual functions of organizational doctrine; instead, they insisted on regarding its emergence as a betrayal of the dialectic and as evidence of the "sclerosis" of the PCF.

Other radical intellectuals have conceded the practical efficacy of a reduced doctrine. Sartre, for example, disagreed with Stalinist materialism but recognized its historical mission as a "working-class myth." Althusser has refused to engage in political analysis and has confined himself to the specifically philosophical issues of Marxism. Both have tried to avoid the wrath of the apparatus by setting forth criticisms of a limited, nonpolitical nature. Sartre concentrated on metaphysical and ethical issues and accepted the practical leadership of Thorez. Althusser tried to differentiate between theoretical practice and political practice—in order to delineate a realm of activity in which the intellectual could expend his creative energies without infringing on the prerogatives of the politician.

Even these partial criticisms and cautious initiatives have been regarded by the Communist leadership as fundamental and dangerous challenges. The PCF has refused to accept any revision of its doctrine or any redefinition of the intellectual's role that might compromise the leadership's absolute ideological authority.

Despite the rebuffs they have suffered, Sartre and Althusser have been reluctant to sever their ties with the Party. They seem to feel that without the Communist movement they are *nothing*—that is, their words lack any practical effect, any real social impact.

In recent years, however, the intellectual has tried to actualize his normative and theoretical visions by turning to another social force, the radical youth. During the Algerian crisis, the existentialists regarded the students as shock troops in the antiwar struggle. During the early sixties, the UEC became the principal spokesman for Italian-inspired revisionism. When Professor Althusser decided to return Marxism to its original purity and vigor, he turned to the Communist students at the Ecole Normale.

Many students have been content to act as the foot soldiers of the radical intelligentsia. The UEC blended Sartre and Gorz with Togliatti; the JCR joined Mandel and Lambert with Castro, Trotsky, and Luxemburg; the M-L groups fused Althusser with Mao.

Others, however, have adopted a position of complete rebellion. They reject the Communist party—but they also reject the "old men" of the intelligentsia. The theoretical systems of Sartre and Althusser are viewed as being just as repressive as the hierarchy of the PCF. The revolution will come, they argue, only through spontaneous, unrestrained revolt. The creativity of the student revolutionaries, their imaginative innovations, and their total affirmation of freedom will inspire the working class and set an example for the masses.

Despite the students' claims that they have broken completely with the past, existentialist, structuralist, and traditional Marxist and anarchist themes continually reappear in their words and acts. Nevertheless, it is clear that the student radicals have moved steadily to the left. In the early sixties the UEC rebels were fighting for more Party democracy, an effective popular front policy, and the gradual reform of social structures. By 1966 the student community had been captured by the militantly revolutionary notions of Ché, Trotsky, and the Chinese. In the spring of 1968 the fashionable theories

were those of the situationists and Cohn-Bendit. A glorification of
the pure act of revolution replaced traditional concerns over theoretical and organizational matters.

While the Party moved to the right and assumed an almost social
democratic posture, the students moved in the opposite direction.
This can be partially attributed to the apparent failure of the established leftist organizations and the traditional intellectual leaders.
During the first decade of the Fifth Republic, the left remained divided
and helpless before the growing power of the Gaullist regime. Sartre
had repeatedly failed in his attempts to show the PCF the error of
its ways, and he had temporarily turned from politics to autobiography
and Flaubert. After his rebuke by the central committee, Althusser
turned to a rigorous but somewhat esoteric study of the concept
of science.

The move to the left must also be viewed within the context of
international communism. The debate between the Party and the
students has frequently expressed itself in conflicting attitudes toward Third World revolutionary movements. The PCF supports the
Soviet position, while the radical students generally share the stands
of the Cubans or Chinese. As far as the Vietnam war is concerned,
the Party stresses the objective of peace through negotiations. As
was the case during the Algerian war, the students call for a complete military victory by the National Liberation Front.

The popularity of the Third World movements is due in large
measure to the fact that they seem to provide an alternative basis
for revolutionary action—an alternative social force with which the
student and intellectual can ally. After Soviet-style communism was
rejected in the late fifties, the major countermodels were those of
the Cubans and the Chinese. After Togliatti's death in 1964, Italian
revisionism no longer seemed a viable substitute. By the mid-sixties,
the reformist policies of the PCI and the PCF were virtually indistinguishable. The revolutionary initiative had shifted to Asia
and Latin America. Ho and Ché were in the front lines of the struggle
against American imperialism.

The remoteness of the Third World was anything but a disadvantage.
Obviously, neither the Cubans nor the FLN could provide real support
in the struggle for French socialism. But neither could they interfere

with the creative initiatives of the students. A Maoist or a Castroite can therefore feel that he is part of a great social movement without suffering any of the confining disadvantages of such an alliance.

Becoming a *chinoise* or a *guévariste* means engaging in "exemplary actions," which inspire the masses and thus prepare the foundation for a Chinese- or Cuban-style revolution in France. From a detached perspective, an attitude of this sort might seem somewhat naive—but it must be remembered that radical movements often thrive on tenuous but attractive illusions.

In the last analysis, however, the success of extreme left notions—anarchism, the cult of spontaneity, direct action, the efficacy of violence—stems from the fact that they correspond to the exigencies of the students' situation. Within the context of the university, *gauchisme* makes sense. If one wishes to mobilize a large and disparate mass of students and intellectuals, for a limited time, in order to impose limited demands on a distant and unresponsive authority, one would do well to follow the example set by Daniel Cohn-Bendit.

DERADICALIZATION

The PCF's commitment to a reformist, popular front government is often interpreted as evidence of its deradicalization. The Party's leaders, it is argued, have become power-oriented pragmatists. They no longer believe in Marxism-Leninism but merely use it to disguise or rationalize the real interests of their organizational empire.

There is little doubt that Communist doctrine fulfills certain ideological functions. It is one of the indispensable tools that the elite uses to preserve the strength and integrity of its bureaucratic apparatus. In fact, it is by virtue of this organizational role that ideology continues to exercise a profound influence on strategic and tactical decision making.

It is difficult to accept the assertion that the PCF is bifurcated into a pragmatic elite and a corps of ideological followers. It is conceivable that the Party leadership strives to maintain the ideological commitment of its followers for practical reasons; but by doing so, it invariably finds itself constrained and influenced by ideology.

Having set forth a particular ideological tenet (such as the "leading role of the Soviet Union"), the Party can depart from it only at the risk of demoralizing its followers. Pragmatic decisions, which blatantly contradict doctrinal assumptions, tend to have a debilitating effect on organizational discipline, spirit, and confidence.

In addition, it should be noted that those at the apex of the bureaucratic pyramid often base their decisions on information that has been passed up to them by individuals in subordinate positions. If ostensible doctrinal loyalty is an important criterion for reward and promotion, then information that travels upward through organizational channels will invariably assume an ideological coloration. If the leadership is pragmatic but its bureaucratic eyes and ears are ideological, then the leadership's perceptions of the world will be shaped by ideology.

The very notion of a pragmatic leader is problematic. Even the most hardheaded realist is not, in the strict sense of the term, a neutral observer. When one views social reality, one does not see "raw data" or "pure sensations"; one's perceptions are always focused, selected, and organized by certain symbolic formations.

When the Party decision maker faces his social environment, he views it *through* the perceptual categories posited by Marxism-Leninism. To assume that Communist doctrine merely provides the raw material for ex post facto rationalizations is to assume that the decision maker has alternative perceptual equipment at his disposal that he can use to organize his *initial* perceptions.

It is not altogether clear where the working-class apparatchik would get alternative equipment of this sort. Having had little formal education, it is doubtful that he has been exposed to a wide variety of non-Marxian explanatory models. When confronted with a confusing welter of social phenomena, he quite naturally turns to the cognitive resources readily at hand: the categories and paradigms of Marxism-Leninism.

It is easy to dismiss Communist doctrine as a set of vulgar simplifications that "fail to do justice" to the complexities of modern industrial society. Nevertheless, even "vulgar" Marxism provides a complete cognitive map, which fragments society into a manageable number of classes and relates their conditions of existence to a wide range of intellectual and political developments. Naturally, it suppresses subtlety and denies ambiguity—but for this very reason it provides those who use it with a serene sense of confident, intellectual mastery.

We can therefore interpret the PCF's immediate reaction to the events of May 1968 as a ritualistic response, conditioned by the Stalinist reduction of Marxism-Leninism. In addition, the Party's long-range strategy is also the product of explanatory paradigms contained in its organizational doctrine. The program of Rochet and Marchais is definitely not a pragmatic response to "new" conditions; on the contrary, it is based on ideological notions developed almost thirty years ago, during the popular front period. De Gaulle and his successors, like the Fascists, represent the large monopolies. To fight them, the PCF must mobilize not only the working class but also the democratic elements of the middle class. The immediate goal of the Communists is not a socialist revolution but the defense of republicanism against the monopolies and their "reactionary stooges."

Given this perspective, the Party could not surrender to the adventurist provocations of the student radicals. To retain the support of the petit-bourgeoisie, it had to stress its respect for legality and parliamentary norms.

It is difficult to fault the Party for refusing to utilize the May uprising to seize state power. As Waldeck Rochet pointed out, an attempt of this sort would have plunged France into a long and bloody civil war. Most of the blood would have been that of the working class. Despite its considerable organizational strength, the PCF was no match for the powerful and apparently loyal military apparatus of de Gaulle. There is little doubt that the ruling class had both the will and the ability to preserve its hegemonic position.

Within the context of the university environment, the tactics of the *gauchistes* made considerable sense. But as techniques for the immediate transformation of the social totality, they left much to be desired. The Party was correct in its insistence that the Latin Quarter and the French nation were two very different political entities.

It is important to note, however, that the Communists conceived of the situation in sharp, "either/or" terms. As usual, its mode of perception was rigidly dichotomous. Either surrender to the *gauchiste*

adventurists, alienate the middle class, and risk organizational assets—
or continue to play the parliamentary game, unequivocally condemn
the students, and preserve as much as possible.

Since it was imprisoned within its organizational doctrine, the Party
failed to consider alternative courses of action—solutions which would
have allowed it to continue to pursue its major strategic objectives
while at the same time permitting it to expand its influence among
the radical students and intellectuals. No effort was made to respond
in an innovative or creative fashion to the developments within the
university. Instead of recognizing the uniqueness of this milieu, the
PCF proceeded to impose upon it dry, doctrinal preconceptions. The
Party fell back on its ritualistic reaction patterns. By issuing a monotonous series of insults ("servants of monopoly capital," "petit-bourgeois adventurists," etc.), the Party seems to have lost much of the
sympathy it once enjoyed in the university; and it also lost the undeniable energy, enthusiasm, and creativity of the student left.

The Party could have escaped its "either/or" dilemma if its student
organization had possessed a significant measure of tactical autonomy.
As it was, the UEC immediately discredited itself by following the
PCF's lead and harshly condemning the Latin Quarter demonstrations.
The Communists should have allowed the UEC to remain *with* the
great mass of the students—even if this meant following them to the
barricades. In general, the UEC should have been permitted to adopt
methods of mobilization appropriate to the terrain of the student
milieu.

Second, the UEC should have been allowed to support the principal university-oriented demands of the students: specifically, the call
for university autonomy and greater student power in university decision making.

Since it was necessary for the Party to continue to proclaim its
support for parliamentary norms, it was also necessary for it to discourage its student organization from taking part in the revolutionary adventures of the *gauchistes*. But it was not necessary to prohibit
the UEC from engaging in militant protests against police brutality
or from participating in forceful demonstrations for university reforms. Nor was it necessary for the Party to engage in tendentious
name-calling with popular student leaders; and it was particularly

unwise to label the students "sons and daughters of the big bourgeoisie."

By allowing its students to participate in activities which trans-
gressed the norms of parliamentary legality, the PCF would have
exposed itself to charges of deceit and duplicity. The right would have
accused it of secretly conspiring against the state while publicly supporting the constitution. But despite the PCF's cautious behavior,
it still managed to evoke precisely this response from the Gaullists
and from the right-wing daily *Le Figaro*. By pursuing its "either/or"
strategy, the Party suffered all of the disadvantages of being associated with the uprising—and gained none of the advantages (such as
possible increases in influence among the students and the radical
intelligentsia).

The May revolt brings into focus the principal ideological and
organizational dilemmas that the French Communist party presently
faces.

First, there is the persistent problem of preserving unity in diversity.
If the Communists are to succeed in their efforts to form a broad
"democratic" front, they must expand their influence among increasingly diversified clientele groups. Thus, their subsidiary organizations must develop tactics of mobilization that correspond to the
particular characteristics of these groups.

For example, France's half million students provide a vast reservoir
of Communist recruits and sympathizers. In addition, the radical
youth is, in itself, an energetic and powerful social force. If the Party
is to increase its support in the university and the lycée, it must come
to grips with the specific internal contradictions of these communities.
Instead of simply regarding the students as potential Party ideologues,
the PCF must make an attempt to understand and respect their particular problems, needs, and aspirations. Instead of imposing a preconceived role upon them, it must attempt to respect them for what,
in fact, they are.

At the same time, as the Party diversifies and creates more and more
subsidiary bodies, the unifying function of its organizational doctrine
becomes increasingly vital. The existence of a plethora of independent
organizations, pursuing distinct tactical objectives, creates a powerful
centrifugal force; this must be counteracted by the centripetal force

provided by the commitment to common strategic goals and shared ideological beliefs.

Yet, one of the reasons that the PCF's reaction to the events of May seemed unimaginative and ineffective was that its decisions were often shaped by its organizational doctrine. While the need for unity necessitates the strengthening of doctrinal commitment, the need for flexible, creative behavior seems to demand that the decision maker free himself from the confining bonds of ideology.

If the Communists are to respond effectively to new challenges, they must set aside the rigid schemas of *doctrine* and utilize instead the more subtle insights of Marxist *theory*. In short, the theorist— the petit-bourgeois intellectual—must assume a new and expanded role. The specialists in economics and sociology should be encouraged to carry out in-depth studies of particular social problems, and on the basis of these studies, they should be permitted to present proposals for strategic and tactical policy to the central committee.

However, any subordination of doctrine to theory tends to undermine the authority of the present Party elite. The formal legitimacy of the apparatchiki's power rests on their supposed mastery of Marxist-Leninist ideology—on their roles as the guardians of the Party's traditional organizational doctrine.

In the last analysis, the PCF's dilemmas express themselves in this conflict: on the one hand, the Party wishes to expand and diversify itself; on the other hand, it wishes to preserve its unity—and also the hegemony within this unity of the proletarian apparatchik.

As Lenin said: "The theory of Marx is all-powerful because it is true." But its truth assumes a different form in different settings and situations. Whose task is it to pursue these separate truths? Must the same individuals who determine the truth also lead the activities that translate it into power? Or conversely, must the specialists in "power" also be specialists in "truth"? Finally, who synthesizes these partial truths into the one, indivisible Truth, which gives the movement its resolve and its will to proceed—and which cements its unity?

Notes

CHAPTER 1

1 Karl Marx and Frederick Engels, *The Communist Manifesto* (New York, 1966), p. 19.
2 Ibid., p. 22.
3 Ibid., p. 19.
4 V. I. Lenin, *State and Revolution* (New York, 1956), p. 76.
5 V. I. Lenin, *What Is To Be Done?* (New York, 1965), p. 33.
6 Ibid.
7 Marx and Engels, *Manifesto,* p. 26.
8 Karl Marx, Preface to the *Critique de l'économie politique* (Paris, 1957), p. 4.
9 Waldeck Rochet, *Les Evénements de mai-juin* (Paris, 1968), p. 29; all translations from French texts are my own unless otherwise noted.
10 Ibid.
11 Waldeck Rochet, *Qu'est-ce qu'un révolutionnaire dans la France de notre temps?* (Paris, 1968), pp. 20-21.
12 Ibid., p. 51.
13 Waldeck Rochet, *Qu'est-ce que la philosophie marxiste?* (Paris, 1966), p. 8.
14 Ibid., pp. 27-28.
15 Rochet, *Qu'est-ce qu'un révolutionnaire,* p. 17.
16 V. I. Lenin, *Selected Works,* vol. 1 (New York, 1967), p. 41.
17 Maurice Thorez, *Son of the People,* trans. Douglas Garman (New York, 1938), p. 63.
18 The PCF's and the PCI's divergent attitudes toward polycentrism were obviously determined by a wide variety of factors, of which the problem of ideological orthodoxy was only one; see Donald Blackmer, *Unity in Diversity: Italian Communism and the International Communist Movement* (Cambridge, 1968).
19 André Barjonet, *La Révolution trahie de 1968* (Paris, 1968).
20 David Caute, *Communism and the French Intellectuals* (New York, 1964), p. 25.
21 Gérard Walter, *L'Histoire du Parti communiste français* (Paris, 1948), p. 378.
22 Caute, *Communism,* p. 28.
23 Laurent Casanova, *Le Parti communiste, les intellectuels et la nation* (Paris, 1949), p. 69.
24 Ibid., pp. 74-75.
25 Ibid.
26 Ibid., p. 12.

27 Ibid., p. 13.
28 Ibid., p. 18.

CHAPTER 2

1 Michel-Antoine Burnier, *Choice of Action,* trans. Bernard Murchland (New York, 1968), p. 44.
2 David Caute, *Communism and the French Intellectuals* (New York, 1964), p. 187.
3 Ibid., p. 87.
4 Arne Naess, *Four Modern Philosophers* (Chicago, 1968), p. 275.
5 Burnier, *Choice of Action,* p. 87.
6 Caute, *Communism,* p. 253.
7 Burnier, *Choice of Action,* p. 86.
8 Ibid., p. 106.
9 For discussions of the relationship between Sartre's original statement of the existentialist position and his later Marxism, see Wilfred Desan, *The Marxism of Jean-Paul Sartre* (Garden City, 1966); Walter Odajnyk, *Marxism and Existentialism* (Garden City, 1965); George Novack, ed., *Existentialism Versus Marxism* (New York, 1966); and Raymond Aron, *Marxism and the Existentialists* (New York, 1969).
10 Simone de Beauvoir, *The Mandarins,* trans. Leonard M. Friedman (Cleveland, 1960), p. 123.
11 Ibid., p. 242.
12 Jean-Paul Sartre, *Nausea,* trans. Lloyd Alexander (Norfolk, n.d.), p. 238.
13 Jean-Paul Sartre, *Literature and Existentialism,* trans. Bernard Frechtman (New York; 1966).
14 Arne Naess, *Philosophers,* p. 182; for a discussion of the relationship between Heidegger's metaphysics and its political consequences, see Karl Loewith, "Les Implications politiques de la philosophie de l'existence chez Heidegger," *Les Temps Modernes,* November 1946.
15 Martin Heidegger, *German Existentialism,* trans. Dagabert D. Runes (New York, 1965), p. 19.
16 Sartre, *Nausea,* p. 73.
17 Desan, *Marxism of Sartre,* pp. 2-3.
18 Jean-Paul Sartre, *Situations,* trans. Benita Eisler (Greenwich, 1964), p. 113.
19 Maurice Merleau-Ponty, *Humanism and Terror,* trans. John O'Neil (Boston, 1969), pp. 111-12.
20 Jean-Paul Sartre, *Literary and Philosophical Essays,* trans. Annette Michelson (New York, 1955), p. 226.
21 Ibid., p. 231.
22 Jean-Paul Sartre, "Les Communistes et la paix," *Les Temps Modernes,* July 1952, p. 33.

23 Desan, *Marxism of Sartre,* pp. 85–90.
24 Burnier, *Choice of Action,* p. 40.
25 Sartre, *Situations,* p. 124.
26 Jean-Paul Sartre, *The Words,* trans. Bernard Frechtman (Greenwich, 1969), p. 159.
27 Simone de Beauvoir, *The Force of Circumstance,* trans. Richard Howard (New York, 1965), p. 6.
28 Quoted by Sartre in *Situations,* p. 183.
29 Beauvoir, *Mandarins,* p. 242.
30 Sartre, *Situations,* p. 86.
31 Beauvoir, *Mandarins,* p. 179.
32 Ibid., p. 222.
33 For a concise history of both "Socialism and Liberty" and the R.D.R. see Burnier, *Choice of Action,* and Beauvoir, *Force of Circumstance.*
34 Beauvoir, *Force of Circumstance,* p. 17.

CHAPTER 3

 1 Pierre Hervé, *La Révolution et les fétiches* (Paris, 1956); see also *Lettre à Sartre* (Paris, 1956) in which Hervé responds to criticisms published in *Les Temps Modernes.* For an English summary of Hervé's position, see François Fejtö, *The French Communist Party and the Crisis of International Communism* (Cambridge, 1967), pp. 69–72.
 2 David Caute, *Communism and the French Intellectuals* (New York, 1964), p. 201.
 3 Ibid., p. 226.
 4 *L'Express,* November 9, 1956.
 5 *Les Temps Modernes,* November–December–January 1956-57.
 6 Ibid., p. 106.
 7 Jean-Paul Sartre, *Situations,* trans. Benita Eisler (Greenwich, 1964), p. 93.
 8 Caute, *Communism,* p. 227.
 9 Ibid., p. 228.
10 Fejtö, *French Communist Party,* p. 71.
11 Ibid., p. 79.
12 Caute, *Communism,* p. 234.
13 Declaration of the Sorbonne-Lettres section of the UEC after its dissolution; *Partisans,* April 1966, p. 52.
14 "L'Union des jeunesses communistes," *Est et Ouest,* May 1957, p. 5.
15 *L'Humanité,* April 3, 1945.
16 "L'Union," *Est et Ouest,* p. 6.
17 Quoted in the refutation of Garaudy's report by Auguste Lecoeur in *France Nouvelle,* 24 November 1951.
18 "L'Union," *Est et Ouest,* p. 5.

19   *L'Humanité,* May 25, 1955.
20   "L'Union," *Est et Ouest,* p. 8.
21   Ibid., p. 8.
22   Léo Figuères, *Le Parti communiste français, la culture et les intellectuels* (Paris, 1962), p. 65.
23   Ibid., p. 68.
24   Ibid., p. 71.
25   Ibid., p. 72.
26   Ibid.
27   "L'Union," *Est et Ouest,* p. 8.
28   Claude Angeli, "Communistes: Tillon accuse," *Le Nouvel Observateur,* 20-26 July 1970, p. 9.
29   Michel-Antoine Burnier, *The Choice of Action* (New York, 1968), p. 168.
30   Simone de Beauvoir, *The Force of Circumstance,* trans. Richard Howard (New York, 1965), p. 130.
31   Quoted by Mona T. Houston in "The Sartre of Madame de Beauvoir," *Yale French Studies,* no. 30, p. 26.
32   Ibid., p. 30.
33   Sartre, *Situations,* p. 88.

CHAPTER 4

1   François Fejtö, *The French Communist Party and the Crisis of International Communism* (Cambridge, 1967), pp. 168-69.
2   Ibid., p. 304.
3   Raymond Guyot, "Le Combat pour le République continue," *Cahiers du Communisme,* October 1958.
4   Theses of the Fourteenth Congress of the PCF quoted in Jean Baby, *Critique de bas* (Paris, 1960), p. 106.
5   Guyot, "Le Combat," *Cahiers du Communisme.*
6   Fejtö, *French Communist Party,* p. 304.
7   Michel-Antoine Burnier, *Les Existentialistes et la politique* (Paris, 1966), p. 31.
8   Ibid., p. 121.
9   Fejtö, *French Communist Party,* p. 100.
10   Michel-Antoine Burnier, *Choice of Action* (New York, 1968), p. 123.
11   "Second Congrès de l'UEC," *Est et Ouest,* April 1958, pp. 4-5.
12   Jean-Pierre Morillon, "Le Conflit des étudiants communistes avec la direction du PCF," *Est et Ouest,* November 1963, p. 5.
13   Jean Piel, "Interventions des congressistes," *Cahiers du Communisme,* June 1961, pp. 207-12.
14   Fejtö, *French Communist Party,* p. 138.
15   Ibid.
16   Burnier, *Les Existentialistes,* p. 152.

17 "Open Letter," *Clarté,* December 1964.

18 Ibid.

19 André Gorz, *Strategy for Labor,* trans. Martin A. Nicolous (Boston, 1967).

20 "Open Letter," *Clarté.*

21 *Démocratie '65,* February 1965.

22 Ibid.

23 "Tribune: La Dissolution du secteur lettres de L'UEC," *Partisans,* April 1966, p. 52.

24 Jeunesse communiste révolutionnaire, *Texte de référence politique,* 1968, p. 5.

25 Claude Harmel, "Les Groupes révolutionnaires de l'extrèmegauche devant la crise révolutionnaire de mai 1968," *Est et Ouest,* June 1968, p. 9.

26 See Mandel's excellent work on Marx's *Capital, Marxist Economic Theory* (New York, 1968).

27 Jeunesse communiste révolutionnaire, *Texte,* p. 26.

28 Ibid., p. 6.

29 Christian Hébert, "Les Etudiants," *Le Nouvel Observateur,* 30 April 1968.

30 Roger Garaudy, *De l'anathème au dialogue* (Paris, 1965).

31 Roger Garaudy, *Marxisme du XXe siècle* (Paris, 1965).

32 Louis Althusser, "Contradiction et surdétermination," *La Pensée,* December 1962.

33 Louis Althusser, "Sur le jeune Marx," *La Pensée,* March-April 1961.

34 Louis Althusser, "Marxisme et humanisme," *Cahiers de ISEA,* June 1964.

35 Louis Althusser, *Lire Le Capital,* tome 2 (Paris, 1968).

36 Garaudy, *Marxisme du XXe siècle,* p. 56.

37 Althusser, *Lire,* tome 1, p. 75.

38 Roger Garaudy, *Peut-on être communiste aujourd'hui?* (Paris, 1968), p. 271.

39 Louis Althusser, "La Philosophie comme arme de la révolution," *La Pensée,* April 1968.

40 Garaudy, *Peut-on être communiste aujourd'hui?* p. 272.

41 See, for example, Louis Althusser, "Sur la dialectique matérialiste," *Pour Marx* (Paris, 1965); this essay is presented as a textual exegesis on Mao's *On Contradictions,* although it is obviously much more.

42 Michelle Perrot and Annie Kriegel, *Le Socialisme français et le pouvoir* (Paris, 1966), p. 214.

43 Claude Harmel, "Vers la création d'un parti français pro-chinois," *Est et Ouest,* December 1967.

44 Ibid.

45 Claude Harmel, "Les Groupes révolutionnaires de l'extrème gauche *Est et Ouest,* June 1968, p. 6.

46 Ibid.

CHAPTER 5

1   Waldeck Rochet, *Le Marxisme et les chemins de l'avenir* (Paris, 1966),
    p. 20.
2   Louis Althusser, *For Marx,* trans. Ben Brewster (New York, 1970),
    pp. 163-217.
3   Ibid.; for Althusser's self-criticism, see the introduction to the English
    edition, pp. 14-15.
4   Rochet, *Le Marxisme,* p. 19.
5   Louis Althusser, "La Philosophie comme arme de la révolution," *La
    Pensée,* April 1968, p. 27.
6   Gajo Petrovic, *Marx in the Mid-twentieth Century* (New York, 1966),
    pp. 63-65.
7   Jean-Pierre Morillon, "Le Conflit des étudiants communistes françaises
    avec la direction du PCF," *Est et Ouest,* November 1963, p. 6.
8   Ibid.
9   J. V. Stalin, *The Problems of Leninism and the Foundations of Leninism*
    (Moscow, 1926).
10 Morillon, "Le Conflit," p. 8.
11 Ibid.
12 Ibid.
13 *L'Humanité Nouvelle,* 20 July 1967.
14 *Die Zeit,* Hamburg, April 9, 1965.
15 The speeches of this conference are reprinted in a brochure entitled,
    "Les Etudiants communistes face aux grands problèmes de l'époque,"
    (Paris, 1963).
16 Ibid., pp. 116-17.
17 Ibid., p. 117.
18 Ibid., pp. 26-27.
19 *L'Humanité,* May 11, 1963.
20 For an account of the Seventh Congress of the UEC, see Richard Cornell,
    "Rebellion of the Young," *Problems of Communism,* September-October
    1965, pp. 11-17.
21 *Unir pour le socialisme,* April 1964.
22 The final issue of *Clarté,* December 1964, gives an account of these in-
    trigues; see also the Trotskyist monthly, *Internationale,* Paris, April 1965),
    pp. 4-5.
23 Cornell, "Rebellion," p. 15.
24 Fejtö, *French Communist Party,* p. 15.
25 *France Nouvelle,* April 17-23, 1965, pp. 5-7.
26 See the article in *l'Humanité* by Guy Hermier, secretary-general of the UEC,
    20 January 1966.

27 Claude Harmel, "Vers la création d'un parti communiste français pro-chinois," *Est et Ouest,* December 1967, pp. 24-25.
28 *L'Humanité,* May 3, 1968.
29 Katia D. Kaupp, "La Lettre des 'trente-six,'" *Le Nouvel Observateur,* June 12-18, 1968, pp. 13-14.
30 *L'Humanité,* May 9, 1968.
31 Ibid.
32 "Of Student Poverty: Considered in its Economic, Psychological, Political and Particularly Intellectual Aspects, and a Modest Proposal for its Remedy," published in an English translation in the *Berkeley Barb,* vol. 5, no. 26, issues 124, 125, 126.
33 Ibid., issue 124, p. 9.
34 Ibid.
35 Ibid.
36 Ibid., issue 126, p. 8.
37 Ibid., issue 124, p. 9.
38 Ibid.
39 "Daniel Cohn-Bendit s'entrient avec Jean-Paul Sartre," a conversation partially quoted in J. Sauvageot, et al., *La Révolte étudiante: les animateurs parlent* (Paris, 1968), p. 92.
40 Ibid.
41 Ibid.
42 Jean-Paul Sartre, *Critique de la raison dialectique* (Paris, 1960), pp. 498-630.
43 Sauvageot, et al., *La Révolte étudiante, p. 95.*
44 Ibid.
45 "Daniel Cohn-Bendit s'entrient avec Jean-Paul Sartre," a conversation published in its entirety in *Le Nouvel Observateur,* 20 May 1968.
46 Ibid.
47 Sauvageot, *La Révolte étudiante,* p. 96.
48 Leon Trotsky, *The Russian Revolution* (Garden City, 1959), p. 199.
49 *L'Humanité,* 3 May 1968.
50 Ibid.
51 Ibid.
52 Léo Figuères, "Le Gauchisme: hier et aujourd'hui," reprint from *Cahiers du Communisme,* June 1968, p. 10.
53 Ibid.
54 Ibid.
55 Claude Prévost, "Les Bases de l'idéologie gauchiste," *La Nouvelle Critique,* June 1968, p. 13.
56 Waldeck Rochet, "Le Parti communiste et les evenements de mai-juin 1968," Numéro spéciale du *Bulletin de l'Elu Communiste,* no. 30, 2nd and 3rd trimester 1968.

CHAPTER 6

1 *L'Humanité Dimanche,* July 7, 1968.
2 *L'Humanité,* May 18, 1968.
3 *L'Humanité,* May 21, 1968.
4 *L'Humanité,* May 19, 1968.
5 *L'Humanité,* May 19, 1968.
6 Claude Harmel, "Le Parti communiste devant la crise révolutionnaire de mai," *Est et Ouest,* June 1968.
7 Roger Garaudy, "La Révolte et la révolution," *Démocratie Nouvelle,* April-May 1968, p. 6.
8 Ibid.
9 Waldeck Rochet, "Le Parti communiste et les evenements de mai-juin 1968," Numero spéciale du *Bulletin de l'Elu Communiste,* no. 30, p. 28.
10 Garaudy, "La Révolte," p. 8.
11 *L'Humanité Dimanche,* July 7, 1968.
12 Garaudy, "La Révolte," p. 8.
13 Frédéric Duchamps, "Communistes: la ligne nouvelle," *Le Nouvel Observateur,* 14 July 1968, pp. 13-14.
14 Ibid.
15 Jean-Marie Vincent, "The PCF and its History," *The New Left Review,* November-December 1968, p. 45.
16 Frédéric Duchamps, "Communistes," pp. 13-14.
17 Ibid.

CHAPTER 7

1 V. I. Lenin, *What Is To Be Done?* (New York, 1929), p. 96.
2 Ibid.
3 J. V. Stalin, *Dialectical and Historical Materialism* (New York, 1940), p. 23.
4 Lenin, *What Is To Be Done?* p. 32.
5 Ibid., pp. 86-87.
6 Ibid., p. 130.
7 Ibid., p. 118.
8 Rosa Luxemburg, *The Russian Revolution* (Ann Arbor, 1967), p. 80.
9 Rosa Luxemburg, *Leninism or Marxism?* (Ann Arbor, 1967), p. 79.
10 Annie Kriegel, *Les Communistes français* (Paris, 1968), p. 132.
11 Waldeck Rochet, *Le Parti communistes et les évenements de mai-juin 1968* (Paris, 1968), p. 36.
12 Ibid.
13 André Gorz, *Strategy for Labor* (Boston, 1967); interview with Palmiro Togliatti, *Nuovo Argomenti,* June 16, 1956.

14 Gérard Walter, *Histoire du parti communiste français* (Paris, 1948),
    p. 48.

15 See, for example, the interview with Palmiro Togliatti, reprinted in
    The Russian Institute's *The Anti-Stalin Campaign* (New York, 1956).

16 Leon Trotsky, *The New Course* (Ann Arbor, 1965).

17 J. V. Stalin, *Short Course in the History of the Communist Party of the
    Soviet Union (bolshevik)* (Moscow, 1952), p. 47.

18 Walter, *Histoire,* p. 162.

19 Ibid., p. 179.

20 Georgio Rovida, *Histoire du parti communiste français* (Turin, 1968),
    p. 213.

21 Cahiers de la fondation nationale des sciences politiques, *Le Communisme
    en France* (Paris, 1969), p. 206.

22 Kriegel, *Communistes français,* p. 147.

23 See Stanley Hoffman, ed., *In Search of France* (New York, 1963);
    Michel Crozier, *The Bureaucratic Phenomenon* (Chicago, 1968); and
    Margaret Mead and Martha Wolfenstein, *Childhood in Contemporary
    Cultures* (Chicago, 1957).

24 Crozier, *Bureaucratic Phenomenon,* p. 222.

25 Jesse Pitts, "Continuity and Change in Bourgeois France," in *In Search
    of France,* ed. Stanley Hoffman (New York, 1963), p. 250.

26 Margaret Mead, *Themes in French Culture* (Stanford, 1954).

27 Pitts, "Continuity and Change," p. 254.

28 Crozier, *Bureaucratic Phenomenon,* p. 222.

29 Rochet, *Le Parti communiste,* p. 36.

30 Daniel Cohn-Bendit, *Obsolete Communism,* trans. Arnold Pomerans
    (New York, 1968), p. 154.

31 "Daniel Cohn-Bendit s'entrient avec Jean-Paul Sartre," a conversation,
    Le Nouvel Observateur, 20 mai 1968.

32 Luxemburg, *Leninism or Marxism,* p. 93.

33 Ibid., p. 94.

34 Cohn-Bendit, *Obsolete Communism,* pp. 170–71.

35 Ibid., p. 173.

36 Luxemburg, *Leninism or Marxism,* p. 91.

37 Cohn-Bendit, *Obsolete Communism,* pp. 249–56.

38 *Le Nouvel Observateur,* 20 mai 1968.

39 Cohn-Bendit, *Obsolete Communism,* p. 253.

40 Seymour M. Lipset and Sheldon S. Wolin, *The Berkeley Student Revolt*
    (New York, 1965), p. 6.

41 Pierre Bourdieu and Jean-Claude Passeron, *Les Héritiers* (Paris, 1964),
    p. 48.

42 Ibid., p. 145.

43 Ibid., pp. 136–37.

44 Ibid., p. 165.

45   Ibid., p. 54.
46   Ibid., p. 56.
47   Pitts, "Continuity and Change," p. 251.
48   Ibid., pp. 255-56.
49   Ibid., p. 257.
50   Crozier, *Bureaucratic Phenomenon,* p. 241.
51   "French Education," *Yale French Studies,* no. 22; 1958-59, p. 57.
52   Cohn-Bendit, *Obsolete Communism,* p. 30.
53   Ibid., p. 32.
54   Maureen McConville and Patrick Seale, *Red Flag, Black Flag* (New York, 1968), p. 22.
55   Ibid., p. 27.

CHAPTER 8

1   Eugene H. Methvin, "Mob Violence and Communist Strategy," *Orbis,* Summer 1961, p. 175.
2   Ibid., p. 169.
3   Ibid., p. 167.
4   Jacques Fauvet, *Histoire du parti communiste français,* tome 2 (Paris, 1965), p. 242.
5   Cyril Black and Thomas Thornton, *Communism and Revolution* (Princeton, 1964), p. 33.
6   Daniel Cohn-Bendit, *Obsolete Communism,* trans. Arnold Pomerans (New York, 1968), p. 190.
7   Franz Fanon, *The Wretched of the Earth* (New York, 1957).
8   J. V. Stalin, *Economic Problems of Socialism in the U.S.S.R.* (New York, 1952).
9   Frédéric Bon, "Structure de l'idéologie communiste," in *Le Communisme en France,* ed. Cahiers de la fondation nationale des sciences politiques (Paris, 1969), p. 111.
10   Ibid.
11   Claude Vernay, "Aspects de la politique économique de pouvoir," *Economie et Politique,* numéro 168-169, July-August 1968, pp. 12-13.
12   Waldeck Rochet, *La Marche de la France au socialisme* (Paris, 1966).
13   Frédéric Bon, "L'Idéologie communiste," p. 113.
14   *L'Humanité,* May 3, 1968.
15   Interview with Claude Lecompte, editor of *Nous, les garçons et les filles,* July 19, 1968.
16   J. V. Stalin, *The Foundations of Leninism and The Problems of Leninism* (Moscow, 1950), pp. 114-16.
17   *France Soir,* June 11, 1968.
18   Peter Brooks, "The Fourth World," *Partisan Review,* Fall 1968, p. 541.
19   *L'Humanité,* June 11, 1968.

20 Ibid.
21 Neil Smelser, *Theory of Collective Behavior* (London, 1962), pp. 247-53.
22 Pierre Bourdieu and Jean-Claude Passeron, *Les Héritiers* (Paris, 1964), p. 55.
23 Christopher Katope et al., *Beyond Berkeley* (New York, 1965), p. 406.
24 Wilfred Desan, *The Marxism of Jean-Paul Sartre* (New York, 1965), p. 130.
25 Ibid., p. 131; see also Jean-Paul Sartre, *Critique de la raison dialectique* (Paris, 1960), pp. 394-431.

CHAPTER 9

 1 Daniel Cohn-Bendit, *Obsolete Communism,* trans. Arnold Pomerans (New York, 1968), p. 170.
 2 "Reflections on the French Upheaval," editorial by Paul Sweezey, *The Monthly Review,* New York, September 1968.
 3 Rosa Luxemburg, *Marxism or Leninism?* (Ann Arbor, 1967), p. 98.
 4 Robert Tucker, *The Marxian Revolutionary Idea* (New York, 1969), pp. 181-98.
 5 Ibid.
 6 Donald W. Treadgold, *Twentieth-Century Russia* (Chicago, 1964), p. 317.
 7 Angelo Rossi, *La Guerre des papillons* (Paris, 1954).
 8 For an alternative view that stresses the unique character of the postwar period of violence and argues that it was initiated to restore membership losses sustained from 1945-47, see Thomas H. Greene, "The Communist Parties of Italy and France: A Study of Comparative Communism," *World Politics,* October 1968.
 9 "D'ésacords publics entre le Parti communiste français et le Parti communiste de l'union soviétique," *Est et Ouest,* 1-15 September 1968, pp. 13-16.
10 Compare the politburo declaration of 21 August 1968 with the central committee declaration of 22 August 1968, both of which were published on p. 1 of *l'Humanité.*
11 The most prominent pro-Soviet dissident was the widow of Maurice Thorez, Jeannette Vermeersch, who made her opposition known at the central committee meeting of August 22 and later resigned from the Party.
12 Annie Kriegel, *Les Communistes français* (Paris, 1968), pp. 145, 221-23; "A Propos des finances du Parti communiste français," *Est et Ouest,* 16-31 July 1967, pp. 2-10. Evidence suggests that during the fall and winter of 1968 the CPSU applied pressure on a number of nonruling parties to expel vocal dissidents. During this time, Franz Marek was expelled from the Austrian Party, the "manifesto group" from the PCI, and Garaudy from the PCF. It seems likely that Moscow brought financial pressures to bear on the reluctant Party leaderships, in order to attain this coordinated international purge.

13   See Robert Tucker on the "radical tendency of mind" in *The Marxian Revolutionary Idea* (New York, 1969), pp. 181-98.

14   *Analyses et Documents,* no. 154, May 1968, p. 7.

15   Marc Kravetz, *L'Insurrection étudiante* (Paris, 1968), p. 177.

16   Interviews with Maoist students, Faculty of Science, Halle-aux-Vins, July 4, 1968.

17   Ibid.

18   *Analyses et Documents,* no. 154, p. 5.

19   *Le Monde,* June 12, 1968.

20   *L'Humanité Nouvelle,* 13-16 May 1968.

21   *Analyses et Documents,* no. 154, p. 5.

22   Cohn-Bendit, *Obsolete Communism,* p. 41.

23   Ibid., p. 47.

24   Ibid., p. 44.

25   Ibid., p. 54.

26   Ibid.

27   Ibid., p. 55.

28   Ibid., 60.

29   Ibid., p. 55.

30   Ibid., p. 56.

31   Mouvement du 22 mars, *Ce n'est qu'un début, continuons le combat* (Paris, 1968), p. 61.

32   *Analyses et Documents,* no. 155, p. 29.

33   Ibid., p. 28.

34   *Mai 1968: première phase de la révolution socialiste française* (special issue of the *Quatrième Internationale,* Paris, 1968).

35   *Analyses et Documents,* no. 154, p. 7.

36   *Analyses et Documents,* no. 155, p. 28.

Bibliography

Albertini, Georges. "Le Parti communiste français dans la crise révolutionnaire de mai 1968." *Est et Ouest,* no. 406, 1 June 1968.

Alia, Josette. "Opposition: les sombres querelles des 'appareils.'" *Le Nouvel Observateur,* no. 186, 7 June 1968.

Almond, Gabriel. *The Appeals of Communism.* Princeton: Princeton University Press, 1954.

Althusser, Louis. "La Philosophie comme arme de la révolution." *La Pensée,* April 1968.

——. *Lénine et la philosophie.* Paris: Maspero, 1971.

——. *Lire Le Capital.* Vols. 1 and 2. Paris: Maspero, 1965.

——. *Pour Marx.* Paris: Maspero, 1965.

Angeli, Claude. "Les Communistes devant l'énigme étudiante." *Le Nouvel Observateur,* no. 185, 15 May 1968.

Andrieu, René. *Les Communistes et la révolution.* Paris: Julliard, 1968.

Antoine, Gérald, and Passeron, Jean-Claude. *La Réforme de l'université.* Paris: Calman-Levy, 1966.

Aron, Raymond. *The Elusive Revolution.* New York: Praegers, 1969.

——. *Marxism and the Existentialists.* New York: Harper & Row, Inc., 1969.

——. *Marxismes imaginaires.* Paris: Gallimard, 1970.

——. *The Opium of the Intellectuals.* New York: W. W. Norton, 1962.

Baby, Jean. *Critique de bas.* Paris: Maspero, 1960.

Barjonet, André. "C.G.T. 1968." *Les Temps Modernes,* July 1968.

——. *La Révolution trahie de 1968.* Paris: Les Editions John Didier, 1968.

Beauvoir, Simone de. *The Mandarins.* Cleveland: Meridian Books, 1960.

Black, Cyril E., and Thornton, Thomas P., eds. *Communism and Revolution.* Princeton: Princeton University Press, 1964.

Blackmer, Donald L. M. *Unity in Diversity: Italian Communism and the International Communist Movement.* Cambridge: MIT Press, 1968.

Borkenau, Franz. *European Communism.* New York: Harper and Brothers, 1953.

Bourdieu, Pierre, and Passeron, Jean-Claude. *Les Hérities: les étudiants et la culture.* Paris: Editions de Minuit, 1964.

Brayance, Alain. *Anatomie du parti communiste français.* Paris: Denoël, 1952.

Brooks, Peter, trans. "The Fourth World: Part II, Documents." *The Partisan Review,* Fall 1968.

Burnier, Michel-Antoine. *Choice of Action.* New York: Random House, 1968.

Cahiers de la fondation nationale des sciences politiques. *Le Communisme en France.* Paris: Armand Colin, 1969.

Cantril, Hadley. *The Politics of Despair.* New York: Collier Books, 1962.

Cantril, Hadley, and Rodnick, David. *On Understanding the French Left.* Princeton, N.J.: Institute for International Social Research, 1956.

Caute, David. *Communism and the French Intellectuals.* New York: Macmillan, 1963.

Casanova, Laurent. *Le Parti communiste, les intellectuels et la nation.* Paris: Editions Sociales, 1949.

"Ceux qui en étaient, ceux qui n'en étaient pas: enquète sur le communisme et les jeunes." *Esprit,* 1 February 1946, pp. 191–260.

Cohn-Bendit, Daniel. *Obsolete Communism; The Left-wing Alternative.* New York: McGraw-Hill, 1968.

Cohn-Bendit, Daniel; Duteuil, J. P.; Geismar, A.; and Savageot, Jean. *La Révolte étudiante.* Paris: Editions de Seuil, 1968.

Comité d'action Censier. *Nous sommes en marche.* Paris: Seuil, 1968.

Cornell, Richard. "Rebellion of the Young." *Problems of Communism,* September–October 1965.

——. *Youth and International Communism.* New York: Walker and Company, 1965.

Coudray, Jean-Marc; Lefort, Claude; and Morin, Edgar. *Mai 1968: la brèche.* Paris: Fayard, 1968.

"La Crise de l'Union des étudiants communistes de France." *Est et Ouest,* no. 297, 1 April 1963.

Crozier, Michel. *The Bureaucratic Phenomenon.* Chicago: University of Chicago Press, 1967.

Daniel, Jean. "Le Grand chambardement." *Le Nouvel Observateur,* no. 184, 22 May 1968.

Déledicq, A. *Un mois de mai orageux.* Paris: Epoque, 1968.

Desan, Wilfred. *The Marxism of Jean-Paul Sartre.* Garden City: Doubleday, Anchor Books, 1965.

Duchamps, Frédéric. "Communistes: la ligne nouvelle." *Le Nouvel Observateur,* no. 191, 1968.

Dutschke, Rudi. *Ecrits politiques.* Paris: Christian Bourgeois, 1968. Paris

Fejtö, François. *The French Communist Party and the Crisis of International Communism.* Cambridge: MIT Press, 1967.

Figuères, Leo. *La Jeunesse et la communisme.* Paris: Editions Sociales, 1963.

——. *La Parti communiste français, la culture et les intellectuels.* Paris: Editions Sociales, 1962.

Le Parti communiste français. *Les Etudiants communistes face aux grands problèmes de l'époque.* Paris, 1963.

——. *Pour une réforme démocratique de l'enseignement.* Paris: printed by *Ecole et la Nation,* 1967.

Garaudy, Roger. *Le Grande tournant du socialisme.* Paris: Gallimard, 1969.

——. *Marxisme du XXe Siècle.* Paris: Editions Plon, 1966.

——. "Révolte et la révolution." *Démocratie Nouvelle,* April–May 1968.

Gluckman, André. *Stratégie et révolution en France.* Paris: Christian Bourgeois, 1968.

Gorz, André. *Strategy For Labor.* Boston: Beacon Press, 1967.

——. "The Way Forward." *New Left Review,* November-December 1968.

Harmel, Claude. "L'Attachment du parti communiste français de l'union soviétique." *Est et Ouest,* no. 395, 16 December 1967.

——. "Les Groupes révolutionnaires de l'extrème gauche devant la crise de mai 1968." *Est et Ouest,* no. 406, 1 June 1968.

Hoffman, Stanley, et al. *In Search of France.* New York: Harper and Row, 1963.

Jeunesse communiste révolutionnaire. *Texte de réference politique.* Paris, 1967.

Joussellin, J. *Les Révoltes des jeunes.* Paris: Les Editions Ouvrières, 1968.

Kaupp, Katia. "La Lettre des 'trente-six.'" *Le Nouvel Observateur,* no. 187, 12 June 1968.

Kravetz, Marc, ed. *L'Insurrection étudiante.* Paris: Union Générale d'Editions, 1968.

Kriegel, Annie. *Les Communistes français.* Paris: Editions de Seuil, 1968.

——. *L'Oeil de Moscou à Paris.* Paris: Julliard, 1968.

Lecercle, Jean-Louis. "Le 'Mouvement' à Nanterre." *La Pensée,* October 1968.

Lefebvre, Henri. *The Explosion.* New York: Monthly Review Press, 1969.

Lenin, V. I. *Left-wing Communism: An Infantile Disorder.* New York: International Publishers, 1940.

——. "The Student Movement and the Present Political Situation." *The New Left Review,* November-December 1968.

——. *What Is to Be Done?* New York: International Publishers, 1929.

Lipset, Seymour Martin, and Wolin, Sheldon. *The Berkeley Student Revolt.* New York: Doubleday, Anchor Books, 1965.

Luxemburg, Rosa. *Marxism or Leninism?* Ann Arbor: University of Michigan Press, 1967.

——. *The Russian Revolution.* Ann Arbor: University of Michigan Press, 1967.

Mao Tse-tung. *Four Essays on Philosophy.* Peking: The Foreign Language Press, 1966.

Maspero, François, ed. *La Grève à Flins.* Paris: Maspero, 1968.

Marx, Karl, and Engels, Frederick. *The Communist Manifesto.* New York: International Publishers, 1966.

McConville, Maureen, and Seale, Patrick. *Red Flag, Black Flag.* New York: Ballentine Books, 1968.

Mead, Margaret. *Childhood in Contemporary Cultures.* Chicago: University of Chicago Press, 1967.

Merleau-Ponty, Maurice. *Humanism and Terror.* Boston: Beacon Press, 1969.

Morin, Edgar. *Autocritique.* Paris: Julliard, 1959.

Micaud, Charles. *Communism and the French Left.* New York: Praeger, 1963.

Mouvement du 22 mars, *Ce n'est qu'un début: continuons le combat.* Paris: Maspero, 1968.

Odajnyk, Walter. *Marxism and Existentialism*. New York: Doubleday, Anchor Books, 1965.

Perrot, Michelle, and Kriegel, Annie. *Le Socialisme français et le pouvoir*. Paris: Grasset, 1966.

Petrovic, Gojo. *Marx in Mid-Twentieth Century*. New York: Doubleday, Anchor Books, 1966.

Reynaud, J.-D. *Les Syndicats en France*. Paris: Armand Colin, 1963.

Rieber, Alfred J. *Stalin and the French Communist Party*. New York: Columbia University Press, 1962.

Rochet, Waldeck. "Les Evenements de mai-juin 1968." numéro spéciale du *Bulletin de l'Elu Communiste,* 2e et 3e trimestre 1968.

——. *La Marche de la France au socialisme*. Paris: Editions Sociales, 1966.

——. *Le Marxisme et les chemins de l'avenir*. Paris: Editions Sociales, 1966.

——. *Qu'est-ce qu'un révolutionnaire dans la France de notre temps?* Paris: Editions Sociales, 1968.

Rossi, Angelo. *A Communist Party in Action*. New Haven: Yale University Press, 1949.

Sartre, Jean-Paul. *The Communists and Peace*. London: Hamish, 1969.

——. *Critique de la raison dialectique*. Paris: Gallimard, 1967.

——. *Literature and Existentialism*. New York: The Citadel Press, 1969.

——. *Literary and Philosophical Essays*. New York: Collier Books, 1955.

——. *Situations*. Greenwich: Fawcette Crest Books, 1969.

Schapiro, Leonard. *The Communist Party of the Soviet Union*. New York: Vintage Books, 1960.

"Le Second congrès de l'Union des étudiants communistes de France." *Est et Ouest,* no. 193, 16 April 1958.

Stalin, Joseph. *The Foundations of Leninism and The Problems of Leninism*. Moscow: The Foreign Language Press, 1926.

Tarrow, Sidney G. *Peasant Communism in Southern Italy*. New Haven: Yale University Press, 1967.

Thorez, Maurice. *Son of the People*. New York: International Publishers, 1937.

Trotsky, Leon. *Le Mouvement communiste en France*. Paris: Les Editions de Minuit, 1967.

——. *The New Course*. Ann Arbor: University of Michigan Press, 1965.

——. *The Russian Revolution*. New York: Doubleday, 1959.

"L'Union des jeunesses communistes." *Est et Ouest,* no. 173, 1 May 1967.

UNEF/SNE-sup, *Le Livre noir des journées de mai*. Paris: Seuil, 1968.

Vincent, Jean-Marie. "Réflexions prévisoires sur la révolution de mai 1968." *Les Temps Modernes,* July 1968.

Walter, Gérard. *Histoire du parti communiste français*. Paris: Somogy, 1948.

Index

205